SILHOUETTES OF THE SOUL

Series Editors: Reina Lewis & Elizabeth Wilson

Advisory Board: Christopher Breward, Hazel Clark, Joanne Entwistle, Caroline Evans, Susan Kaiser, Angela McRobbie, Hiroshi Narumi, Peter McNeil, Özlem Sandikci, Simona Segre Reinach

Dress Cultures aims to foster innovative theoretical and methodological frameworks to understand how and why we dress, exploring the connections between clothing, commerce and creativity in global contexts.

Published:

Delft Blue to Denim Blue: Contemporary Dutch Fashion
edited by Anneke Smelik

Dressing for Austerity: Aspiration, Leisure and Fashion in Post War Britain
by Geraldine Biddle-Perry

Experimental Fashion: Performance Art, Carnival and the Grotesque Body
by Francesca Granata

Fashion in European Art: Dress and Identity, Politics and the Body, 1775-1925
edited by Justine De Young

Fashion in Multiple Chinas: Chinese Styles in the Transglobal Landscape
edited by Wessie Ling and Simona Segre Reinach

Modest Fashion: Styling Bodies, Mediating Faith
edited by Reina Lewis

Niche Fashion Magazines: Changing the Shape of Fashion
by Ane Lynge-Jorlen

Styling South Asian Youth Cultures: Fashion, Media and Society
edited by Lipi Begum, Rohit K. Dasgupta and Reina Lewis

Thinking Through Fashion: A Guide to Key Theorists
edited by Agnes Rocamora and Anneke Smelik

Veiling in Fashion: Space and the Hijab in Minority Communities
by Anna-Mari Almila

Wearing the Cheongsam: Dress and Culture in a Chinese Diaspora
by Cheryl Sim

Fashioning Indie: Popular Fashion, Music and Gender in the Twenty-First Century
by Rachel Lifter

Revisiting the Gaze: The Fashioned Body and the Politics of Looking
edited by Morna Laing and Jacki Willson

Reading Marie al-Khazen's Photographs: Gender, Photography, Mandate Lebanon
by Yasmine Nachabe Taan

Wearing the Niqab: Muslim Women in the UK and the US
by Anna Piela

Fashioning the Modern Middle East: Gender, Body, and Nation
edited by Reina Lewis and Yasmine Nachabe Taan

Fashion, Performance, and Performativity: The Complex Spaces of Fashion
edited by Andrea Kollnitz and Marco Pecorari

Silhouettes of the Soul
edited by Otto von Busch and Jeanine Viau

Reina Lewis: reina.lewis@fashion.arts.ac.uk
Elizabeth Wilson: elizabethwilson.auth@gmail.com

SILHOUETTES OF THE SOUL

MEDITATIONS ON FASHION, RELIGION, AND SUBJECTIVITY

edited by Otto von Busch and Jeanine Viau

BLOOMSBURY VISUAL ARTS
LONDON • NEW YORK • OXFORD • NEW DELHI • SYDNEY

BLOOMSBURY VISUAL ARTS
Bloomsbury Publishing Plc
50 Bedford Square, London, WC1B 3DP, UK
1385 Broadway, New York, NY 10018, USA
29 Earlsfort Terrace, Dublin 2, Ireland

BLOOMSBURY, BLOOMSBURY VISUAL ARTS and the Diana logo are trademarks of Bloomsbury Publishing Plc

First published in Great Britain 2022

Selection, editorial matter, Introductions © Otto von Busch and Jeanine Viau, 2022

Individual chapters © their Authors, 2022

Otto von Busch and Jeanine Viau have asserted their right under the Copyright, Designs and Patents Act, 1988, to be identified as Editors of this work.

Series design: BRILL
Cover image © Sandra Samuelsson/EyeEm/Getty Images

All rights reserved. No part of this publication may be reproduced or transmitted in any form or by any means, electronic or mechanical, including photocopying, recording, or any information storage or retrieval system, without prior permission in writing from the publishers.

Bloomsbury Publishing Plc does not have any control over, or responsibility for, any third-party websites referred to or in this book. All internet addresses given in this book were correct at the time of going to press. The author and publisher regret any inconvenience caused if addresses have changed or sites have ceased to exist, but can accept no responsibility for any such changes.

A catalogue record for this book is available from the British Library.

A catalog record for this book is available from the Library of Congress.

ISBN: HB: 978-1-3501-7990-5
ePDF: 978-1-3501-7991-2
eBook: 978-1-3501-7992-9

Typeset by Deanta Global Publishing Services, Chennai, India
Printed and bound in Great Britain

To find out more about our authors and books visit www.bloomsbury.com and sign up for our newsletters.

CONTENTS

List of Figures   vii

Introduction *Otto von Busch and Jeanine Viau*   1

Section One Interfacing the Divine *Otto von Busch and Jeanine Viau*   15

1   The Future Body as Ultimate Dress *Fiona Dieffenbacher*   19

2   No One Can Tell: On the Silent Glamour of Meher Baba *Nicola Masciandaro*   37

3   Embodiments of Shakti: Cosmic Power Displayed by Kumārīs, Incarnate Goddesses of Nepal *Liz Wilson*   51

4   Interview with Kodo Nishimura *Otto von Busch and Mark Larrimore*   65

Section Two Practices of Emulation and Transformation *Otto von Busch and Jeanine Viau*   73

5   Naked or Nude?: Reading the Threads, the Bare, and the Threadbare in Ancient Indian Religion *Joseph Walser*   77

6   Empowered Entrepreneurs: Women of Muslim Faith and the Modest Fashion Movement in the United States *Hassanah El-Yacoubi*   91

7   Fashioning the Subject: Black Queerness, Identity, and an Ethic of Honor *Benae Beamon*   106

8   From the Medieval Christ to Fashion's Heroin Chic: The Sublime Emulation of the Emaciated Paradigm in Secular and Religious Iconography *Tanya White*   117

9   In and Out of One Another's Closets: A Dialogue *Jeanine Viau with Shekinah Morrison*   134

Contents

Section Three The Radiance of the Concealed *Otto von Busch and Jeanine Viau*   143

10   Making Islamic Masculinities: Clothing Traditions in African American Islam *Michael Muhammad Knight*   147

11   Holly Woodlawn, Trash Queen: Queer Agency and Resistance in the Pursuit of Glamour *Jared Vázquez López*   162

12   Fashioning a Glamour: Magical Embodiment in Contemporary Witchcraft *Kristen J. Sollée*   176

13   Interview with Damcho *Otto von Busch*   188

List of Contributors   195
Index   198

FIGURES

1.1	Fashion editor Lynn Yaeger leaving Anna Sui fashion show	21
1.2	Lady Gaga attends ELLE's 25th Annual Women in Hollywood Celebration	22
1.3	Fashion designer Thom Browne poses backstage at the Thom Browne Spring 2016 fashion show	23
1.4	Diagram of the Holy Trinity (Father, Son, and Holy Spirit)	26
1.5	Fashion-dress-embodied soul: An integrated model of identity	26
1.6	A Christian theological framework of embodiment	30
1.7	Three bodies (physical, social, and future)	30
1.8	Three states of "dress" in 2 Cor. 5:1-4	31
1.9	Dress from Viktor and Rolf's "Russian Doll" Autumn/Winter '99 couture collection	33
2.1	Meher Baba, 1925	38
5.1	Sculpture showing drapery of the Buddha	83
8.1	Crucifix, seventeenth century, Spanish	120
8.2	Model walks Prada's Spring 1997 RTW (pret a porter) collection	121
8.3	Figures 8.1 and 8.2 Digitally superimposed during research process (2020) by Tanya White	122
8.4	Tanya White, *Deathly Form Wearing Textile* (2019)	123
8.5	Tanya White, *Precarious Deformity Wearing Textile* (2019)	124
8.6	Tanya White, *Formlessness Wearing Textile* (2018)	128

INTRODUCTION
Otto von Busch and Jeanine Viau

In "Romanesque Arches," one of Tomas Tranströmer's (2011) most famous poems, he suggests a view into the depths of being human. The Nobel Prize–winning author does so by reference to the vaults of church architecture:

> Inside the huge Romanesque church the tourists jostled in the half darkness.
> Vault gaped behind vault, no complete view.
> A few candle flames flickered.
> An angel with no face embraced me
> and whispered through my whole body:
> "Don't be ashamed of being human, be proud!
> Inside you vault opens behind vault endlessly.
> You will never be complete, that's how it's meant to be."
> Blind with tears
> I was pushed out on the sun-seething piazza
> together with Mr and Mrs Jones, Mr Tanaka, and Signora Sabatini,
> and inside them all vault opened behind vault endlessly.

With more than a million and half visitors jostling through *Heavenly Bodies* at the Metropolitan Museum of Art in 2018, this exhibition became the most visited in the museum's history, exceeding prior masterpieces such as Treasures of Tutankhamun in 1978 and the visit of the Mona Lisa to the museum in 1963. At both the Fifth Avenue and the Cloisters locations, *Heavenly Bodies* was arranged according to the Catholic imagination's overlapping architectures of church interior, liturgy, and the sojourn of the human soul. Like Tranströmer's meditation, visitors were affected by and invited to locate themselves (or not) within these architectures, to see themselves reflected in the glass surfaces, in the aspirations expressed in the intermingled garments and art objects, and in the other people making their way through the exhibition.

The success of *Heavenly Bodies* points to a clear public interest in the intersection between fashion and religion, if not into their endless depths. The fascination of the intersection of these fields is not least mirrored by current trends in the academy, such as the American Academy of Religion's seminar on Religion, Attire and Adornment in North America and several published volumes examining this relationship in recent years (Arthur 2000; Bucar 2017; Hume 2013; Neal 2019). Commentary on *Heavenly Bodies* by theologians and religious studies scholars celebrates the ingenuity of creative projects and conversations that manifest the sacred in the sartorial (Moore 2018; Delgado 2018). However, critics also call for an interrogation of the establishment. In the case of *Heavenly Bodies* this means challenging the Catholic hierarchy's monopoly on Catholic identity, the high fashion houses' power over industry standards, and the tyranny of ecclesiastical beauty that hides all manner of sin without the careful stitches of amendment. As Catholic studies scholar Robert Orsi (2018) observes, the sexual abuse crisis and other uglier sides of clericalism were nowhere to be found at the Met's exhibition, which at its heart was a pageant of priestly and courtly finery.

Perhaps the most glaring sin of *Heavenly Bodies* was its omission of divergent embodiments, aesthetic sensibilities, and interpretations of Catholic subjectivity. Emma McClendon (2019), associate curator of costume for the Museum at the Fashion Institute of Technology, describes the scene of the exhibition: "Almost all of the garments were installed on white, waifish mannequins with distinctively Caucasian, doll-like features and blonde, red, or brown wigs that imitate Caucasian hair. Together, these curatorial choices served to whitewash the exhibition, presenting a biased view of the fashion industry and the Catholic church." McClendon along with several other commentators noted the absence of any Afro-diasporic, African, Latin American, or Latinx designers in the exhibition, ironic exclusions considering the largest and fastest-growing populations of Catholics globally belong to these cultures. McClendon also stresses the closeting of gay designers showcased in the exhibition, observing that many have complicated relationships with the church that might have contextualized and enlivened the ways that Catholicism is explored in their design work if their stories had been part of the curation. Similarly, there was an absence of institutionally critical theological perspectives among the curatorial essays and explanatory materials installed throughout the exhibition, such as feminist, queer, Black, and liberationist approaches.

These critiques reveal the need to continue expanding and diversifying deliberations at the intersections of religion and fashion, a need that the particularity of the case studies in this volume responds to. The question of spirituality and dress has become more urgent in a time when religious dress is up for discussion in elections and legislative bodies, and not least across the media. In public, dress is a contested expression of cultural, traditional, and moral values and practices, mixed with anxiety over what kind of soul resides under the contested garments. As discussed by Homi Bhabha (1994), wearing traditional dress in modern contexts can reveal the wearer's refusal to mimic colonial subjectivity. Denying the colonist's desire for a reformed, recognizable Other, dress comes to signal a clash where colonial domination has not created the desired hybridity of subordinates: that their soul has not become "Western enough."

On a parallel track, in the "temples of consumption," there is an ethical reckoning about the social and environmental impacts of the fashion industry. Calls for more sustainable practices mimic moralistic dogma, echoing Victorian sermons of what constitutes consumer respectability, often leading to the privileged preaching abstinence to the poor. Influencers, evangelizing guiltless aesthetic asceticism or minimalist regimes of monastic cleansing, are lining up to save lost subjects and the planet. Battle lines cut through haul videos and deceptive Instagram filters, shame and repent turn into medialized procedures of public soteriology: the authentic soul of the subject can only be saved if they repent, or at least meditate over their unsustainable missteps. Just as monolithic claims about religious and cultural identity need to be questioned, there is also a need to disconnect the concept of fashion from "mere" consumerism, dismantle the pipeline from runway to museum, and attend to the patterns of agency and divine intimacy that dress makes possible.

In a time when cultural iconoclast Kanye West runs masses during Paris Fashion Week under his label Sunday Service, featuring his Sunday Service gospel choir, fully cloaked in his YEEZY uniforms, there is a need to see the intersection between fashion and religion under a new light. In the iteration of March 2020, at Théâtre des Bouffes du Nord, high-profile designers, musicians, and influencers attended, not least social media icons Kim Kardashian West and Kourtney Kardashian (dressed in latex bodysuits by Balmain). Here, a ninety-minute religious ceremony is much more than a catwalk show: it speaks of an ongoing rearticulation of the interface between contemporary fashion and spirituality.

Putting the Soul Out in Public

We suggest to approach fashion as a devotional regime or religion of our time. We can think of religion as a form of evolving expression (or fashion). In this case, what tools, concepts, and methods would we need in order to unpack the intersection between these two phenomena? Is fashion always frivolous and religion always sanctimonious? What is the relationship between dress and the existential depths of the experiencing subject? What across everyday language is called "the soul?"

Oscar Wilde famously argues in *The Picture of Dorian Gray*, "It is only shallow people who do not judge by appearances. The true mystery of the world is the visible, not the invisible." This is Lord Henry's counsel to the young Dorian Gray, and it speaks of the desire to grasp the profound depth of shallowness and exposes the superficial vacancy persistent within the practices of "deepness." Along these lines, our aim with this volume is to move beyond traditional, social scientific, and historical analysis of religious attire and adornment to an examination of conscience through fashion, style, and dress. Our focus reflects the movement of religious and theological discourses outside institutional spaces and dogmatic vocabularies (Knight 2009; Keller and Schneider 2011; Wilcox 2018; Bidwell 2018), just as it favors the new perspectives on fashion studies as an autoethnographic becoming inside complex creative, social, and economic systems (Jenss 2016).

There exists a rich literature on the anthropology of religious dress (Arthur 1999, 2000; Hume 2013), and not least the emerging field of modest dress and cultural approaches to the spectrum of ethnic and religious attire in contemporary society (Tarlo 2010; Lewis 2015). However, a lacuna is apparent in the understanding of the inner experiences of religion and fashion, the connection between the soul and what anthropologist Terance Turner (1980) famously calls "the second skin." In such examinations, it is imperative to think of fashion not as a cover but as a membrane between imaginal realities, surface and depth, body and soul, temporal and contextual domains of aspiration and devotion. Unpacking the relation between the soul and surface is an opportunity for seeing boundaries and substances (not least body and identity) as fluid and transgressive—that they seep into each other, codependent, energizing each other. Speaking of "silhouettes" of the soul highlights a possibility of definition, tracing outlines, seeking contours, draping an immaterial aspect of selfhood as if it has a material body, as well as casting a shadow and speaking of an "ill fit."

Also, most accounts of sacred dress focus on what is explicitly religious or at least literally referential, such as the use of religious symbolism and iconography on clothing. Several of the chapters in this volume transgress the boundaries of what is deemed "religious" and signal an emerging avant-garde in theology and religious studies that is tired of reliance on the dress form—the soul—and is more interested in saying what cannot be articulated, the aporia of identity, an unmaking of the soul toward the making of justice, honor, and difference. Fashion is a catalyst for unmaking the boundaries of religious experience and disciplinary regimes, thereby opening the field to fresh material interlocutions and awareness.

While not all these questions can be answered in this volume, the inquiries collected here do illuminate new vistas across vertical and horizontal axes of experience, from the surface to the depths, between inner and outer reaches. Religious language shines new light on the existential fissures of why dress matters so much to people, even those who profess that all that really counts is the soul. We must ask, does surface and depth, ephemeral becoming and established lineages necessarily stand as opposites, or how are they related?

A Depth of Fashion?

Fashion, in similarity to soul, is an expansive and complex term, yet also all too common in everyday language. And like most fashion scholars, the authors in this volume would probably not agree on one single definition. The term captures paradoxical claims, connoting both originality and copying, difference as well as repetition, novelty as well as echoes from the past. Avoiding the narrow scope of a definition framed by the industry or the "system," the common trope across the contributions in this volume points toward the dressed expression of the time. While such expression gives reference to social stratification, the authors point toward how it also anchors inner beliefs and positions. In this way, fashion is socially meaningful but also mirrors and helps form deeper held convictions and principles.

It is not self-evident, however. In its everyday use, most would agree fashion connotes something ephemeral and shallow. And this may not be surprising. That clothes have little permanence and depth is an everyday experience most of us share. We change clothes across contexts and times of the week, yet still we remain the same person underneath. Surely clothes only act as cover, over a more permanent substance that is our body. On top of that, fashion is a layer of social signification that shuffles clothes in and out of popularity. As a temporal expression manifested in the style of apparel, fashion seems even further removed from the perennial experience of selfhood.

It is not a new thing to challenge the perception of fashion being shallow and trivial. A common trope in probing the meaning of fashion is to highlight its use in the formation, expression, and communication of identity (Barnard 1996). Taking place in the tension between how we perceive ourselves and how others perceive us, identity suggests expression more than introspection and offers little understanding on matters of subjective experience and meaning. Sloterdijk (2013) notes how identity connotes an expression that claims its subject. Like a property, it is something deposited inside oneself. While this may be a simplification of a constructive and formative concept, Sloterdijk points out how identity puts emphasis on preservation and inertia and offers little light and guidance on depth, practice, and refinement. To Sloterdijk, identity requires no cultivation, and it offers little help in the practice of life, or what he calls "anthropotechnics."

> While the Stoics of antiquity devoted their lives to the goal of erecting within themselves, through constant practice, the statue that crafted its best self from invisible marble, the moderns find themselves as finished inertia sculptures and set themselves up in the park of identities, regardless of whether they prefer the ethnic wing of the individualistic open-air space. (Sloterdijk 2013: 188)

Perspectives on fashion emerging from affect put the spotlight on the emotional life in dress. Effectively social and contagious, even if embodied in each individual, the lines traced through affect raises questions on how people tune in to the emotional echoes and desires within (Blackman 2012). In the vivid lives of desire, how can we take into account the ways people practice restraint and self-direction on their journeys toward self-knowledge?

Spiritual experience cannot be reduced to language, and similarly, the experience of fashion can neither be narrowed down to expression or communication. Fashion scholarship is underserved when it comes to frameworks to probe the more existential depths of dress. We could seek to articulate the odysseys down the abyss of inner experience, while not necessarily needing to anchor this in incorporeal essence. The idea is not to "animate" fashion by giving clothes the properties to possess any distinct spiritual essence but to use fashion to navigate our innermost topographies. To do so, we will be using the many maps available of these landscapes in religious traditions, the ones referring to it as something like "soul."

A Language to Excavate Inner Life

On the one hand, the term "soul" is ubiquitous and utterly recognizable. It signifies impulses across cultures to name animating powers and sentience, to understand desires for immortality, identity, and moral integrity, and to speak of inner experience. However, while some spiritual and religious traditions define the soul by the experience of "the human as two" (Kripal 2014: 275), as in the Cartesian split between body and mind or the distinction between material and metaphysical experience, many cultures offer more integrated or polycentric views of subjectivity. The five aggregates of Buddhist anthropology, for example, combine sensory experience with feelings, voluntary and involuntary reactions, recognition, and consciousness in an integrated mechanism of self-making. Some cultures view the body as enlivened and inhabited by multiple presences, such as ancestors and other entities, and in many ontological systems, souls are not limited to human beings or even just sentient beings. The Ancient Greeks recognized both accompanying powers (*daimon*) and multiple animating aspects within the body, such as Aristotle's three souls (*psyches*): the nutritive, the sensitive, and the rational. In many cultures, the inner life has a body, not a physical one but a dream-body, a "subtle" body, or an "ethereal" or "astral" body in some esoteric doctrines. It inhabits the realm of shapeshifters and other liminal types of being, animating dreams, visions, fantasies, and the imaginal realms, realms that border the reality of fashion.

Because of this variety, soul can be a fraught and contested reference. The term's cultural specificity does not always reflect the varieties of ontological or existential speculation elaborated by unique religious traditions and individuals; acts of translation and analogy are not neutral. Soul comes from the Old English *sáwol*, which became the vernacular gloss for the high Latin *anima* after early translations of the biblical literature and Christianized transcriptions of Old English epic poetry in the Middle Ages. Prior to this, as Christianity spread in elite Roman circles, *anima* replaced the Hebrew *nephesh* and the Hellenic *psyche*. These translations inevitably erased cultural particularities and were acts of Christian domination and transmission as much as understanding. The Christian supremacist predilection for analogy continued under European imperialism and colonialism and all but obliterated the sacred languages of indigenous and enslaved peoples. Hence, in the field of religious studies today, perennialist and comparative approaches are being questioned because of their tendencies to universalize and adopt shared terms by which to analyze all spiritual and religious experiences (Masuzawa 2005).

The soul is subject to context, both theoretically and experientially. As Owen Barfield (1988: 78) points out about even premodern perspectives, the world does not necessarily extend away from the subject like a stage but is instead a garment worn about the body. Contextualization is especially important for those struggling to articulate their personhood in dehumanizing social conditions. In *The Souls of Black Folk*, for example, W. E. B. Du Bois describes the "twoness" experienced by Black Americans: "It is a peculiar experience, this double-consciousness, this sense of always looking at one's self through the eyes of others, of measuring one's soul by the tape of the world that looks on in amused contempt and pity" ([1903] 2008). Du Bois is not describing the metaphysical divide between body and soul. He is describing the experience of being "torn asunder" by the incongruence between the desire for true and free self-consciousness, and the imposition of how the world sees Blackness. Du Bois also names the dual cultural consciousness further articulated by postcolonial theorists (Fanon [1952] 2008; Bhabha 1985). He describes the striving to reconcile two souls, one belonging to and protective of African ancestral culture, and another desiring belonging and opportunity in America.

Our aim in this collection, then, is not to offer a static theory of or even shared definition of "the soul." We, along with several of the authors in the volume, resist the monotheistic tendency of our culture that holds oneness as an ideal. Rather, we present a familiar pattern, a flexible concept that helps to mediate interactions between fashion-style-dress, inner experience, and what Georg Simmel called "the unlimited itself" ([1904] 1957: 542). This leaves us to consider how we are to speak of the consistency of the inner world as it relates to fashion. What useful conceptual tools could we use to unpack the inner experience of dress practices, the emotional echoes within, the existential domains that are animated by imagination or curtailed by shame and agony? If we acknowledge that dress practices can vivify the bowels of emotion, what spiritual techniques and discourses are used across faiths and cultures?

The Poetics of Dressing Deeply

As a tentative response to these questions and a connecting thread among the meditations collected in this volume, we propose the notion of *dressing deeply*. Dressing deeply queries the realness of the inner life and the potential for dress to disclose and even be a mode of examination for the mysteries of subjectivity. Like religion, fashion then can be understood as a method for excavating and displaying inner experience, and speculating about the ways human beings touch into divinity or, as the French creative Romain Rolland described it in a letter to Sigmund Freud in 1927, "the feeling of the eternal (which can very well not be eternal, but simply without perceptible limits, and like oceanic)" (Parsons 1999: 36). Also, the intimacy of dress makes it personally revelatory, a very poetics of the soul, mediating some of the most challenging and meaningful conflicts of human life.

Thinking of both the soul and dress as poetic enterprises opens to the emotional strata of connections between inner and outer life. "Two truths approach each other," the poet Tomas Tranströmer (1987) posits, "One comes from inside, the other from outside, and where they meet we have a chance to catch sight of ourselves." Tranströmer's observation recalls paradoxes at the heart of founding projects in both the disciplines of religious studies and fashion studies. Georg Simmel, for example, presented his seminal study of fashion as an inquiry at the meeting of the individual soul and society, where the perennially conflicting forces of uniformity and differentiation interact to create change. Simmel proposes that this interaction "constitutes the whole wealth of our development, the whole incentive to advancement, the possibility of grasping a vast proportion of all the infinite combinations of the elements of human character, a proportion that is approaching the unlimited itself" ([1904] 1957: 542). However, even though Simmel glimpses "the infinite combinations of the elements of human character," his rigid dualism keeps him, and his views of the soul and fashion, subject to troubling social hierarchies—sexism, classism, racism, and European supremacy.

Looking to the origins of religious studies offers a more pluralistic vision, albeit also mired in the intellectual and cultural Eurocentrism of modernity. One of the central aporia for the philosopher-psychologist of religion William James, for example, is the tension between empirical and spiritual convictions. On the one hand, James insists on the impossibility of proving the realness of a "substantial soul" (1899), thus his refusal to discuss "immortality" or "eternity" at length calling these secondary concerns to matters of consciousness ([1902] 1994: 569). On the other hand, James tirelessly probes the depths of inner experience, the outer reaches of which he speculated might border on the "mother-sea" of consciousness (1899: 27). He locates and defends religious experience as occurring in the individual "recesses of feeling, the darker, blinder strata of character . . . the only places in the world in which we catch real fact in the making" ([1902] 1994: 545). For James, prioritizing individualized consciousness explains and accepts the world in its pluralistic form, rather than some "absolutely unitary fact" ([1902] 1994: 149), allowing each to pursue their unique spiritual destiny.

Something clear from both Simmel and James' meditations is the persistence of the experience of the inner life and how this consciousness involves the individual in some greater mystery. To "be oneself" one must also surrender the self, that is, attune to and follow something that is larger than oneself. This also becomes visible in the "laws of imitation" of sociologist Gabriel Tarde (1903), where the psycho-social phenomena of imitation and invention hold harmony and conflict in tension, fashions and beliefs being examples. To expose the emergence of shared inner values, not only behaviors, Tarde uses concepts from physics such as "waves" and "rays" of imitation, pointing to forces that transgress the individual through the intimate poetics of passionate interests. Yet simultaneously, Tarde's perspective points to the poetics of desire where the "inner life," as the nexus of experience, is an episode of transgression, of passionate ecstasy; to fully be oneself, one must be outside or beyond oneself, immersed and drawn into the oceanic currents of sensualities.

So how does one do transgression, thereby moving beyond the limits of oneness or duality to the possibilities generated by paradox? Simmel, James, and Tarde each grasp at these outer reaches with a poetic utterance: "the unlimited itself," "mother-sea," "waves." Approaching the movements between inner and outer experience poetically through fashion-style-dress allows for the suspension of resolution. It embraces tension as the possibility for articulation locating the soul squarely in generative conflict from which any destiny, any outfit is possible. In this way, the poetic grounding in experience also allows us to take the edges off the colonizing tyrannies of oneness and dualism in exchange for an array of possibilities. Fashion is, as Elizabeth Wilson (2004: 383) suggests, a tool through which users can "escape into re-enchanted worlds."

Dressing deeply, then, is a mode of diffraction in the way that Donna Haraway describes. Diffraction as a mode of inquiry, rather than seeking one conclusive format or harmony, allows patterns of difference and subjective standpoints to emerge and so "offers us a way of putting emphasis on practice, on process, on ways to do things rather than in finding a conclusive meaning: it is the interference and conflicts that are the forces under investigation" (von Busch 2016: 185). Haraway offers diffraction as an antidote to "the reproduction of the sacred image of the same, of the one true copy" (1992: 299). Her cyborg navigates pluralistic even competing locations, aims, and commitments and works creatively with any materials and nonmaterials available, humans and nonhumans, methods and systems.

In this unending process of articulation, nothing and no one is off-limits according to some predetermined dogmatic scheme—scientific, religious, or cultural.

> This cyborg does not have an Aristotelian structure; and there is no master-slave dialectic resolving the struggles of resource and product, passion and action. S/he is not utopian nor imaginary. S/he is virtual. Generated along with other cyborgs, by the collapse into each other of the technical, organic, mythic, textual, and political, s/he is constituted by articulations of critical difference within and without each figure. (1992: 330)

Dressing deeply is part of this eternal creative process joining oceanic speculation with material articulation similar to Haraway's cobbling together of poetic syntax and pragmatic applications. As she observes, "Lives are built; so we had best become good craftspeople with the other worldly actants in the story" (1992: 300). Dressing deeply gives the soul texture, layers, and shape in the world. It is an attempt to make negotiations between the inner life, dress practices, and the unlimited itself real, deliberate, and manifest. Along these lines, this volume is organized according to three aspects of dressing deeply, themes that help us frame the variety of cultural subjectivities, approaches to fashion-style-dress, and methods of excavation introduced by the contributors.

Exploring Deep Dress

This book began with a session at the 2017 American Academy of Religion Annual Meeting. Panelists examined the interplay of religious, ethical, and sociohistorical dimensions of subject formation as assembled and expressed through clothing and in relation to fashion. The papers focused on the generative potential of tensions and transgressions in the interplay between inner spiritual techniques and their outer representation or the performative elements of identity production. What became obvious was how the paradox between conformity and innovation happens in everyday lived practices and individual experience, whether preparing a sermon or tying a scarf, and how "inner" spiritual practices were deeply entangled in appearances and practices of adornment. The topic asked for more thorough investigations and cross-disciplinary engagements.

While the case studies collected here represent a diverse array of cultural expressions and analytical approaches, most of them emerge from and are situated within the American context. This reflects the interests and locations of the contributors and editors as scholars working and teaching mainly in the US academy. This gives some of the approaches taken throughout this volume a bend that is distinct from perspectives and interpretations found in the locales where some of the examined religious and dress practices originated. We realize there are significant trends and innovations happening at the intersection of religion and fashion in other regions, such as Japan and Africa, for example. We also noted limits to the religious traditions and themes covered in the volume, for example, the absence of studies focusing on Jewish fashions, eco-spirituality, and sustainability and not least indigenous perspectives. Our hope, then, is that this volume will be an invitation to other projects that expand the scope of inquiry into the richly textured landscapes and depths of spirituality and fashion-style-dress.

The chapters in this book are organized in three sections, where each part presents one aspect of entanglement between inner life and outer representation. Section One, "Interfacing the Divine," examines how clothes explicitly imagine and even assist with divine incarnations and destinies. Here, the distinction between divine entities and the human being, between the worldly and the extraordinary appears not as a clear boundary but as a membrane or a misty landscape. Dress is a medium through which to explore this mystery and permeability. Deep dress becomes a liminal realm of avatars and inner experience where divine revelation happens through the means of body and adornment.

Section Two, "Practices of Emulation and Transformation," brings attention to the techniques of ascetic training and elaborate becoming, where the soul is not a readymade substance or inherently aligned with vows or precepts, but a continuous process of transformation. The soul is impressionable, and deep dress practices help to discern and display affect, day to day, moment to moment. Not unlike alchemical practices, such metamorphoses happen in tandem between realms of experience, in disciplined procedures conjoining the inner and outer, and by the inevitable accidents of self-making. Learning to dress deeply is also done in collaboration with others, whether by emulating or resisting existing trends, joining movements, or forming intimacies. Deep dress as a method for examining inner and outer, individual and social, subject and object interactions reveals that the refinement of spiritual practices takes place simultaneously with changes in the world of appearances.

In Section Three, "The Radiance of the Concealed," the chapters explore the depths of poetic allure and expressive possibility in dress. The hidden inner life aches to be revealed and communicated; it calls and lures, plays with attention, but remains partially concealed or not yet finished. Revelation is always partial because of the limits of dress, as with language, lack of means, and because the possibilities are indeed infinite, the well of mysteries bottomless, the process of disclosure endless. Like the world of glamour, dressing deeply involves mystical attraction and conjuring of lived practices that generate curiosity and open worlds between subjects, attuning attention and behaviors to shared experiences. Curiosity thrives in partially knowing, somewhat revealing, leaving something to the imagination, things left unsaid. It is excited by surprising and transgressive utterances. Deep dress is a poetic technique uniquely situated to both conceal and surprise, to demur or make an entrance.

What we present to the reader is a collection of perspectives, from spiritual practices seeking guidance or assurance in the world of appearances to fashions listening inwards for the spiritual workings of materialization. It is a world of drag. For the perspectives more incarnationally inclined, it is a world of the divine in drag, whether venerating shakti's avatars or approximating the transfigured body through dress.[1] Drag is an apt analogy for deep dress because it is a highly disciplined and revelatory practice. Through play and experimentation, drag develops rigorous regimes of concealment and self-making through surface mediums, such as makeup, clothing design, and embodied gesture. Drag mystifies rigid binaries between genders, between inner life and outer world, between substance and experience, performer and audience as it reveals that all of us are already always in drag.

Rainer Maria Rilke expresses similar anxiety over the danger of limiting ourselves to rigid, perhaps ill-fitting silhouettes, in the poem "God's True Cloak":

> We must not portray you in king's robes,
> you drifting mist that brought forth the morning.
> Once again from the old paintboxes
> we take the same gold for scepter and crown
> that has disguised you through the ages.
> Piously we produce our images of you
> till they stand around you like a thousand walls.
> And when our hearts would simply open,
> our fervent hands hide you. (*Book of Hours*, I 4)

While some might point out Rilke's warning against dressing the divine as a form of idolatry, we think the more significant insight is the juxtaposition between the singular wardrobe of a king and the drifting mist which opens our hearts and keeps our hands fervent. The real danger, as Haraway points out, is in the foreclosure of curiosity and creativity for the sake of reproducing the sacred image of the same, the one true copy (1992: 299). In response, this collection moves beyond the regal monotone of the Met's *Heavenly Bodies* exhibit, as discussed at the start. The diffractive poetics of dressing deeply that we propose opens onto the multitude, to the endless current of self-articulation, an array of inner wardrobes where vaults open behind vaults endlessly.

Note

1. Using drag as a way to talk about divine manifestation in the world is attested to in multiple religious and spiritual traditions. See, for example, approaches in Christian theology applying queer theory, including drag as a transgressive interpretation of and challenge to assumptions about God's human appearance in the world (Althaus-Reid 2000); or the instruction popularly attributed to spiritual teacher Ram Dass, "Treat everyone you meet like God in drag" (Newton 48: 2014).

References

Althaus-Reid, Marcella (2000), *Indecent Theology: Theological Perversions in Sex Gender and Politics*, London and New York: Routledge.
Arthur, Linda B. (ed.) (1999), *Religion, Dress and the Body*, Oxford: Berg.

Arthur, Linda B. (ed.) (2000), *Undressing Religion: Commitment and Conversion from a Cross-Cultural Perspective*, Oxford: Berg.
Barfield, Owen (1988), *Saving the Appearances: A Study in Idolatry*, Middletown, CT: Wesleyan University Press.
Barnard, Malcolm (1996), *Fashion as Communication*, London: Routledge.
Bhabha, Homi K. (1985), "Signs Taken for Wonders: Questions of Ambivalence and Authority under a Tree Outside Delhi, May 1817," *Critical Inquiry*, 12(1), 144–65.
Bhabha, Homi K. (1994), *The Location of Culture*, London: Routledge.
Bidwell, Duane R. (2018), *When One Religion Isn't Enough: The Lives of Spiritually Fluid People*, Boston: Beacon Press.
Blackman, Lisa (2012), *Immaterial Bodies: Affect, Embodiment, Mediation*, London: Sage.
Bucar, Elizabeth (2017), *Pious Fashion: How Muslim Women Dress*, Cambridge, MA: Harvard University Press.
von Busch, Otto (2016), "Action! Or, Exploring Diffractive Methods for Fashion Research," in Heike Jenss (ed.), *Fashion Studies: Research Methods, Sites and Practices*, London: Bloomsbury, 181–97.
Delgado, Jessica (2018), "Refashioning gender and modern visual theology," *The Immanent Frame*, November 2. https://tif.ssrc.org/2018/11/02/refashioning-gender-and-modern-visual-theology/ (Accessed January 5, 2021).
Du Bois, W. E. B. ([1903] 2008), *The Souls of Black Folk*, Project Gutenberg. https://www.gutenberg.org/files/408/408-h/408-h.htm (Accessed January 13, 2021).
Fanon, Frantz ([1952] 2008), *Black Skin, White Masks*, trans. Richard Philcox, New York: Grove Books.
Haraway, Donna (1992), "The Promises of Monsters: A Regenerative Politics for Inappropriate/d Others," in L. Grossberg, C. Nelson and P. Treichler (eds.), *Cultural Studies*, New York: Routledge, 295–337.
Hume, L. (2013), *The Religious Life of Dress*, London: Bloomsbury.
James, William (1899), *Human Immortality: Two Supposed Objections to the Doctrine*, 2nd edn, Cambridge: The Riverside Press.
James, William ([1902] 1994), *The Varieties of Religious Experience: A Study in Human Nature*, New York: The Modern Library.
Jenss, Heike (ed.) (2016), *Fashion Studies: Research Methods, Sites, and Practices*, London: Bloomsbury.
Lewis, R. (2015), *Muslim Fashion: Contemporary Style Cultures*, Durham: Duke University Press.
Keller, Catherine, and Laurel Schneider (2011), *Polydoxy: Theology of Multiplicity and Relation*, London: Routledge.
Knight, Michael (2009), *Journey to the End of Islam*, New York: Soft Skull Press.
Kripal, Jeffrey J. with Ata Anzali, Andrea Jain, and Erin Prophet (2014), *Comparing Religions : Coming to Terms*, West Sussex, UK: Wiley Blackwell.
Masuzawa, Tomoko (2005), *The Invention of World Religions, Or, How European Universalism Was Preserved in the Language of Pluralism*, Chicago: University of Chicago Press.
McClendon, E. (2019), "Heavenly Bodies: Fashion and the Catholic Imagination," *CAA.Reviews*, 1. https://search.ebscohost.com/login.aspx?direct=true&db=edb&AN=133902687&site=eds-live&scope=site (Accessed January 5, 2021).
Moore, Brenna (2018), "The Soulful, Comic Defiance of *Heavenly Bodies*," *The Immanent Frame*, September 21. https://tif.ssrc.org/2018/09/21/the-soulful-comic-defiance-of-heavenly-bodies/ (Accessed January 5, 2021).
Neal, Lynn S. (2019), *Religion in Vogue: Christianity and Fashion in America*, New York: New York University Press.

Newton, David E. (2014), "Alpert, Richard (Ram Dass, 1931-)," in Nancy E. Marion and Willard Oliver (eds.), *Drugs in American Society: An Encyclopedia of History, Politics, Culture, and the Law*, vol. 1, Santa Barabara, CA: ABC-CLIO, LLC, 47–9.

Orsi, Robert (2018), "Something old, Something New, Something Borrowed, Something Blue, Something Dead," *The Immanent Frame*, September 21. https://tif.ssrc.org/2018/09/21/something-old-something-new-something-borrowed-something-blue-something-dead/ (Accessed January 5, 2021).

Parsons, William B. (1999), *The Enigma of the Oceanic Feeling: Revisioning the Psychoanalytic Theory of Mysticism*, Cary: Oxford University Press.

Simmel, Georg ([1904] 1957), "Fashion," *The American Journal of Sociology*, LXII(6): 541–58.

Sloterdijk, Peter (2013), *You Must Change Your Life*, Cambridge: Polity.

Tarde, Gabriel (1903), *The Laws of Imitation*, New York: H. Holt.

Tarlo, Emma (2010), *Visibly Muslim: Fashion, Politics & Faith*, Oxford: Berg.

Tranströmer, Tomas (1987), "Preludes," in Robert Hass (ed.), *Selected Poems, 1954–1986*, 3, New York: Ecco Press.

Tranströmer, Tomas (2011), *New Collected Poems*, Hexham: Bloodaxe Books.

Turner, Terence (1980), "The Social Skin," in J. Cherfas and R. Lewis (eds.), *Not Work Alone*, London: Temple Smith, 112–40. Reprinted in Hau 2(2), 2012: 486–504.

Wilcox, Melissa M. (2018), *Queer Nuns Religion, Activism, and Serious Parody*, New York: New York University Press.

Wilson, Elizabeth (2004), "Magic Fashion," *Fashion Theory*, 8(4): 375–86.

SECTION ONE
INTERFACING THE DIVINE
Otto von Busch and Jeanine Viau

Scholars of fashion, body, and dress recurringly contemplate clothing as a "second skin." This conceptual playfulness has analytical and metaphorical consequences, but it is also grounded in the everyday use of clothes: we change layers of clothing throughout the day, yet still, what remains underneath, the flesh of our self, remains the same. There is an immediate experience that clothes only touch the surface of life.

Yet, simultaneously, we feel deeply about our clothes. Even the most confident or sartorially apathetic person may agonize about what to wear for a certain situation. We can get uncomfortable in our second skin, the context may not be right, and a stain or fray may be a nuisance. The image we see in the mirror is at friction with what we see inside. This membrane between "me" and the world does not do its job. It gets even more complicated when we think of what it is that is at work "inside" ourselves, of what it is we long to reveal.

One aspect of dressing deeply is interfacing with something within, giving shape to an experience that is more than the ego or the self. This can take different forms and meanings across spiritual techniques. Some speak of the feeling of the eternal, a portal that opens beyond the self, a passage inward that may well open outward. Others call out for or are possessed by a specific divine presence, such as the Kumārī, young girls in Nepal who are incarnations of shakti as Liz Wilson describes in her chapter. Fashion plays a role in such interfacing, whether as a membrane between the inner and outer realms or as a mode of communion with divine powers. The texture of these connections is not necessarily smooth but made of tensions, folds, and wrinkles of concrete and mystical experience.

Theologian Dorothee Soelle (2001: 27) posits, "mystical experience happens when the I steps forth from its self-imposed and imagined limits. The I leaves the everyday world and, at the same time, leaves itself as the being defined by that world." Soelle draws parallels to the Sufi mystic Rumi's strophe "Why, when God's world is so big, / did you fall asleep in a prison / of all places?" (2001: 30) Soelle places Rumi's words in relation to the individualization processes under the modern standardized economic order, with its limited scope of what it means to be human.

Here we can think of mystical anthropotechnics toward the divine; how the divine opens itself to draw attention toward something more than the self, a breaking out of the prison we have fallen asleep in, a doorway opening to the deeper chambers of experience, or as Fiona Dieffenbacher explores in her chapter, a future ultimate reality. As in many faiths, this expedition is led by poetic language, in shrouds and robes of vagueness, as the map cannot be universal. In such poetics of inner wayfinding, we may also think of the mystical potential of fashion, where dress is so much more than communication and conformity; it is a search for depth and meaning in a world of appearances. Deep dress is a quest to handle attire and adornment as vehicles, waymarkings, or the path itself on this inner odyssey or toward the infinite horizon. Here, fashion is the magic of glamour surfacing; as Elizabeth Wilson (2007:100) points out, glamour is sublime, it signifies the magic and allure of appearances, and it "depends on what is withheld, on secrecy, hints, and the hidden."

In everyday language, a wearer's "style" connotes something deeper, more stringent, more truthful than the fluctuations of trends or dressing up for a specific occasion. Style is here a constant, an anchor held fast beneath the currents of the moment. Take, for example, Nicola Masciandaro's study in this volume of the affective constancy and charm of Meher Baba's silence. To reference someone's style is a way to speak of a search for a steadfastness inwardness beyond the oscillations of the everyday. Life is continuous change, and to be human is to adapt, yet the pursuit for expressing "how I feel inside" echoes of a desire to keep one room as a source of stability, even if this darkness is in itself a process of metamorphosis.

The chapters in this section explore how the divine I might use deep dress to move between the world of appearances and ultimate longings. Fiona Dieffenbacher makes a direct correlation between a relational Trinitarian theology and the tripart interplay between fashion-style-dress, a process of subject formation patterned after divine self-articulation. Her Cartesian I longs for the transfigured body promised in Christian scripture, completed in and by the resurrected Christ. Fashion-style-dress becomes a process by which the soul participates in imagining this future body as ultimate dress, lavishly wrought, the clothing of salvation. In counterpoint to the exuberance of Dieffenbacher's ultimate dress, Nicola Masciandaro's inquiry into the "avataric normcore" of Meher Baba notes the sage's intent to blend into the multitude, a style amplified by silence, a clearly monistic utterance. Masciandaro presents an example of how divine incarnation is recognizable in the style of Meher Baba, and how paradoxically, the body is only another "clothing" of spiritual reality, as experientially rich, real, and multifaceted as all other forms of appearance.

Appearances have the power to make divinity real, as with the Kumārī, young girls in Nepal who are vessels of divine presence on earth. In her examination of this phenomenon, Liz Wilson shows how surface mediums such as dress, makeup, comportment, and choice of colors manifest the goddess and signify the worthiness of her avatar beneath, showing the possibility of divine disclosure in all aspects of human character and charisma. Here, it is through the surface, through the medium of dress, that the onlooker gains access to the material embodiments of shakti, the divine force animating the world.

Finally, for queer Buddhist monk Kodo Nishimura, makeup is part of spiritual practice and a service entangled with that of the spiritual guidance of the monk. Here, makeup on the body comes in alignment with the makeup for a deeper sense of self, or a makeup of the mind, the process of developing beauty for the appearance of a more true self. Beauty is more than just looks; it is people putting on god. It connotes Madison Moore's (2018) notion of the eccentricity of being free from the limitations of selfhood to finally expand, to blossom as "fabulous." Across these inquiries, the glamour of fashion is more than surface. It is a poetics that expands inward, and dressing gives both wearer and onlooker a glimpse of the divine within.

References

Moore, Madison (2018), *Fabulous: The Rise of the Beautiful Eccentric*, New Haven, CT: Yale University Press.
Soelle, Dorothee (2001), *The Silent Cry: Mysticism and Resistance*, Minneapolis: Fortress.
Wilson, Elizabeth (2007), "A Note on Glamour," *Fashion Theory*, 11(1): 95–108.

CHAPTER 1
THE FUTURE BODY AS ULTIMATE DRESS
Fiona Dieffenbacher

Introduction

In existing fashion studies scholarship, religion is primarily dealt with at two ends of the spectrum in the context of material culture—via ethnographic studies of situated religious dress practice or the spectacularization of religious iconography within fashion design practice. Current fashion and cultural theorists acknowledge the relationship between the body and dress as an embodied practice and discuss the social, dressed, or "fashioned" body in the context of the present world in which we live. While these are valuable perspectives, they don't fully represent the complicated relationship between the material, the "spiritual" and the philosophical, or the body, soul, and dress within the wider system of fashion. Throughout fashion theory, many scholars reference the Cartesian split as being problematic in their recognition of the disconnect between interior/exteriority. This disconnect between body and soul warrants further discussion, and in this chapter, I hope to offer a more integrated approach that seeks to reconcile these seemingly disparate domains.

It is important to state from the outset that I am neither a religious scholar nor a theologian. My approach in this chapter is that of a lay practitioner, fashion studies scholar, and design practitioner seeking to integrate Reformed Protestant theologies of the body and soul with contemporary fashion theories of subjectivity. I argue that religious belief fundamentally changes one's perception and experience of the situated practice of being and having a "dressed" body in the present and future tense. As a research practitioner who embraces belief in the supernatural and the natural world this impacts one's concept of the earthly body, soul, and ergo dress. From this perspective, I aim to present an integrated approach via a fashion-dress-embodied soul model that offers a more unified view of present embodiment, alongside an inclusive framework that seeks to represent the future states of dress, bodies, and environments. I will utilize the term "embodied soul" versus body/soul throughout the text as I feel this represents the human being and personhood from a unified standpoint as a totality versus body and soul as separate entities, which is central to my position.

What Are We Dressing—The Body or the Soul?

This question may appear to be somewhat of an oxymoron, given the platonic legacy of the hierarchical relationship between these two entities—one that elevates the immortal soul over the lowly, material body thwarted by death. However, the reconciliation of these two entities is critical if we are to navigate beyond the perceived ontological assumptions about the embodied practice of materiality (body/soul & dress) in the context of fashion, and if we are to have any hope at moving beyond the issues associated with their disconnect that complicates the relationship between the body, dress, and identity.

The eighteenth-century English essayist William Hazlitt cautions: "Those who make their dress a principal part of themselves, will, in general, become of no more value than their dress" (1818). However, three centuries later the capacity of clothing to communicate the deepest sense of ourselves or indeed to become part of us is a recurring theme within the discourse of fashion studies and material culture. For example, a quick Google search of the question "Can clothing tell us who we are?" yields 5,490,000,000 responses in a matter of seconds with articles running the gamut declaring, "You are what you dress!" "Our clothes can change who we are," or asking if the clothing we wear reflects what is inside us. These internet articles merely scratch the surface (no pun intended) of the topic from various perspectives—psychological, physiological, or emotional. No matter where you stand in response to this question, it is clear that the discussion of the role clothing plays in communicating who we are to the world around us is ongoing and widespread.

Vogue editor Lynn Yaeger states, "The way that we present ourselves to the world comes from a very deep psychological place. It's hard to know why something looks so right to me that clearly doesn't look right to other people" (Scatturo 2013: 50; Figure 1.1). Memorably, Lady Gaga in her award acceptance speech at the ELLE Women in Hollywood event in October 2018 spoke about her choice to wear a Marc Jacobs menswear suit after trying on multiple designer dresses to no avail. She felt the suit provided the appropriate visual compliment to her message: "This was an oversized men's suit made for a woman. Not a gown . . . In this suit, I felt like me today, I felt the truth of who I am well up in my gut. And then wondering what I wanted to say tonight became very clear to me" (Okwodu 2018; Figure 1.2). When discussing the instincts that led to the creation of his own label during an interview with GQ, fashion designer Thom Browne described his desire and commitment to wearing wool flannel suits in the heat of LA when nobody else was dressing up, explaining that "he wore gray flannel because gray flannel was the way he felt on the inside" (Pappademas 2008). His subsequent adoption of uniform dressing leads to a curated visual identity represented by a wool flannel suit, deliberately crumpled white shirt, skinny tie and cable knit sweater vest edged with the iconic Thom Brown striped ribbon trim (Figure 1.3).

What is the *deep psychological place* that Yaeger refers to when describing the presentation of ourselves to the world? What is this *inside* that Browne speaks of, and why does flannel succeed in communicating this to the outside? Why did the Marc Jacobs suit make Gaga feel like herself? It would appear that clothing helps us articulate the *truth of who we are* that she describes as a physical sensation *welling up in her gut*. In each of these examples, the wearer views clothing as a means to express their internal feelings and sense of themselves to the world, yet we must acknowledge that these Western

The Future Body as Ultimate Dress

Figure 1.1 Fashion editor Lynn Yaeger leaving Anna Sui fashion show during New York Fashion Week, September 11, 2017. Photo by Gilbert Carrasquillo/Getty Images.

examples of celebrity figures represent a particular level of privilege and economic status to do so—one not afforded to everyone. However, the sentiments expressed by Yaeger, Gaga, and Browne reflect the widespread online discussion that points to clothing as the key agent of communication responsible for articulating an inner sense of self. I would argue that they also point to a deeper ontological recognition of the human condition and identity by their use of terms "inside" and "outside," and the sense that (in Gaga's case) what is inside is coming out. This speaks to the idea that clothing can reconcile who we are on the "inside" (soul or self) with the representation of "outer" ourselves (body) to the world.[1] The thoughts articulated by Yaeger, Gaga, and Browne point us back to the ancient platonic dichotomy representing a disconnect between insides and outsides.

In attempting to address this dichotomy of interiority and exteriority, responses from the following three scholars are worth considering. Daniel Miller describes clothing as a kind of "pseudo-language that could tell us about who we are, but questions what and where this real self is that clothing represents that lies deep within us," referring to this

Silhouettes of the Soul

Figure 1.2 Lady Gaga attends ELLE's 25th Annual Women in Hollywood Celebration presented by L'Oréal Paris, Hearts on Fire and CALVIN KLEIN in Beverly Hills on October 15, 2018. Photo by Neilson Barnard/Getty Images for ELLE Magazine.

as something we imagine whether philosophically or via our experience of everyday life (2010: 12–13, 17). He uses the terms "self" and "soul" interchangeably and declares, "we won't find a soul by cutting deep into someone, though I suppose we might accidentally release it" (Miller, Stuff 2010: 12–13, 17). Miller turns to semiotics and the role of objects as signs and symbols that represent us but runs into another issue as he feels the problem with this is that we presume a certain relationship between the interior and exterior. He sees no reason why we should view our "real being" to be deep inside and the falsity on the outside and views this as a cultural construction not an inherent truth. Miller is on to something as I would agree that our "real being" doesn't reside inside of us in the sense that there is this immaterial smaller, yet more important entity residing deep within me that is the "real me."

Malcolm Barnard articulates the relationship between fashion and identity as one of representation; that fashion represents identity, stands for us, or something about us. He acknowledges the commonly held assumption that *who you are*, your personality or

The Future Body as Ultimate Dress

Figure 1.3 Fashion designer Thom Browne poses backstage at the Thom Browne Spring 2016 fashion show during New York Fashion Week. Photo by Mireya Acierto/Getty Images.

identity on the inside, is represented by what you wear on the outside and the assumption that one has an identity that is represented or externalized by what one wears: "It is as though one's identity were self-sufficient, existing without any relation to anything else except the clothes and fashions that represent it on the outside" (Barnard 2014: 91). However, Barnard argues that if something represents something else, then the thing doing the representing (clothing in this case) cannot be the thing that is represented. Susan Kaiser describes this experience of articulating *who we are* through fashion as a collective experience of *becoming*. She acknowledges that this process of expressing who, when, and where is an ongoing challenge: one associated with various ambiguities and contradictions—between the tension between desiring to fit in and express uniqueness within the world, and the ever-changing interplay between freedom and constraints.

> Fashion is not a thing or an essence. Rather, it is a social process of negotiation and navigation through the murky and yet-hopeful waters of what is to come. Fashion involves *becoming* collectively with others. . . . Fashion materializes as

bodies move through time and space. Time and space are both abstract concepts and contexts: the process of deciphering and expressing a sense of who we are (becoming) happens in tandem with deciphering and expressing *when* and *where* we are. (Kaiser 2013: 1)

Cartesian Dualism with its platonic roots is often referenced by theorists as being the main culprit in the mind/body split that subsequently leads to a disconnect when navigating the space between the body and dress.[2] In her chapter "Minding Appearances" in *Body Dressing*, Susan Kaiser asks, "to what extent does my appearance, style represent or create truths about who I am?" She states that linking style, truth, and subjectivity together "seems almost heretical" recognizing that these "age-old questions inevitability frame the interiority of being in opposition to the exteriority of appearing" (Kaiser 2001: 79).[3] Here, these oppositional terms point to an assumption of duality as Kaiser treats "truth" as "knowledge production" that individuals use to negotiate a sense of meaning or purpose with others referencing sociologist, Steven Shapin's term "collective judgment" (1994: 4). She equates style with appearance seeing it not merely as an image but more like a process that becomes a means of entering the discourse of being and becoming in the world. Kaiser notes that the Cartesian split between the mind and the body results in a problematic disconnection between subjectivity and style; that this split results in a devaluation of the body, nature, and inevitably style.

The platonic legacy still holds a preeminent position in thinking about the body and soul relationship. Plato reasoned that the human mind or soul could not be identified with the physical body, and that the mind is a nonphysical and therefore nonspatial substance. Believing that the soul was eternal and exists prior to the body, he viewed the body as the *prison of the soul*, furthering the idea that the primary goal is to escape the material world. Platonic thinking crept into Gnosticism and the early Christian church via Saint Augustine and centuries later found its way into the writings of sixteenth-century French theologian and protestant reformer John Calvin, a principal contributor to the development of the system of reformed theology (later known as Calvinism).[4] Consequently, Christianity absorbed this Cartesian dualistic concept of the body/soul hierarchy into its doctrine (Cooper 2009: 32).

However, I would argue that to continue speaking about "insides" and "outsides," or the body and the soul in platonic separatist terms is problematic from a Christian reformed theological perspective. In Gen. 2:7 the breath of God animates the body to life, and this view of the human being as an embodied soul points to the concept of personhood and the body as a totality not separate entities at odds with one another. The lived embodied experience of the human condition is not one where we can distinguish between this sense of an *inside* and *outside*. I would argue that we are dressing our body and our soul simultaneously when we put on clothing in the present that feels like "us." For example, one might say, "I dressed myself this morning," the simultaneity of this action speaks to the unity of being in this activity. In the next section I will propose an integrated model that demonstrates this simultaneity and the interactive relationship between entities engaged in acts of dress, representation, and identity formation.

Fashion-Dress-Embodied Soul: An Integrated Model

> Our clothes are too much a part of us for most of us to be entirely indifferent to their condition: it is as though the fabric were indeed a natural extension of the body, or even of the soul. (Bell 1976: 19)
>
> Dress in everyday life is always more than a shell, it is an intimate aspect of the experience and presentation of the self and is so closely linked to the identity that these three—dress, the body and the self—are not perceived separately but simultaneously as a totality. (Entwistle 2015: 10)

While still speaking in separatist terms of the body and soul (or self), these two quotes from Quentin Bell and Joanne Entwistle point toward the concept of simultaneity or totality and an integration of entities. The model I seek to present builds on this concept toward uniting the body/soul (embodied soul) in relationship to fashion and dress as interactive agents participating in identity formation and representation. Fashion theorist Carol Tulloch articulates fashion-style-dress as a system of concepts and uses hyphens between each term to propose whole-and-part relationships (361–86). My proposed model follows her nomenclature for the same reasons. She describes style as agency—the construction of self through the assemblage of garments and accessories and views this process of "self-telling" as aiding in further articulation. The *fashion-dress-embodied soul* model of identity I propose is analogous to the structure of the Holy Trinity and speaks to the relationship between these interrelated yet unique entities.

In an attempt to offer a philosophical, speculative framework by which we can view the temporal embodied soul and its relationship to dress and identity within the fashion system, I generated the models in Figures 1.4 and 1.5. Built upon the biblical concept of the Holy Trinity (Father, Son, and Holy Spirit), they represent the relationships between these entities and the totality of the whole. The diagrams are based on the *trinity knot* also called the *Triquetra*.[5] The original design is one of the best-known symbols in Celtic culture, adapted by the Celtic Christian church to represent the Holy Trinity. This form is appropriate to adopt for a fashion context given its reference to the craft of textiles and the symbolism of eternity represented by the *Trefoil* shape created by joining together the two loose ends of a common overhand knot, resulting in a continuous knotted loop. Traditionally, the interlocking pattern signifies the interdependent relationships between Father, Son, and Holy Spirit as three persons of the Godhead.[6]

In the Holy Trinity diagram (shown in Figure 1.4), the "three in one" concept refers not to three parts that together constitute one God (1/3+1/3+1/3 = 1), nor to a God with multiple personalities, but rather to three equal, yet distinctive, persons that together in community act as one entity (Godhead) (1+1+1 = 1). John Frame's pedagogical technique, *triperspectivalism* articulates the roles of each person in the Trinity in the context of a systematic theology of three perspectives of God's lordship over all knowledge (1987). Each perspective takes on a specific role: Father = Normative (Authority—the understanding of the world as a revelation of God, Son = Situational (Accomplisher—understanding of the world as factual situations that God has brought to pass), and the

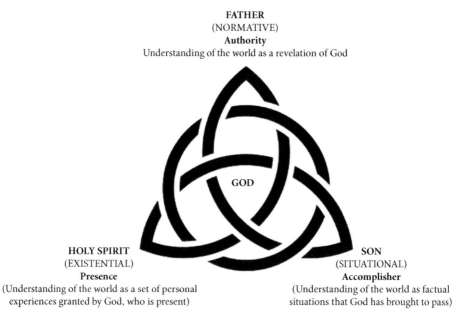

Figure 1.4 Diagram of the Holy Trinity (Father, Son, and Holy Spirit).

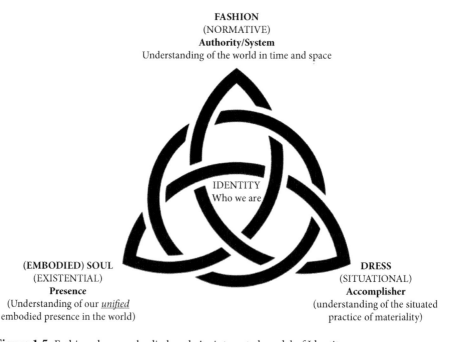

Figure 1.5 Fashion-dress-embodied soul: An integrated model of Identity.

Holy Spirit = Existential (Presence—the understanding of the world as a set of personal experiences granted by God, who is present).

As shown in the comparative diagram in Figure 1.5, fashion represents the normative authority or overarching system correlating to the role the Father and the embodied soul takes on the existential role of our embodied presence in the world with dress as the situational accomplisher or agent that facilitates the process of representing us to the world. Following the model of the Trinity all three entities have unique roles that together contribute to identity formation. The embodied soul and dress work within the system of fashion to contribute to our clothed, social presence in the world. This aligns with current perceptions presented within the discourse but reconciles the disconnect presented by the Cartesian body/soul split in that the concept of the embodied soul offers a unity that is missing. The role of dress as situational accomplisher points to its capacity or agency for reconciliation in the process of representation, navigating between the materiality of our embodied presence in the world within time and space.

Unclothed (Naked): Clothed: Reclothed

From a philosophical standpoint, addressing concerns around the issue of change, Karen Hanson concedes that clothing is in some way a necessity of life, yet acknowledges that for philosophers, uneasiness persists on matters of appearance and describes the perception of the changing modes of dress as "worse than worthless for this serious thinker" (2019: 107–21). Referencing what she calls the "nostalgia for the Eden before self-consciousness" Karen Hanson explains the ongoing frustration we experience in the act of dress: "Clothing is a part of our difficult, post-Edenic lives, and dress, stationed at a boundary between self and other, marking a distinction between private and public, individual and social, is likely to be vexed by the forces of border wars" (2019: 191). She articulates that fashion depends on being recognized, that one is seen, among other things, as an *object* of others' sight, others' cognition. From a Christian position, her remarks resonate with the Creation account, where the first humans in their unclothed state were *seen* by God and lived in complete freedom under the gaze of the divine. The text states: "And the man and his wife were both naked and were not ashamed" (Gen. 2:25, ESV).[7]

Scholar of comparative literature Peter Stallybrass notes, "Nakedness conflates the Edenic state, the shame that follows the Fall, and the moment of expulsion, thus bringing together three moments of time into a single image" (2011: 82, 86). In the Creation account, the sequence of dress moves through three states: unclothed (naked), clothed, and reclothed. In the first instance, humanity is "dressed by God," in Gen. 2:7 when God breathed life into the inanimate (naked) body and it becomes an embodied soul; "then the Lord God formed the man of dust from the ground and breathed into his nostrils the breath of life, and the man became a living creature" (ESV). Second, in Gen. 3:7 after the fall when Adam and Eve make their own coverings, "Then the eyes of both were opened, and they knew that they were naked. And they sewed fig leaves together and made themselves loincloths" (ESV). And lastly, in Gen. 3:21 when God reclothed Adam and Eve, physically covering their shame in nakedness as an act of grace and mercy, "And the Lord God made for Adam and for his wife garments of skins and clothed them." Stallybrass reminds us that throughout the Middle Ages an iconographic tradition existed of depicting God's reclothing of Adam and Eve, "From the church fathers to the Reformation and counter-Reformation, it was God's reclothing of Adam and Eve, not the fig leaves behind which Adam and Eve previously hid, that was the primary focus of biblical exegesis" (2011: 83).

It is important to distinguish the initial act of covering as a response to shame versus one of modesty. Emmanuel Mounier states that modesty can be articulated as meaning my body (physical) turned toward the world (social) (1989: 79). In shame, existence is disclosed in its nothingness; it's being held captive by the gaze which sees the human in its body as nothing more than a function of its need. Biblical scholar Felix Ó Murchadha states that it is only through the fall that the human feels itself naked, because it is only then that the difference between sarx (parts or flesh) and soma (the whole body) arises (2013: 147). In its dress the human being conceals its corporeal self in its fullness from the world. Shame, then, is feeling the lack of worth in relation to an imperious gaze, which lays claim to the whole of the human. It is overcome not primarily through a reversal of the transcending act of the other's gaze but by a reassertion of modesty through the (literal or metaphorical) covering of oneself in clothes (Ó Murchadha 2013: 37). Clothing, then, in the context of the fall takes on the dual role of covering both the inner condition of shame brought on by the realization of the naked state of being and the external physical reality of nakedness itself. From a biblical perspective, this accounts for the ongoing quest to reconcile interiority and exteriority of being and offers context to the role of clothing in this activity.

From a contemporary perspective, Anne Hollander describes the relationship between the corruptibility of the body in relationship to the corruptibility of nakedness post-fall like this: "For Christians the corruptibility of the body, dressed or undressed lies in its fragile susceptibility to decay and sin, but the special corruptibility of nakedness among naturally clothed humans lies in its readiness to seem not only erotic but weak, ugly, or ridiculous" (1993: 84). She states that no matter how creative we are in clothing's conception, it is always "less beautiful than the sacred living body it conceals; or as a protective and deceptively beautiful cloak, required to hide man's wretched original state, which had been perfect, but became shameful after his fall" (Hollander 1993: 85). Hollander's comments point to the incomplete capacity of clothing in a temporal sense to compensate for the break between what we conceive of as an internal sense of being and the perpetual need to represent and reconcile this to the world around us.

In his seminal work, *Ways of Seeing*, John Berger proposes that nudity itself is a form of clothing: "To be nude is to be seen naked by others and yet not recognized for oneself. . . . To be on display is to have the surface of one's own skin, the hairs of one's own body turned into a disguise which, in that situation, can never be discarded. The nude is condemned to never being naked. Nudity is a form of dress" (1972: 54). Berger's concept points us back to the creation narrative and our original state, before shame entered and nakedness was not seen as "being on display." In the fall, humans moved from an incorruptible to a corruptible state; from naked to clothed; from immortal embodiment to embodied mortality. Clothing, post-fall with the body now imbued with death and decay, took on the role of representation for the first time—left with the task of reconciling borders as Hanson suggests between self and other. Perhaps this is what we feel when attempting to assimilate this activity when dressing ourselves or communicating ourselves to others via our dress practice. The temporal act of dress here and now is often filled with frustration as we attempt to reconcile these two entities: body and soul (or self). It is incomplete and often anxiety-producing for many people. However, in the moments when we feel most "like ourselves" (whether in layers of petticoats, a man's suit or wool flannel) is when all the entities are working together in collaboration: fashion-dress-embodied soul. We feel momentarily "complete," but the feeling is elusive and the process of achieving this seems relentless.

From the believer's perspective, there is an acknowledgment that clothing in the temporal world will never make us feel truly like ourselves, only God can complete or "dress" us in the ultimate sense. For the Christian there is the promise of the restoration to come—a renewal of all things—not only of the earth itself but of our own physical body and identity. The incorruptible, glorious state of perfection we seek in the present is attainable in the future when we "put on" the future body.

The Future Body as (Ultimate) Dress

The proposed Christian theological framework of embodiment shown in Figure 1.6 represents three states of "dress" (naked, clothed, and more fully clothed), bodies (physical, social, and future or "spiritual"), environments (human, world, and "heaven on earth") in time present and future. The domains circled represent areas yet to be addressed in the current discourse. In 1 Cor. 15:53-54, the apostle Paul provides us with an exposition of two different types of bodies, the *present body*, corruptible, decaying, and doomed to die, and the *future body*, incorruptible, undecaying, never to die again.

> For this perishable body must put on the imperishable, and this mortal body must put on immortality. When the perishable puts on the imperishable, and the mortal puts on immortality, then shall come to pass the saying that is written: "Death is swallowed up in victory."

The language of physicality challenges our sense of what we perceive to be matter or immaterial, real or unreal. Here we begin to grasp the idea that the body we inhabit now is perishable and mortal and, in that sense, less material or less physical than the imperishable/immortal one promised to believers in the future.

Awaiting the New Body | 2 Cor. 5:1-4

> For we know that if the *earthly tent (skēnos)* we live in is destroyed, we have a *building (oikodomē) from God*, an *eternal house (oikia) in heaven*, not built by human hands.

Silhouettes of the Soul

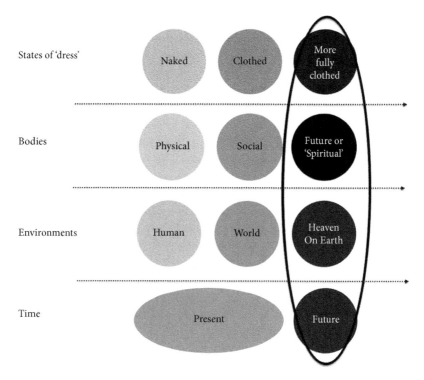

Figure 1.6 A Christian theological framework of embodiment.

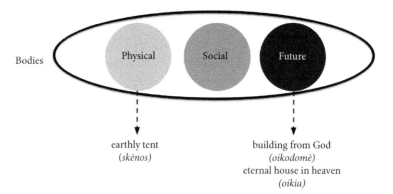

Figure 1.7 Three bodies (physical, social, and future). The Greek term *skēne* (or masculine *skēnos*) for (earthly) *tent* in 2 Cor. 5:1 and 5:4 translates the Old Testament Hebrew term *ōhel* to refer to a temporary or mobile tent. It is permanent in the sense that it serves as a home or house, but not in terms of its material structure. This is especially true in contrast to *baît*, "house," which primarily has the meaning of home or family, but, when it refers to a physical dwelling, it denotes a building that is made of more durable materials than a tent.

The Future Body as Ultimate Dress

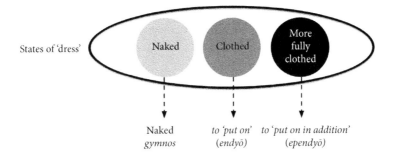

Figure 1.8 Three states of "dress" in 2 Cor. 5:1-4.

> Meanwhile we groan, longing to be *clothed instead (ependyō "put on in addition")* with our heavenly dwelling, because *when we are clothed (endyō "put on"), we will not be found naked (gymnos).*

> For while we are in this tent, we groan and are burdened, because *we do not wish to be unclothed but to be clothed instead (ependyō "put on in addition") with our heavenly dwelling*, so that what is mortal may be swallowed up by life. (Emphasis added by author)

According to biblical scholar Luis Iván Martínez-Toledo, Paul applied the verbs ἐνδύω *(endyō) to "put on"* and ἐπενδύω (ependyō), to *"put on* in addition" to earthly or heavenly habitations as illustrated in Figures 1.7 and 1.8 (2016: 1–3). There is an implicit change from one to another; moreover, v. 4 seems to parallel the habitations with death or life, in this case death being swallowed up by life, as inferring that one garment or habitation is being changed for another. The references to different habitations show that the issue refers to two physical natures, one before *ependyō* and the other after. Here, Martínez-Toledo provides us with theological underpinnings for the meaning and use of the term "nakedness" found in this passage—the Greek term Ὑυμνός (*gymnos*) is commonly translated as "naked" in 2 Cor. 5:3 and has been understood to refer to the state of the human being between death and resurrection. Martínez-Toledo states that in this passage Paul is focusing on the change from one existence into another, through the hope provided by the resurrection of Jesus. Nakedness for him is an "undesirable absence of a house" (Martínez-Toledo 2016: 39).

Similarly, New Testament scholar N. T. Wright comments that where Paul speaks of the new *tent* or *tabernacle* that is waiting for us, he is referring to the new "house," dwelling, a new body, waiting within God's sphere ("heaven"), ready for us to put it on over the present one so that what is mortal may be swallowed up with life.[8] He acknowledges that this concept requires Westerners to make a huge leap of the imagination and that it also requires us to be open to new interpretations of materiality beyond platonic concepts:

> We have taken for granted Plato's ontological contrast between "spirit" in the sense of something immaterial and "matter" in the sense of something material,

solid, physical. We think we know that solid objects are one sort of thing and ideas or values or spirits are a different sort of thing. We know that bodies decay and die; and so, we assume that to be bodily, to be physical, is to be impermanent, changeable, transitory, and that the only way to be permanent, unchanging, and immortal is to become nonphysical. (Wright 2008: 153)

Wright emphatically states that Paul's point here is not so. The dominant cosmology of his day was Stoic rather than platonic, and he posits that what Paul is asking us to imagine is that there will be a new mode of physicality, which stands in relation to our present body as our present body does to a ghost.[9] It will be much more real, more solid, more *bodily* than our present body. Wright states that what Paul is suggesting here is that a Christian in the present life is a mere shadow of their *future* self. Essentially, this will be a new state of incorruptible physicality. For the scholar and layperson alike the concept and language are challenging to understand. Here, the "spiritual" body does not mean we will be shadows or immaterial spirits; but rather, "spiritual" is a suggestion about what will be animating our bodies—namely the Holy Spirit.[10] Wright admits that this new mode of embodiment is hard to describe and proposes a new label for it—*transphysical*:

The early Christians envisaged a body which was still robustly physical but also significantly different from the present one. If anything, we might say *not that it will be less physical*, as though it were some kind of ghost or apparition, but more. *Not unclothed, but more fully clothed*. (Wright 2003: 477; emphasis added by author)

Here, for believers, we begin to see more articulated language around three states of embodiment; "unclothed," "clothed," and "more fully clothed" that challenges us to invert our conception of physical embodiment and our everyday experience of the physical world. Wright suggests from a close interpretation of the text that what we are experiencing now on earth is less physical than what is to come in the future in terms of bodies or the world we will one day inhabit as believers.

More Fully Clothed

Viktor and Rolf's Autumn/Winter '99 Couture show entitled *Russian Doll* (on view at the Met's Heavenly Bodies Exhibition in 2018) offers us a visual representation of the concept presented by Wright of the future body being "more fully clothed." In the original performance by Viktor and Rolf the model Maggie Rizer stood on a rotating platform dressed by the duo in successive layers of clothing similar to the stacking nature of Matryoshka dolls.[11] Viktor comments, "Transformation is always a very important word in our world, and we try to express transformation in different ways. That was one way of playing with that idea" (Bateman 2017). After the performance, Viktor and Rolf equated the care and devotion they lavished upon Rizer as a form of icon worship.

The Future Body as Ultimate Dress

Figure 1.9 Dress from Viktor and Rolf's "Russian Doll" Autumn/Winter '99 couture collection, on display at the "Heavenly Bodies" exhibition at the Met Cloisters, New York, September 2018 Gallery View, Romanesque Hall. Image: © The Metropolitan Museum of Art.

For our purposes, this performative act of fashion is symbolic on two levels: first, for the representative stages of embodiment that correlate to the various "clothed" states we encountered in the Corinthian texts and second, from the perspective of the materiality itself. Viktor and Rolf's use of burlap is intriguing, for the basic sheath dress Rizer wears in the first look, one could argue, points to a state of "nakedness" in both the simplicity of the unadorned silhouette and in its materiality. Subsequent layers utilize increasingly more elaborate fabrication and embellished techniques—moving from lace to sparkling rhinestones to encrusted paisley motifs on linen to silk beaded appliqué. The scale of clothing builds throughout, with the last three garments almost swallowing Rizer's diminutive frame entirely; the shoulders rise dramatically, reaching her ears and in the end the clothing wears the subject—superseding her body. In the penultimate piece (Figure 1.9), the humble linen covered in rhinestones is elevated to a more glorious state via its materiality, that one could argue represents the transition from the corruptible mortal body to the future, glorious, eternal body.

Concluding Comments

This chapter has attempted to address a series of dichotomies: first, the hierarchy and disconnect between the body and soul; second, the ongoing navigation between interiors and exteriors, as well as the tension between clothing and its role in the representation of identity. By writing from the dual positions of faith and fashion, my goal is to present an integrated perspective from this simultaneous vantage point in order to offer a unique perspective on the topic of body, dress, and soul—one that seeks to revisit and re-situate ancient beliefs in a contemporary context, responding to existing themes across the field of fashion studies, philosophy, and material culture.

The integrated model of *fashion-dress-embodied soul* is offered in response to the problematic Cartesian split referenced by many theorists across the discourse on dress and the body. The Trinitarian comparison provides us with descriptors for the roles each entity plays in relationship to the other as a collective, not unlike the terms Kaiser utilized in speaking of the collective act of "becoming." This model speaks to the activity and role of clothing in a universal sense, regardless of one's position on religious belief. Clothing as communication and representation is widely recognized and experienced by anyone who engages in the daily act of dressing.

In its role of situational accomplisher clothing acts both temporally and temporarily to reconcile the disconnection one feels between this sense of the "inside" versus the "outside" articulated by Yaeger, Gaga, and Browne as "real me" inside and the "social me" outside. I would argue that the deep psychological place referenced by Yaeger points to a recognition of an integrated sense of embodiment that is reconciled in the concept of the embodied soul.

In terms of the concept of the future body as ultimate dress, this builds on ideas expressed by contemporary scholars (most prominently Berger) that nudity can be considered as a form of dress. I posit that the future, glorious body the believer "puts on" is the ultimate "eternal" form of dress; and that subsequently, clothing in the interim is attempting to achieve what God will do ultimately. To be unclothed, seen, and not ashamed one could argue is the ideal state of being and embodiment that is not yet (fully) possible here on earth. To be fully clothed in our nakedness, in our subjectivity in the presence and under the gaze of the divine creator then, could be considered as the ultimate dress for the embodied soul.

Notes

1. While I recognize that for many the term "self" may be interchangeable for the "soul," for the purposes of this chapter I will differentiate "self" as a secular term used in the context of oneself in relationship to the world.

2. Dualism is an ancient concept that was deeply rooted in Greek thought. Plato and Aristotle reasoned that the human mind or soul could not be identified with the physical body and holds that the mind is a nonphysical—and, therefore, nonspatial—substance. Rene Descartes (1641) reinforced this concept and gave it a name, dualism. The word "Cartesius" is the Latin form of the name Descartes, hence the term "Cartesian Dualism."

3. The term "subjectivity" is a central philosophical concept related to consciousness, agency, personhood, reality, and truth and refers to an individual being a "subject," one who possesses conscious experiences, such as perspectives, feelings, beliefs, and desire. This entity has agency or meaning that it acts upon or wields power over another entity (an *object*).

4. Gnosticism (after *gnôsis*, the Greek word for "knowledge" or "insight") is the name given to a loosely organized religious and philosophical movement that flourished in the first and second centuries CE. https://www.iep.utm.edu/gnostic/

5. The *Triquetra* was originally used to symbolize and honor the Mother, Maiden, and Crone of the neo-pagan triple goddess. It signifies the three life cycles of a woman in relation to the phases of the moon.

6. The term "person" in this instance refers to the use within the biblical text of the three components of the trinity: God the Father, God the Son, and God the Holy Spirit as personified beings or entities.

7. The English Standard Version of the Holy Bible is used as it adheres to an "essentially literal" translation philosophy, taking into account the differences of grammar, syntax, and idiom between current literary English and the original text. It is the preferred translation for these reasons among many reformed denominations.

8. The tabernacle refers to the portable dwelling of Yahweh (God). It was used by the children of Israel from the Exodus from Egypt until the conquest of Canaan/entering into the Promised Land. Moses received instruction from God at Mt. Sinai on its construction and transportation (Exodus 25–31 and 35–40).

9. Stoicism is an ancient Greek school of Hellenistic philosophy founded at Athens by Zeno of Citium in early third century BC. The school taught that virtue, the highest good, is based on knowledge; the wise live in harmony with the divine Reason (also identified with Fate and Providence) that governs nature and are indifferent to the vicissitudes of fortune and to pleasure and pain.

10. For the majority of Christian denominations, the Holy Spirit or Holy Ghost is the third person (hypostasis) of the Trinity: the Triune God manifested as God the Father, God the Son, and God the Holy Spirit.

11. The traditional set of wooden Matryoshka Russian nesting dolls decreases in size and stacks inside one another. Viktor and Rolf employed this technique in the reverse in their performance of dressing model Maggie Rizer in ever-increasing layers of clothing to symbolize the consumptive cycle of fashion during their Autumn/Winter '99 Couture show.

References

Barnard, Malcolm (1996), *Fashion as Communication*, Routledge.
Barnard, Malcolm (ed.), (2007), *Fashion Theory, A Reader*, 1st ed., London: Routledge.
Barnard, Malcolm (2014), *Fashion Theory: An Introduction*, 1st ed., London: Routledge.
Bateman, Kristen (2017), "How Viktor & Rolf Interrogated Consumption Through Couture," *AnOther.com*, January 3. http://www.anothermag.com/fashion-beauty/9370/how-viktor-and-rolf-interrogated-consumption-through-couture (accessed March 3, 2019).
Bell, Quentin (1976), *On Human Finery*, London: Hogarth Press.
Berger, John (1972), *Ways of Seeing*, London: Penguin.
Entwistle, Joanne (2015), Addressing the Body, *The Fashioned Body: Fashion, Dress and Modern Social Theory*, Cambridge: Cambridge University Press.
Frame, John M. (1987), *The Doctrine of the Knowledge of God, (A Theology of Lordship)*, P & R Publishing.
Hanson, Karen (1990), "Dressing Down Dressing Up-The Philosophic Fear of Fashion," *Hypatia*, 5(2), Feminism and Aesthetics (Summer, 1990), 107–21. Published by Wiley on Behalf of Hypatia, Inc.

Hazlitt, William (1818), *"On the Clerical Character,"* in *Political Essays with Sketches of Public Characters*, London: Printed for W. Hone.

Hollander, Anne (1993), *Seeing Through Clothes*, University of California Press.

Kaiser, Susan (2001), "Minding Appearances: Style, Truth, and Subjectivity," in Joanne Entwistle and Elizabeth Wilson (eds.), *Body Dressing*, 79–102, London: Berg

Kaiser, Susan B. (2013), *Fashion and Cultural Studies*, London: Berg.

Martínez-Toledo, Luis Iván (2016), *The Naked State of Human Being, The Meaning of Gymnos in 2 Corinthians 5:3 and its Theological Implications*, Wipf & Stock.

Miller, Daniel (2010), *Stuff*, Cambridge and Malden, MA: Polity.

Mounier, Emmanuel. *Personalism*, University of Notre Dame Press, 1989.

Okwodu, Janelle (2018), "In an Oversized Suit, Lady Gaga Delivers a Powerful Speech," *Vogue.com*, October 16. https://www.vogue.com/article/lady-gaga-marc-jacobs-suit-women-in-hollywood-event

Ó Murchadha, Felix (2013), *A Phenomenology of Christian Life, Glory and Night*, Indiana University Press.

Pappademas, Alex (2008), "Designer of the Year: The Incredible Suit-Shrinking Man," *GQ.com*, November 1. https://www.gq.com/story/designer-of-the-year-thom-browne-menswear

Scatturo, Sarah (2013), "Fashion Criticism as Political Critique: An Interview with Lynn Yaeger On Fashion Criticism," *Fashion Projects*, 4: 47–54.

Shapin, Steven (1994), *A Social History of Truth*, The University of Chicago Press.

Stallybrass, Peter (2011), "Visible and Invisible Letters, Text Versus Image in Renaissance England and Europe," in Marija Dalbello and Mary Shaw (eds.), *Visible Writings, Cultures, Forms and Readings*, Rutgers University Press.

Tulloch, Carol (2015), "Style-Fashion-Dress: From Black to Post-black," *Fashion Theory* 14(3): 273–303.

The Bible, New International and English Standard Versions. Various Publications.

Wright, N. T. (2003), *The Resurrection of Son of God, Vol 3: Christian Origins and the Question of God*, Minneapolis, MN: Fortress Press.

Wright, N. T. (2008), *Surprised by Hope, Rethinking Heaven, the Resurrection, and the Mission of the Church*, New York: Harper Collins Publishers.

CHAPTER 2
NO ONE CAN TELL
ON THE SILENT GLAMOUR OF MEHER BABA
Nicola Masciandaro

Silence is the element in which great things fashion themselves together; that at length they may emerge, full-formed and majestic, into the daylight of Life.

—Professor Diogenes Teufelsdröckh

Divinity is not devoid of humanity. Spirituality must make man more human. It is a positive attitude of releasing all that is good, noble and beautiful in man. It also contributes to all that is gracious and lovely in the environment.

—Meher Baba

We want selfless design in life.

—Princess Norina Matchabelli

Throughout his dynamic and multiphased life, Meher Baba (1894–1969) used various kinds of dress, both Eastern and Western, and exhibited distinctive manners, most conspicuously his signature pink coat, unique sign language, and 44-year-long silence.[1] In 1929, four years into that silence, Meher Baba commented on the importance of his external style for his spiritual work:

> [M]ark my mode and taste for dressing. I wore that black [kamli] coat with a hundred patches for years. I also wore the chappals until the last moment when their original material had been totally replaced. And now you see that I have had a new coat sewn and wear it with new shoes and stockings, keeping myself well-dressed, spruce, and tip-top—quite the reverse of what I had been doing. And who knows, perhaps I may one day give up all these clothes and remain only in a langoti, or even stark naked! *No one can tell.* Sadgurus and Perfect Masters, even though Realized, have their own ways of living and working. . . . So each one maintains some definite mode for a long time. My style is quite different. I often change my food and attire, and there are reasons behind it. Even this external mode of living has connection with my inner working for the world. (Kalchuri 1985: 1050, my emphasis)

To speak of Meher Baba's style, in the absence of any "definite mode," means especially to attend to his silence and the presence of the spiritual "inner working" for the sake of which it was maintained. As Meher Baba explained to the Dutch filmmaker Louis van

Silhouettes of the Soul

Figure 2.1 Meher Baba, 1925. Public domain image. Public domain image, source: https://commons.wikimedia.org/wiki/File:Meher_Baba_1925.jpg.

Gasteren in 1967, "My outward silence is not a spiritual exercise; it has been undertaken and maintained solely for the good of the world. God has been everlastingly working in silence, unobserved, unheard—except by those who experience his infinite silence" (Kalchuri 1985: 5288).[2]

Focusing on this silence, this chapter will consider Meher Baba's style in order to think fashion in the direction of a divinely inverted selfishness wherein the fashion statement works less to uphold than to undo separative identities, suspending us in a mirror within the silent unity of reality—a no-one-can-tell fashion wherethrough the visible speech of glamour is folded through itself into the intimate horizon of limitless silence that silences no one and is never afraid to speak. At the same time, I am aware of the futility of trying to capture Meher Baba's style in words. As Chanji, Baba's secretary for twenty years, wrote in his diary near the end of his life, "Baba's greatest hold on all is his love. Something indefinable and inexplicable that attracts all to him. . . . What is that subtle charm? . . . None can define nor explain, yet it is a fact of facts!" (Kalchuri 1985: 2389). I hope to show that the silent mystery of Meher Baba's style has everything to do with an extraordinary naturalness, the divine transparency of someone who can truly say, "He who knows everything, displaces nothing. To each one, I appear to be what he thinks I am" (Baba 1957: 3).

Who Am I?

Meher Baba loved to play hide and seek, a silence-requiring game to which he likened "the whole of life . . . in which you must find your real self" (Baba 1971: 179). Analogously, the *je ne sais quoi* quality of his presence was such that he normally concealed himself during his movements, which were frequent and extensive, not to avoid being recognized but *to prevent arousing wonder as to who he is*.[3] As Eruch Jessawala, the lifelong interpreter/translator of Baba's alphabet board and gestures recalls,

> His personality or presence was so arresting that people would single him out amidst the crowds and just stop and gaze at him. So Baba would cover his face with scarves, wear goggles or wear a turban or a felt hat; he would wear the headgear that suited the conditions and fashion of that area. In this way he remained incognito. (Le Page 1978: 17)[4]

Especially telling are Meher Baba's encounters and connections with persons of glamour. In 1933, aboard the *SS Conte Verde*, Meher Baba, failing not to attract interest while out for a walk in Western clothes, was greeted by Sanyogita Devi, the Mahrani of Indore, one of the chicest style icons of her day, famous for her (and her husband's) avant-garde tastes and beauty, as captured in portraits by Bernard Boutet de Monvel and Man Ray.[5] To her Baba explained,

> As I do not wish to meet anyone while outside on deck, I dress like an ordinary man to avoid being recognized. No one knows me as I really am. For those who want to know my Real Self, I have no need to put on such a show. But I am afraid of those who have no longing to know me truly and have to hide my identity from them. (Kalchuri 1985: 1549)

This admission of fear is fascinating in light of the conventional mode of celebrity glamour as the projection of image and not the person as they really are, and thus the need for personal space without the burden of maintaining the image. Meher Baba's concern seems to be precisely the reverse, a desire to be recognized only by individuals with a sincere interest to know him "as I really am," for an encounter in the silent language of the heart, such as Sir Anthony Brooke, after unexpectedly arriving to see Baba in 1965, recalls: "[The] meeting with beloved Baba was quite beyond words. It was the briefest possible, but everything was in it. He is Pure Love" (Kalchuri 1985: 5125).

The no-one-can-tell quality of Meher Baba's presence is reflected most dramatically in the experience of Princess Norina Matchabelli, the celebrated cosmopolitan silent film actress (aka Maria Carmi) and perfume designer for whom, as Anita de Caro observed, "everything . . . had to have style" (Frederick 1983: 17). Speaking of her first meeting with Meher Baba in New York in 1931, Norina wrote,

I doubt whether that experience can be expressed in words. I had heard about him, but I remained skeptical. . . . I entered the room in which Baba was sitting surrounded by followers and disciples. That very moment, an experience began, full of wonder and beauty. Suddenly I had to run across the room and I found myself weeping on the floor at his feet. Weeping, weeping! Oh, how I was weeping! But I also began to laugh, and the streams running down my cheeks and the outbursts of laughter became one. I was resting my head on Baba's hand, and my whole body was shaking with terrific sobs of liberation. Eventually, I quieted down. Baba then took my face between his hands and looked at me for a long time into one of my eyes, and then into the other, and then back into the first eye. Then he spoke to me via the alphabet board. His first words were: "I am man and woman and child. I am sexless." He then paused for a while, brought his face nearer to mine and spelled out, "Have no fear." (Landau 1935: 112)

It was a profound turning point in Norina's life, inwardly and outwardly. As Jean Adriel observed, "The old hauteur of sophistication was replaced by child-like wonder" (Adriel 1947: 17–18).[6] Norina, nicknamed Noorjehan ("Light of the World") by Baba, returned to New York in a black dress, the only one of fifty she did not leave in India, explaining to a reporter, "Once I couldn't sleep on a bed unless it cost a certain price. Now, I turn as a flower toward the sun" (Matchabelli 1997: 23). The silent actress renowned for performing a thousand times a statue of the Virgin Mary that comes to life warmed in the love of one who, in the words of her *Manifesto* (1936), "imparts the Light in Silence and in Action" (Matchabelli 1997: 117), now steps into the heliotropic rhythm of a freer, spontaneous glamour. Abandoning the trappings of elegance only intensifies her elegance, glowing in a speaking silence: "Even her eyes and her hands were vocal" (Landau 1935: 112). As Meher Baba's sister Mani recalled, "she could melt a stone, if it was for Baba" (Irani 1987).

Spelling Silence

The prism of Meher Baba's appearance points to the mystery of style as a gestural power at the boundary of speech and silence, a visible language grounded in the palpable presence of the invisible. As Max Picard writes, "silence is not visible yet its existence is clearly apparent. It extends to the farthest distances, yet is so close to us that we can feel it as concretely as we feel our own bodies" (Picard 1952: 2). Meher Baba's silence, as the primary medium of his supremely active life and "usual lightning speed" (Kalchuri 1985: 932), presents a similar paradox—so natural and close as to pass unseen, so deep and vast as to astonish. Silence is the style of his style, the cloak of his fashion. As C. B. Purdom, Meher Baba's first biographer, observes in *The God-Man*, "Is it not terrifying that Baba should have maintained silence all these nearly forty years? For silence is the abyss, or the very edge of the abyss. In the ordinary way, in silence, we come dangerously near the gap of meaninglessness, in which nothing has a name or a rightful place. To me it is astonishing that a man should look into the darkness so long, and should live; it *shrouds* Baba with the deepest mystery" (Purdom 1964: 413, my italics).

In the world of high fashion, around the mannequin silence of the model, absence of speech serves to foreground appearance, subsume individuality within the cosmopolitan power of a look, and guard the overall spell of *glamour*, which archaically means, as Sir Walter Scott said, "the magic power of imposing on the eyesight of the spectators, so that the appearance of an object shall be totally different from the reality" (Moser 2015: ix).[7] As the mission statement of Silent Models reads, a top New York agency, "Each and every one of our models is carefully selected by our international team, who ensure that each contributes in a significant and unique way to our aesthetic."[8] Here silence is the sound of "glamour labor," the captivated and captivating work of allure—an arachnid silence of enchantments spun in threads of relation, as Otto von Busch observes: "The fashionista is no victim of fashion, no slave, but a subservient and laboring worshipper of sensual esoterrorism with a beast stalking in pleasant guise. . . . The allure, moment pierced, the silent stream of dark webs" (von Busch 2016: 13).

Like *spell* (from **spel-*, "to say aloud, recite"), glamour (cognate with *grammar*), and allure (from **lothran*, "to call") both concern the threshold of speech. Their concepts reflect the nature of fashion's magic as grounded in the silence through which images speak, precisely by being both existent and nonexistent, betweenly outside both subjects and objects, elsewhere.[9] Such is the "grand secret of . . . mirrors," that "every image—a sensate form as such—is *the existence of a form outside of its proper place*" (Coccia 2016: 18). The imaginal topology of fashion, as desire for lovely forms forever out of place (cf. Narcissus), for the ecstasy of being *in* fashion, is bound by the desire for beauty not accidentally or simply because beauty is desirable, but more precisely because beauty fills the space between silence and language: "Images are silent, but they speak in silence. They are a silent language. They stand on the frontier where silence and language face each other closer than anywhere else, but the tension between them is resolved by beauty" (Picard 1952: 80). As every image, speaking in silence, both is and is not, so "Fashion's question is not that of being, but rather it is simultaneously being and nonbeing; it always stands on the watershed of the past and the future and, as a result, conveys to us, at least while it is at its height, a stronger sense of the present than do most other phenomena" (Simmel 1997: 192). The extra presentness of fashion, the newness of its place, is possible only through a silent forgetting or tacit ignoring of the difference between the elsewhereness of images and the otherworldliness of beauty, in other words, the magical illusion—so easily broken—that this extra present moment, rapt in the glow of glamour, is eternal.

As surely in some fashion it is! The divinity of fashion, its putative "timelessness," is a species of negative eternity bearing like a shadow or trace the true presence of the eternal as *actus purus*, the infinite actuality of reality itself. Thus Nietzsche, praising the profound superficiality of the Greeks, calls us back in *The Gay Science* to the paradoxically divine height of appearances: "They knew how to *live*: what is needed for that is to stop bravely at the surface, the fold, the skin; to worship appearance, to believe is shapes, tones, words—in the whole Olympus of appearance!" (Nietzsche 2001: 9). And Meher

Baba: "If you don't want to be old before you really ought to become old, be cheerful in deed, thought, word and in appearance—*most of all in appearance*.... It is a divine art to look always cheerful. It is a divine quality. It helps others" (Duce 1975: 625, my italics). Fashion is forever, temporally eternal and eternally temporary, an irreplaceable medium whereby the world never ceases renewing itself in ways we can never properly anticipate.

Highest of the High Fashion

In the atmosphere of Meher Baba's silence, withholding of speech indexes an unaccountable and hyper-relational order of fashion, the style of an absolute identity, of the One who is and tells all: "I tell you all with my Divine authority, that you and I are not 'We,' but 'One'" (Purdom 1964: 223). This silence is also the sound of a labor, not of absorption into an aesthetic but of an all-inclusive behind-the-scenes universal activity which connects inner and outer, apparent and hidden: "I speak eternally. The voice that is heard deep within the soul is my voice, the voice of inspiration, of intuition, of guidance. Through those who are receptive to this voice, I speak" (Kalchuri 1985: 5288). Indeed the overall energy, attentiveness, and expressiveness of Meher Baba's activity and manner, all the ways he communicated without speaking, often gave the impression that he did, and there are many stories of people who "hardly noticed he was silent,"[10] just as Baba himself said, "How can I be silent? I don't speak with my tongue. I speak continuously with my heart" (Frederick 1963: 21).[11]

The triple form which Bachelard identifies as the substance of the Nietzschean life, "cold, silence, height [*hauteur*]—three roots for the same substance" (Bachelard 1943: 161), is mirrored in the cold silence of high fashion and, more approachably, in the *coolness* of style.[12] Meher Baba also elevated himself in a sense, claiming to be neither an ordinary human being nor a holy man, but the avatar (from *avatāra* "descent") or God-Man who age after age *descends*, "suffer[ing] Himself to be persecuted and tortured, to be humiliated and condemned by humanity for whose sake His Infinite Love has made Him stoop so low, in order that humanity, by its very act of condemning God's manifestation in the form of Avatar should, however indirectly, assert the existence of God in His Infinite Eternal state" (Natu 1984: 106). And this descent, of course, is no less an elevation of the human into the divine: "You say to yourselves, 'How can I, a lowly human, be God Himself.' You are afraid of the very idea that you are God! But it is a fact" (Kalchuri 1985: 649). At the same time, Meher Baba's identity took the form of a kind of divinely playful distance from himself. Months after his first public declaration, in 1954, of being the avatar, he stated, "I asked myself whether I was the Avatar, and the clear and definite answer was, 'Yes, I am the Ancient One, the Highest of the High'" (Kalchuri 1985: 3620). So of "Meher Baba," given by his early disciples, Baba said that "my name is more powerful than I am!" (Arjani 2015). From this supremely human position of descended divinity, as the living conscious presence of ordinary unconscious divinity, Meher Baba warmly refused to hold himself apart from anyone: "To me saint and sinner, high and low, rich and poor, man and woman, young and old are all just the same. Why?

Because I am in everyone. No one should hesitate to embrace me and to meet me with all love" (Kalchuri 1985: 4301).

Let us compare the silence of high fashion to that of the Highest of the High. The silence of the former promises to elevate identity via participation in a transhistorical cultural medium that elitely speaks for it, as if selecting the subject from the noisy crowd of so many who are not so destined: "Not only is the consumer going to be reborn into a higher personal manifestation, but as the narcissist L'Oreal slogan goes, it is "because I'm worth it" (and implicitly that means others are not). With each new fashion I am reborn, reincarnated into a higher form; more pure, more perfect. And only I am truly worth it" (von Busch 2018: 71).[13] The silence of the latter, working to liberate one from illusory phenomena of births and deaths, reverberates with the imminent emergence of the divinity within *every* subject: "When I break my silence, the impact of my love will be universal and all life in creation will know, feel and receive of it. It will help every individual to break himself free from his own bondage in his own way. I am the Divine Beloved who loves you more than you can ever love yourself" (Purdom 1964: 344). The silence of the former is an invisibility whose presence tends toward disappearance, neither extending "to the farthest distances" nor felt concretely "as we feel our own bodies" but rather compressed and woven into the luminosity of the glamorous image or event whose texture and effect the breaking of silence threatens to unravel: "When models break their silence, their testimonies 'dispel' glamour as a carefully crafted fiction" (Soley-Beltran 2012: 115). Moreover, insofar as silent models and their images exist as aesthetic selections, their silence (as emblematized in the photo chosen for its perfectly parted/pouting mouth) echoes with the virtual noise of a sea of counter-actualities, just as every attempt at sprezzatura or spontaneous naturalness is haunted by its own intentionality and artifice. But the silence of the latter, of One beyond number, is absolutely natural, being identical with the true and actual silence of all images and identities, in unity with the essential unspeakability of the real self in all, the one only the breaking of *that* silence will reveal: "I am the Ancient One. When I break my silence, the world will know who I am. Let us play now!" (Kalchuri 1985: 4001). This may also explain why it is impossible to find a bad photo of Meher Baba, because no camera ever caught him talking. High fashion silence promises itself to remain unbroken, but never does, always breaking its promise. Highest of the High fashion silence promises to break itself, yet never does, paradoxically keeping its promise alive by not keeping it, by letting the promise itself forever speak.

The difference is felt. In contrast to the austere silence of the fashion exemplar, whose affect is characteristically cold—"Style is a wave of frozen silence, the lamentation caused by the mating of humanity and eternity" (Sato Sato 2016: 21)[14]—Meher Baba's silence flows with the sweetness of a being who stands freely at the center of all activity, inside and outside of time, who *holds the line* of the true boundary of all human talk:

> If you were to ask me why I do not speak, I would say I am not silent, and that I speak more eloquently through gestures and the alphabet board. If you were to ask me why I do not talk, I would say, mostly for three reasons. Firstly, I feel that

through you all I am talking eternally. Secondly, to relieve the boredom of talking incessantly through your forms, I keep silence in my personal physical form. And thirdly, all talk in itself is idle talk. Lectures, messages, statements, discourses of any kind, spiritual or otherwise, imparted through utterances or writings, is just idle talk when not acted upon or lived up to. (Kalchuri 1985: 3555–6)

In considering the fashion/silence intersection, we must always keep in mind the kind and degree of activity that moves through it, remembering that the nature of one's appearance or *species* is itself vital to existence, that "living beings could almost be defined as the entities that constitute themselves in the medium of [self-presentation]" (Coccia 2016: 80).[15] In turn, self-presentation has everything to do with how one speaks and how one is silent, with the design of the heart which appears, however worn, on your sleeve.

All Are Me and I Am You

One of the most salient aspects of Meher Baba's style of action was the deep sensitivity and sheer human warmth of his presence. An illustrative anecdote is provided by Don Stevens in his introduction to *God Speaks*: "God has never spoken to me, but I am sure that I have seen Him act in human form. That is the only manner in which I can explain the incredible sensitivity of action and reaction which characterized Meher Baba during those brief periods on a Saturday afternoon in New York when I first saw him in action" (Baba 1973b: xi). He goes on to describe how, in the midst of a busy and changing scene, Baba inexplicably mirrored a hand gesture (the circular sign of perfection) which Don had made three times outside of Baba's line of sight, confirming in each instance his responding gesture with a more direct gaze, expressing his awareness of Don also when his back was turned. Far beyond the apparent magic, the moment indexes Meher Baba's "complete ability not only to understand but, in some manner, to *be* one's own self" (Baba 1973b: xii). So *God Speaks*, which Meher Baba dictated letter by letter in silence "to appease the intellectual convulsions of the mind of man" and dedicated "To the Universe—the Illusion that sustains Reality," begins: "All souls (*atmas*) were, are and will be in the Over-Soul (*Paramatma*). Souls (*atmas*) are all One. All souls are infinite and eternal. They are formless" (Baba 1973b: 1, 190). In the formless light of infinite individuality, all forms reflect each other. Or as Ibn Arabi says, "O marvel! a garden amidst fires! / My heart has become capable of every form" (Arabi 1911: 67).

Here we find a supreme form of "*fanera* . . . the secret capacity of every animal to transform its nature into fashion, to overturn its own substance into mannerism" (Coccia 2016: 81), a manner so divinely and lovingly complete that it gives itself to the other as the sensitivity of one's own infinite self. Far beyond his charm, Meher Baba's style is one that awakens into unfathomable affective unity seer and seen, as in an infinite mirror of recognition: "You and I remain divided by no other veil than you yourself, that is, the 'I' in you" (Baba 1969: 63). How to tell the silent power of style to spell this unity, to reveal in the reflection of vision the fact of oneself as veil of the one in all? The answer lies somewhere in the *being* of the image as that which binds from within externally appearing subjects or bodies. "[F]ashion acts simultaneously as a prosthesis of the imagination and a physical extension of the body" (von Busch and Hwang 2018: 16), a medium wherethrough seeing and being seen interface and play each other's position around the simultaneously extro- and intromissive energy of the *look*. Sounding the depth of this specularity, Meher Baba's look effects a gravitational order of attraction free from the duality of acceptance/rejection, one where the winner and loser of the fashion gamble both win because each is no less lost to the unitary play of life: "Is it anybody's fault if one finds oneself on the right side of things or the wrong side of things? No! Every human being has come to serve and achieve a definite purpose, and by playing his part to perfection he automatically works out his own salvation" (Baba 1972: 3).

Soul at Play

Given that fashion is a gamble, a game in which "my sense of self changes as it is set to play, from the deep body-schema of proprioception to the socialized ideal self" (von Busch and Hwang 2018: 55), the whole game itself is forever open to be being played on par with life and gambled upon its ultimate horizon. There is no threshold separating fashion's game from the impossible and inevitable limit where becoming what you are converges with being God: "When the soul comes out of the ego-shell and enters into the infinite life of God, its limited individuality is replaced by unlimited individuality. The soul knows that it is God-conscious and thus preserves its individuality" (Baba 1973a: II.174). The unboundedness of fashion, the impossibility of saying where fashion begins or ends, is of a piece with the divine unity of life and the correlative interconnectedness of all things: "there is no unbridgeable gulf separating the finer aspects of nature from its gross aspect. They all interpenetrate one another and exist together" (Baba 1973a: III.55). More specifically, there is no definitive separation in the sensible life of beings between clothing and embodiment: "Clothing does not stand opposite the body. It is merely a second or minor body, in the same way that the organic body, according to ancient Platonic theology, is the first clothing of the soul. . . . The anatomical body and clothing . . . are two poles of the same reality" (Coccia 2016: 92). Likewise there is no limit to the life of fashion, which is interwoven with the evolution of individualized consciousness or the soul as it undertakes the endless adventure of realizing itself via identification and disidentification with innumerable forms. As Krishna tells Arjuna on the battlefield, "Just as you throw out used clothes / and put on other clothes, new ones, / the Self discards its used bodies / and puts on others that are new" (*Bhagavad Gita* 2000: 2.22). The universe is a fashion show.

The more fashion penetrates technically into anatomical bodies, the more visible and actualized this ancient analogy becomes, above all in the imaginal sphere wherein the "boundary, ostensibly dividing body and clothing, is permanently dissolved" (de Perthuis 2008: 176). In this present age where, as Baba says, "the mirror literally and figuratively has become such a seemingly indispensable part of modern life" and "the best that most can do is to try to look the part they play" (Kalchuri 1985: 4350), fashion itself is revealed as a phantasmagoric reflection of the authentic, avataric narcissism of the divine. As Karen de Perthuis observes,

> There can be no doubt as to the narcissism of fashion's project: this is an image of fashion incarnate... the synthetic ideal in the fashion photograph is the apotheosis of fashion, and from its deified position it creates an avatar of itself... it turns to itself as the ideal and creates something "nearer to its heart desire." Something that is beyond perfection. (de Perthuis 2008: 180)

Yet to take seriously this insight, to do more than flirt with the terms of fashion's divine, one need follow glamour's glow beyond itself and step boldly into the mirror, beyond fashion's circumscribed—and into its uncircumscribable—*me-ness*: "The fact that God being One, Indivisible and equally in us all, we can be nought else but one, is too much for the duality-conscious mind to accept. Yet each of us is what the other is" (Kalchuri 1985: 3555).

Seeing that "to engage in fashion is to go for a quotidian adventure, challenge the world for a small quake of the soul" (von Busch and Hwang 2018: 23), we must affirm all the more the spiritual infinity of fashion's gamble. The spontaneous power of style is of a piece with the universal nature of life as the play of a divinely sovereign Self for whom quality so rules over quantity such that everything is simultaneously totally expendable and utterly precious:

> Spiritual infinity includes in its scope all phases of life. . . . Being greater than the greatest, spiritual infinity is also smaller than the smallest, and it can equally express itself through happenings irrespective of whether they are outwardly small or great. Thus a smile or a look stands on the same level as offering one's life for a cause. (Baba 1973a: I.168)

Above all, as entities divinely embodied in fashion by the miracle of existence—"Never was there a time / when I did not exist, or you, / or these kings; nor will there come / a time when we cease to be" (*Bhagavad Gita* 2000: II.16)—all are called by the very fact of this embodiment to live fearlessly and honestly in one's best carefree style. As Meher Baba said with reference to a longtime disciple who habitually preferred his old tattered and patched clothes,

> People die in all sorts of ways but it is nothing to be upset about; they are born again and again in different gross bodies. But during one's lifetime, one should do whatever one honestly feels without getting attached to actions. Changing bodies between lifetimes is similar to changing a coat. Some die young . . . some live long lives. They do not change their coats often, like Gustadji. But when Gustadji was with me on the recent trip to the West, he became well dressed and maintained a neat and clean appearance. (Kalchuri 1985: 3163)

The nature of eternal existence is simply such that it demands fashion, fresh styles, new manners of appearing.

The One Who Provokes the Question

In *God Speaks*, Meher Baba explains how the universe and its innumerable forms of life are conceived in a spontaneous question, described as "the original whim of God" or the soul's "first urge to know Itself" (Baba 1973b: 109, 8). It is this infinite impulse, concealed in all experience, that destines every individual to universal self-knowledge, when "the final answer of 'I am God' is obtained to the first word 'Who am I?'" (Baba 1973b: 109). Following suit, Meher Baba's style dramatizes the specular infinity of eternal self-recognition, reflecting the self's own appearing, impossible to pin down, at once the direct evidence its own impossibility and the mirror image of beauty itself, beautifully defined by Simone Weil as "experimental proof that the incarnation is possible" (Weil 1999: 150). With inexplicable sprezzatura, his manner exhibited the divine, sublimely comic proportions of human identity. When asked by Eruch, on behalf of a bewildered group of Baba lovers, how to explain to others who Baba is, Baba was amused and replied, "tell them that when someone asked, 'Who is Meher Baba?' they should reply, 'He is the one who provokes this question in you—the being of all beings'" (Jessawala 1995: 178). Here the paradoxical specularity of spiritual naturalness comes into view, just as a mirror always both never and only lies, pointing both beyond itself and back at the viewer. "The mirror is changeless, immovable and always steady. I, too, am like a mirror. The change you observe is in you—not in me. I am always so constant and still that it cannot be imagined" (Kalchuri 1985: 1062). As mirror between humanity and divinity, Meher Baba wore his own form as fashion, like an image in the universal mirror of cosmic illusion: "All this is imagination and exists only in imagination. What you see physically is not Baba; it is only my body—a mere piece of clothing!" (Kalchuri 1985: 3971). The mysteriously captivating naturalness of Meher Baba's manners and movements is thus no less perceivable as a form of perfect ordinariness, a mere-ness reversely reflected in the fashion-being of the model who comports herself as a simple wearer of clothes and becomes a kind of living image of no one in particular. As top model Clotilde once said, "I am an optical illusion" (Soley-Beltran 2012: 106). But whereas behind the supermodel there lurks (the illusion of) a human being presumably more or less like ourselves, behind Baba's form is something so real one cannot be oneself and see: "I am bliss personified. This five-foot, six-inch physical form you see is not real. If you could see my Real Form, you would not be yourself" (Kalchuri 1985: 1039).

Moving between being the only one present and being totally elsewhere, the trace of Meher Baba's style silently spells out a space for fashion that may be conceived as a kind of *avataric normcore*. Correlatively, Meher Baba set "no precepts"—"I have come not to teach but to awaken. Understand therefore that I lay down no precepts"—and emphasized above all the practice of honesty in the midst of ordinary life: "The best way to cleanse your heart and to prepare for the stilling of the mind is to lead a normal life in the world" (Purdom 1964: 343, 286).[16] In the spirit of Professor Diogenes Teufelsdröckh, the great mystical clothing-philosopher of Thomas Carlyle's *Sartor Resartus* for whom the "beginning of all Wisdom is to look fixedly on Clothes . . . till they become *transparent*" (Carlyle 1831: II.9), any fashion that wakes one to the silence of honesty with oneself and others deserves our everlasting yes.

Notes

1. On Meher Baba's silence and his methods of communication, see Purdom (1964: 407–14), Sanjinés (2014), and Schwartz (2011: 620–5).
2. See also Gasteren's *Beyond Words* (1997) and *Nema Aviona Za Zagreb* (2012), which contain footage of Baba gesturing these words.
3. On Meher Baba's movements, see Fenster (2018), which lists approximately 2,700 trips.
4. Cf. the account of Baba's trip aboard the SS *Conte Rosso* in 1932: "Almost all who saw him wanted to know who he was and insisted upon being told. . . . The ship's Italian stewards, sailors, purser and other officers especially seemed to 'scent' Baba's presence. . . . They vied with one another to render assistance and tried to approach Baba on one pretense or another whenever an opportunity arose. As the voyage continued, in spite of trying to keep Baba's identity a secret, he became known to most of the passengers, officers and crew, who looked at him with a sort of reverence which perhaps they themselves hardly understood or could explain" (Kalchuri 1985: 1549). And concealment may also reveal, intensifying the question of identity by calling attention to its secrecy, making the fashion-play of Meher Baba's incognito presence no less visible as a spiritual hide-and-seek game perfectly suited to spin heads and capture hearts: "That night, Baba went to Monte Carlo with the mandali, Norina, and Elizabeth to see the casinos. Dressed incognito, he looked stunning; wearing a cape of Norina's and a French beret of Mercedes' [de Acosta]" (Kalchuri 1985: 1860–1).
5. See Ganapathi (2018) and Jhala (2018: 147).
6. See also Matchabelli (1997).
7. "The perception of models as 'dumb' or mute objects has been a common theme in scholarly work on visual culture" (Entwistle and Wissinger 2012: 4).
8. https://www.silentmodelsny.com/About
9. Ibn Arabi uses the example of a man looking into a mirror: "He is neither a truth-teller nor a liar in his words, 'I saw my form, I did not see my form.' . . . So the cosmos only became manifest within imagination. It is imagined in itself. So it is, and it is not" (Chittick 1989: 118).
10. https://meherbaba.eu/his-silence/
11. For an explanation of Baba's gestural language and the inimitable style of its expressive flow, see "Mandali Moments: Meher Baba's Gestures," https://www.youtube.com/watch?v=WphnDsCLpDI.
12. See Giacomotti (2017).
13. von Busch (2018).
14. Cf. Brown (2016).
15. Hence, fashion's internal war with being fashionable, the inevitable impossible fight to fashionably free fashion from fashion as such, which only intensifies the problem of

fashionableness as the mode of self-presentation wherein the fact of self-presentation supervenes over its substance, as if breaking the silence of every fashion statement with *I am fashionable*.

16. The former statement is especially important, being the first sentence of Baba's "Universal Message," given in 1958.

References

Adriel, Jean (1947), *Avatar: The Life Story of the Perfect Master Meher Baba: A Narrative of Spiritual Experience*, 2nd ed., Santa Barbara: J. F. Rowny Press.
Arabi, Ibn (1911), *Tarjuman al-Ashwaq*, trans. Reynold A. Nicholson, London: Royal Asiatic Society.
Arjani, Mehera (2015), "The Transformative Power of Taking Baba's Name," *Meher Gazette*, 5. https://myemail.constantcontact.com/-Archival-edition--Meherabode-Gazette----Spring-Issue-No--5--April-2015-.html.
Baba, Meher (1957), *Life at Its Best*, ed. Ivy O. Duce, New York: Dutton & Co.
Baba, Meher (1969), *Life Is a Jest*, ed. A. K. Hajra, Jabalpur: R. P. Pankhraj.
Baba, Meher (1971), *Listen, Humanity*, ed. Don E. Stevens, New York: Colophon.
Baba, Meher (1972), *Meher Baba on War*, ed. K. K. Ramakrishnan, Pune: Meher Era Publications.
Baba, Meher (1973a), *Discourses*, 6th ed., 3 vols, San Francisco: Sufism Reoriented.
Baba, Meher (1973b), *God Speaks: The Theme of Creation and its Purpose*, 2nd ed., New York: Dodd, Mead & Co.
Bachelard, Gaston, (1943), *L'air et l.es songes: essai sur l'imagination du movement*, Paris: Librairie José Corti.
Brown, Vanessa (2016), "Why Fashion Models Don't Smile," *The Conversation*, January 26. http://theconversation.com/why-fashion-models-dont-smile-53658
von Busch, Otto (2016), *Moda Maleficarum, or, The Dark Allure of Fashion*, New York: Self-Passage.
von Busch, Otto (2018), *Vital Vogue: A Biosocial Perspective on Fashion*, New York: Self-Passage.
von Busch, Otto and Daye Hwang (2018), *Feeling Fashion: The Embodied Gamble of Our Social Skin*, New York: Self Passage.
Carlyle, Thomas (1831), *Sartor Resartus: The Life and Opinions of Herr Teufelsdrockh*, London: Chapman and Hall.
Chittick, William C. (1989), *The Sufi Path of Knowledge: Ibn al-Arabi's Metaphysics of the Imagination*, Albany: State University of New York Press.
Coccia, Emanuele (2016), *Sensible Life: A Micro-ontology of the Image*, trans. Scott Alan Stuart, New York: Fordham University Press.
Duce, Ivy O. (1975), *How a Master Works*, Walnut Creek, CA: Sufism Reoriented.
Fenster, David (2018), *Chronology of Meher Baba's Movements*, Ahmednagar: Meher Nazar Publications. https://www.ambppct.org/Book_Files/CHRONOLOGY.pdf.
Entwistle, Joanne and Elizabeth Wissinger (2012), "Introduction," in Joanne Entwistle and Elizabeth Wissinger (eds.), *Fashioning Models: Image, Text and Industry*, 1–14, London: Berg.
Frederick, Filis (1963), "Notes on the East-West Gathering of Baba Lovers In Poona, India, November, 1962," *The Awakener*, 9: 1–59.
Frederick, Filis (1983), "Heroines of the Path," *The Awakener*, 20: 12–50.

Ganapathi, Meera (2018), "How the Last King of Indore Left a Mark on the World of Style and the Arts," *Scroll*, November 13. https://scroll.in/magazine/899359/how-the-last-king-of-indore-left-a-mark-on-the-world-of-style-and-arts.

Giacomotti, Fabiana (2017), "Cool and the Gang: The Everlasting Fashion of an Unfashionable Word," in Giovanna Motta and Antonello Biagini (eds.), *Fashion Through History: Costumes, Symbols, Communication (Volume 1)*, Newcastle Upon Tyne: Cambridge Scholars, 460–8.

Irani, Mani S. (1987), "Norina Can Charm a Stone," *Mandali Hall Talks*, August 8. https://www.mandalihall.org/man-870808/ [audio recording].

Jessawala, Eruch (1995), *That's How It Was: Stories of Life with Meher Baba*, Myrtle Beach, SC: Sheriar Foundation.

Jhala, Angma Dey (2018), *Courtly Indian Women in Late Imperial India*, London: Pickering & Chatto.

Kalchuri, Bhau (1985), *Lord Meher: Online Edition*, Ahmednagar: Avatar Meher Baba Perpetual Public Charitable Trust. http://www.lordmeher.org.

Landau, Rom (1935), *God is My Adventure: A Book on Modern Mystics, Masters, and Teachers*, London: Faber and Faber.

Le Page, William (1978), *It So Happened . . . : Stories from Days with Meher Baba*. Bombay: Meher House Publications.

Matchabelli, Norina (1997), *Norina's Gift: Messages from Meher Baba, Received Through Princess Norina Matchabelli*, ed. Christopher Wilson and Charles Haynes, Myrtle Beach, SC: EliNor Publications.

Mitchell, Stephen (2000), *Bhagavad Gita: A New Translation* (2000), trans. Stephen Mitchell, New York: Harmony.

Moser, Benjamin (2015), "Glamour and Grammar," in Clarice Lispector (ed.), *The Complete Stories*, trans. Katrina Dodson, New York: New Directions.

Natu, Bal (1984), *Glimpses of the God-Man, Vol. 4*, Myrtle Beach, SC: Sheriar Press.

Nietzsche, Friedrich (2001), *The Gay Science*, trans. Josefine Nauckhoff, Cambridge: Cambridge University Press.

de Perthuis, Karen (2008), "Beyond Perfection: The Fashion Model in the Age of Digital Manipulation," in Eugénie Shinkle (ed.) *Fashion as Photograph: Viewing and Reviewing Images of Fashion*, 168–81, London: I. B. Taurus.

Picard, Max (1952), *The World of Silence*, trans. Stanley Godman, Chicago: Regner.

Purdom, C. B. (1964), *The God-Man: The Life, Journeys, and Work of Meher Baba, with and Interpretation of his Silence and Spiritual Teaching*, London: George Allen & Unwin.

Sanjinés, José (2014), "Meher Baba's Silent Semiotic Output," *Signs and Society*, 2: 121–59.

Sato, Sato (2016), *Style and Steel: Fashion and the Endurance of Supremacy*, New York: Self Passage.

Schwartz, Hillel (2011), *Making Noise: From Babel to the Big Bang and Beyond*, New York: Zone.

Simmel, Georg (1997), "The Philosophy of Fashion," in David Frisby and Mike Featherstone (eds.), *Simmel on Culture: Selected Writings*, 187–206, London: Sage.

Soley-Beltran, Patrícia (2012) "Performing Dreams: A Counter-History of Models as Glamour's Embodiment," in Joanne Entwistle and Elizabeth Wissinger (eds.), *Fashioning Models: Image, Text and Industry*, 97–115, London: Berg.

Weil, Simone (1999), *Gravity and Grace*, trans. Emma Crawford and Mario van der Ruhr, London: Routledge.

CHAPTER 3
EMBODIMENTS OF SHAKTI

COSMIC POWER DISPLAYED BY KUMĀRĪS, INCARNATE GODDESSES OF NEPAL

Liz Wilson

At the height of the annual autumn festival of Indra Jatra, the streets of Kathmandu teem with people. Huge carts rumble through the crowded streets surrounded by musicians and masked dancers. One of the giant carts contains a little girl who is thought to embody the power of the Nepalese state. Each year, on the last day of the festival, the little girl dips her finger in vermilion power and decides whether the ruler kneeling before her is worthy. If she deems the ruler adequate to the task of leading the nation, she places a mark on the forehead of the ruler. This little girl is called *Kumārī* ("young woman," in English), and her physical form is a vehicle for Durgā-Taleju, a powerful warrior goddess, to be present on earth. The goddess regularly takes the form of little girls in the Kathmandu valley; a little girl represents the goddess in each of the three city-states that were historically powerful in the Kathmandu valley. The Kumārī who reigns in Kathmandu is known as the royal Kumārī; she has been the focus of state rituals ever since Kathmandu became the center of power when the region was unified into a single state in the mid-eighteenth century. It is the royal Kumārī who rides in the chariot during Indra Jatra and who decides the fate of the ruler at the end of the festival.

While accompanying students on a study abroad program in 1992, I was fortunate to be able to stand in close proximity to the cart bearing the royal Kumārī during Indra Jatra. Doing follow-up research in 1995, I met the reigning Kumari of Patan and interviewed her family and some neighbors who lived on her street. Since that time, there have been significant changes to the political system in Nepal. Consequently, it is unclear what the future holds for royal Kumārīs. This chapter takes a close look at how the presentation of self that is typical of Kumārīs has expressed central ideas about righteous statecraft in Nepal. I will explore in particular notions about the soul conveyed by the Kumārīs and the relationship between the Hindu philosophical concept of three *guṇa*s or strands of existence and the three colors that Kumārīs wear on their foreheads and on other ornaments. Wearing gold, red, and black, young women designated as Kumārīs visually proclaim messages about divine power through their physical appearance. They are always seen in public wearing gold, red, and black. The tripartite color symbolism accords with Hindu philosophical thinking about achieving balance in the world as a basis for ethically grounded state power. The colors gold,

Silhouettes of the Soul

red, and black represent many things about the goddesses that manifest themselves in the form of young girls for the sake of undergirding the power of the state in Nepal. These colors represent the girls' virginity, their potential fertility, and their power as embodiments of the goddess.

The tricolor presentation of self that is typical of these female figures carries messages about the formidable power of the state. Religious fashion and political subjectivity go hand in hand with royal power and national identity embodied in these young girls and their adherence to a strict code of religious fashion. While the young girls chosen as Kumārīs today look the same as their predecessors, the nature of their divine office has changed over time. For many years, the royal Kumārīs were associated with kingship. Living in the palace complex in Kathmandu, the royal Kumārīs maintained dharma or righteous order and provided justification for Hindu monarchs to rule over Buddhists and other ethnic groups in this fertile valley of Nepal. Kumārīs were visited by the kings of Nepal on festival occasions and performed rituals that suggested that it was the power of the warrior goddess Durgā-Taleju that enabled the dynasty of kings to rule. Kumārīs were linked with the army in that they embodied the martial power of the Nepalese warrior goddess. In short, Kumārīs provided legitimacy for the rule of Hindu monarchs of Nepal. Much changed when the monarchy was overthrown in the twenty-first century. In 2008, a constitutional change ended the monarchy and constituted Nepal as a secular nation. Today, there are still young girls treated as living goddesses in Nepal. The royal Kumārī of Kathmandu still lives in the palace complex and still has a relationship with state power in Nepal, but the terms of the relationship are not as clear as before. Change is inevitable for the girls who represent state power in Nepal now that the government is led mainly by leaders associated with communist political parties. This chapter not only will reflect on the history of the Kumārī institution but will discuss new challenges and ways that the institution is changing in response to those challenges.

How the Kumārīs Operate in a World Informed by Visual Exchanges of Information

Clothing and the presentation of self constitute crucial aspects of visual communication in all cultures. Through clothing, one presents such aspects of identity as social class, occupation, gender, sexual orientation, and the like. Clothing has played a crucial role in the articulation of national identity, as Susan Kaiser indicates in her work on fashioning the national subject (2012: 52–74). Certain forms of rural and ethnic dress have held special significance as conveyors of national identity, such as the French beret, the Scottish kilt, the Japanese kimono. Such forms of dress help to create a sense of belonging capable of bringing together disparate ethnic groups who may have little in common except for shared membership in a nation. In this way, key items of dress help to create what Benedict Anderson (2006) calls "imagined community." Thus it is no surprise that nations where revolution has overthrown governments seen as backward and corrupt, new forms of dress have been designed to convey a sense of solidarity with revolutionary forces. Thus after the French Revolution swept the monarchy off the throne, a new style of dress came to represent the national subject. In contrast to the decadent outfits characteristic of the pre-Revolutionary French royal court, this new look featured simple working-class trousers (*sans culottes*) (Kaiser: 65). Likewise, in post-Revolutionary China, a simple style of dress developed that suggested a person's allegiance to the Communist Party and its egalitarian vision of the future. Inspired by military outfits of the Red Guard, it became very common for people of all ages, genders, and walks of life to dress in simple green, blue, and gray garb that suggested affinity with the goals of the state, especially during the period of the Cultural Revolution (Kaiser: 70–1).

Examples of dress that represents the character of the nation could be multiplied. Clearly, dress has an important role to play in the visual communication of identity in places all over the world. But in some places and times, clothing and the presentation of self are particularly freighted with meaning. In South Asia, those imbued with divinity make themselves available to their devotees through the process of *darshan* (Eck 1996). "Darshan" is a Sanskrit term that means simultaneously seeing and being seen. To take darshan of a deity means entering a temple or other sacred space where you view the icon of a deity and, through the medium of the icon, that deity views you in return. The sacred is transmitted through the charged medium of the gaze. Visual information about the nature of the deity and the deity's intentions is conveyed by the clothing that the icon wears and the various types of powders and other substances that ornament the icon. Many icons have their clothing changed every day, with the understanding that the deity's clothing constitutes a medium of grace. For example, in the Minakshi temple of Madurai, South India, the icons of Minakshi and her consort have their old clothing and garlands removed from their images, then the icons are bathed with various liquid substances such as sesame seed oil, yogurt, and milk, and finally the icons are dried and dressed in new clothes, sprinkled with perfume, and adorned with new garlands and expensive jewelry (Fuller 1992: 64–5). Looks are extremely important in this context: it is paradoxically through the surface medium of dress that one gains access to the soul of the other. Surfaces in this context do not connote superficiality but rather depth. In South Asia, many people are extremely adept at the visual exchange of information due to the regular practice of taking darshan of sacred beings. One who is adept at reading clothing and other aspects of the presentation of self can visually take in a great deal of information about a person's age, gender, social status, clan and family relations, and political affiliations in just a quick glance. Dress is an expressive means of communication within the religious culture of South Asia. This is the background in which the triadic color symbolism of the three *guṇas* works to convey information about the power of the divine feminine and power of the Nepalese state. Glancing at the kumārī adorned in red, gold, and black, one communes with the balance of forces that constitutes the power of the goddess. Looking at the carefully composed surface, one can read a message about the commitment of the divine to the flourishing of life in the Himalayan kingdom.

Shakti: The Power of the Divine Feminine

In Hinduism, *shakti*, divine female power, is understood as the force that runs the world, animating and maintaining the manifest aspect of a supreme reality that also has an immaterial, unmanifest aspect (Kinsley 1988: 133–9). It is shakti that gives life to all creatures and animates all things. In order to accomplish specific tasks like creation and destruction, shakti takes the form of specific female deities. All female deities are material embodiments of shakti, and even the male deities venerated by Hindus are said to be animated by shakti. Shakti works through them too. That should come as no surprise. Shakti accomplishes all things: it is the energy that brings the world into being and keeps the world going. Kumārīs are identified as individual manifestations of the *shakti* that is behind all embodied existence. They are specifically thought by Hindus to incarnate the Hindu warrior goddess Durgā in her wrathful form as Taleju, a tutelary deity of the Malla dynasty. Buddhists identify Taleju with the goddess Vajra Devi. Through embodiment in young girls, the goddess defends the Nepalese people and keeps invaders from taking over this crossroads Himalayan country. Nepal is a place where commerce has gone on between different ethnic and cultural groups for millennia: it is a common marketplace for Indian merchants who bring spices and other goods up from the sun-baked expanses of southern Asia and for Tibetans who come down from high altitudes of the north with mountain products. It is a place that is vulnerable to takeover by the many groups that consider Nepal a meeting ground and a place to interact with others.

There are various legends about how the practice of venerating girls as living goddesses began in Nepal (Allen 1996; Glowski 1995; Hume 2013; Majupuri and Roberts 2007; Sakya 2013). One version says that the goddess Durgā-Taleju used to come down to earth and play dice with a particular Hindu king who ruled in the Kathmandu valley. She came night after night until one evening the king could not control his lust and attempted to have sex with her. Durgā left the palace in anger (manifesting herself as the wrathful Taleju) never to return again. But she later revealed to the king that he could still enjoy the benefit of her patronage. Henceforth, the goddess declared that she would take the form of human girls who belong to a Nepalese Buddhist ethnic group, the Newars, and in that form she would henceforth provide protection for the Nepalese people. The Newars have a long history in the Kathmandu valley, where they constitute over half of the population. Newar Buddhists practice a Tantric form of Buddhism that meshes with the Hinduism brought to Nepal by Hindu kings from India. Thanks in part to the common veneration of a goddess who incarnates in the form of human girls, Buddhists and Hindus have built a society together and cemented their alliances by reference to a common stock of deities and sacred powers.

Rituals That Govern the Lives of Kumārīs

There are many Kumārīs who incarnate divine female power in Nepal. At one time, the Kathmandu valley was divided into three kingdoms with three capital cities. Each city was protected by its own Kumārī. In time, the kingdom was consolidated by one dynasty of Hindu rulers who built their royal complex in the city of Kathmandu. The Kumārī of the city of Kathmandu came to outshine the others, but there are still important living goddesses venerated in places outside the city of Kathmandu. And in fact, the worship of prepubertal girls takes place in many locales throughout Nepal and North India. The veneration of girls recognizes them as portals of auspiciousness. Not yet married, but on the cusp of adult female fertility, they represent the bounty that is to come and the idea that if the divine is venerated with appropriate ritual gestures, human devotees will be rewarded with abundance.

To be selected as a royal Kumārī, a girl must undergo an exacting selection process that is done by five senior Buddhist priests known as the *Pancha* (five) Buddha. The horoscope of each candidate is checked for signs that indicate bad luck or aspects of fate contrary to the life of a living goddess. The Kumārī should exhibit bodily perfection; she must have no physical blemishes, such as scars and birthmarks, and should be healthy. If a girl has shed blood, lost any teeth, or been afflicted with disease, she is ineligible to serve as a vehicle of the goddess. In addition to these aspects of physical wholeness, she is expected to have auspicious physical endowments such as a chest like a lion's. The girl must also exhibit gentleness and modesty. Her character should be a good one. She should have a peaceful temperament with no indication of a tendency to fidget, preen, or be a show-off. The Kumārī of Kathmandu is selected when very young (usually around the age of three) and proves herself a worthy vessel of the warrior goddess by showing perfect discipline during a long period of observation and invincible courage during her installation ceremony. The young girl undergoes a month-long period of observation in which she is closely watched for any behaviors incommensurate with those expected of a living goddess.

The final moment in the process of becoming a Kumārī involves taking the girl to a temple for a ritual of installation that removes all previous life experience from the little girl's body so as to offer the goddess a pure vessel in which to enter into human life and Nepalese politics. Having had all previous life experience removed, we might compare the newly installed Kumārī to a vessel that is to be filled with shakti. Her great virtue is her emptiness. We might also compare the perfect emptiness of the Kumārī-elect to the perfect emptiness of fashion models before donning the costumes that they will display. Models are successful in their role, it can be argued, because they can make themselves devoid of qualities that would give them a life of their own. They are "human coat hangers" who give life to the clothing they wear but are themselves devoid of anything that would mark them as distinctive and unique. This suggestion that the more empty a Kumārī is, the more successful she will be is consonant with Buddhist and Hindu concepts of the soul. (Kumārīs are chosen from among the Buddhist community to serve a Hindu goddess, so both theologies are relevant.) Buddhists deny the existence of a permanent soul or other essence within the phenomenal person. To them, emptiness is the best way to describe what constitutes a person. For Hindus, there is an eternal soul (called the Atman) within the phenomenal person, but this soul is devoid of anything distinctive and unique. So the installation ritual that removes a little girl's life experience would thus serve to reveal the true nature of her soul, which is of the same essence as the soul of the universe: empty of particularity.

When the Kumārī is ready to begin performing her duties, one of the first is a ceremony that is performed on the eighth night of a fall festival in celebration of the goddess, a "black night" in which hundreds of buffaloes, goats, sheep, chickens, and ducks are sacrificed at goddess temples throughout the country. The ritual is held on the evening that celebrates the famous military exploit in which Durgā killed a demon in the form of a buffalo, a demon that none of the gods were able to slay. A few hours after midnight, the Kumārī is brought to the Taleju temple to participate in an important annual ceremony. The girl walks by herself around a courtyard that has been strewed with the decapitated heads of buffaloes. The buffalo heads represent the demon vanquished by the goddess Durgā-Taleju. Each head has been made visible by a lighted wick placed between the horns. The Kumārī shows her moxie by walking fearlessly along a raised edge on the border of this bloody courtyard. Although her emptiness is valued, the young girl's fearlessness shows that she carries the courage of the goddess within.

In such ceremonies and in daily life, the Kumārī's life is bound by discipline. State Kumārīs live cloistered lives following a strict regimen of rules that regulate how they eat, sleep, bathe, and comport themselves in daily life. Regulations govern where they go and with whom they interact. Once installed as living goddesses, they stay sequestered most of the time. When they do go out in public for important festivals (thirteen days out of the year), their feet must not touch the ground: they are carried through the streets by attendants or they ride in chariots. The little girls who embody the goddess are expected to be virgins. They avoid not only sex but also going out in public places and meeting people who are not close relatives. They must avoid spending time with men who are not brothers, fathers, uncles, or cousins. They eat a restricted diet of unspiced foods. They must avoid eating certain taboo items, such as hen's eggs and chicken. Everything they touch has to be kept ritually pure. They must avoid coming in contact with a person who wears leather.

Their bodily discipline is formidable. They are to sit without fidgeting on a throne or a cushion for hours at a time. Visiting the living goddess is an important aspect of the religious life of the people of the Kathmandu valley. If she is approached properly, she can fulfill the wishes of devotees. She can impart protection and prosperity to those who come and make offerings to her. It's believed that she can even impart good emotions (such as the loving kindness that is cultivated by Buddhists). She is thought to be prescient and is also thought to have the power to heal visitors, especially those with diseases that affect the blood. For several hours each day, a royal Kumārī sits upon her throne, receiving visitor after visitor. Each day, she may receive up to a dozen visitors. Her movements must be very controlled, since the movements of the goddess during audiences with her devotees are seen as omens. She needs to keep her face free of emotion. She is not to smile. If she should smile while being venerated by a devotee, that would be a declaration of something unsavory in the fate of that person. It is thought that if the Kumārī laughs loudly or cries, the devotee venerating her may take ill. The devotee could even die as a result of a bad omen during an audience with a living goddess. If the goddess rubs tears from her eyes, this is a very bad sign that heralds the imminent death of the devotee. If nothing untoward happens during an audience with a Kumārī, the person's wish will come true. So the daily life of a living goddess involves an incredible amount of discipline to keep her body and her emotions in check.

Just as the Kumārī must be disciplined in how she moves her body, so too there is much expected of her in the way of dress and presentation of self. The ways that a Kumārī wears her hair have great significance for the well-being of the nation. Like other aspects of her self-presentation, the Kumārī's haircare is a matter of complete discipline. She is to wear her hair in a topknot adorned with a red headdress when in public. Anything that deviates from tradition indicates something serious. There simply cannot be any bad hair days for living goddesses. Indeed, problems with haircare are indicative of future disaster; disruptions in the Kumārī's body are tokens of disruptions in the body politic. Isabella Tree tells of how the royal Kumārī Rashmila Shakya's body reacted to anti-monarchy demonstrations in Nepal in 1989–90. For two years in the run-up to democracy, the caretaker who groomed the Kumārī had difficulty tying up the girl's hair in a topknot (Tree 2015: 214). Letting the hair stay down would not be an option. The topknot of the Kumārī is like the cranial mound or *uṣṇīṣa* of the Buddha: it signifies the cosmos in its entirety. This same Kumārī also had fever, headaches, and fits of crying during the time when anti-monarchy and pro-democracy protesters gathered and protests led to violence in Nepal (Shakya and Berry 2007: 61–3). It was only after months of rioting, nightly curfews, and other indications of civil unrest that the king finally announced his agreement to accept a constitutional basis for rule. That very day, the Kumārī's mental and physical distress ceased.

As with the hair, so with the clothing of a Kumārī. At no time will you see them lounging about in sweatpants. Looking smart is part of the job description. They typically wear red clothing. Red, the color of creative energy, is normally not part of a little girl's repertoire. It is a color that one associates with married women. But the living goddess always wears red, indicating her potential fertility. She also wears gold jewelry in significant amounts every day. On their chests, for example, Kumārīs display gold snake necklaces and sacred amulets. On ritual occasions, special attention is given to the forehead. Kumārīs bear a large *bindī* or sacred mark on their forehead. The bindī is worn by married women as a sign of love and prosperity; it is also associated with the mode of life enabled by the third eye, the eye of wisdom that is described in texts on the subtle body as located between the eyes or just above the space between the eyes. The Kumārī's forehead is marked with vermilion and other substances thought to give protection to the eye of wisdom. It's important to take the time to adorn the forehead, especially on festival days. The forehead markings represent shakti, the cosmic energy of the universe. The elaborately constructed forehead marking also signifies wealth, good fortune, and unalloyed success for the nation. It takes a long amount of time to prepare the forehead mark; among the substances that are used are vermilion powder, rock crystal powder, a mixture of powdered turmeric and limestone called "kumkum," and sesame seed oil.

In Kathmandu, the royal Kumārī lives an especially sequestered life enshrined in the heart of the city. She lives in a square building that is called her home (Kumārī Chen), a three-story building by the old royal palace in Kathmandu. The Kumārī's own family lives elsewhere. They may visit her, but they are not to hug her or speak to her. Her family must treat the royal Kumārī with the utmost respect, just like the other people who visit her in her capacity as a living goddess. Like ordinary devotees who worship the goddess in the hope of things like recovery from illnesses, success in business and school, and other forms of good fortune, her parents must visit the Kumārī in her home. They show her honor with the ritual gesture of putting their forehead on her feet, a gesture often seen in South Asian religious life as a way of showing respect for superiors: even the lowly feet of a superior are more pure than the highest and purest part of one's own body, the head. The Kumārī receives her parents and other visitors in a shrine room; on upper floors of her house, there is a throne room for the king and meeting rooms where men of her clan and caste group gather to settle disputes. Most of the time, the Kumārī stays "at home" receiving worship at set times of the day. She does not leave her home to go to school but instead receives visits from tutors. She remains sequestered there unless needed to perform at state rituals. Other nonroyal Kumārīs (such as the Kumārī of Patan whom I visited in 1995) live with their parents but lead cloistered lives, maintaining purity through isolation from situations that could threaten their state of purity. Their dress, makeup, and comportment are similar to that of the royal Kumārīs.

When the royal Kumārī leaves her home for state rituals, she is carried by male relatives so that her feet do not touch the profane ground and bring her ritual impurity. She is to exhibit extreme self-control on these ritual occasions. For example, once a year the royal Kumārī goes out on a chariot procession around the city of Kathmandu. She is not allowed to eat or drink or leave her chariot to go to the bathroom. She is expected to radiate a supernatural calm while, during the chariot procession, the city of Kathmandu erupts in festive merriment. Her placid demeanor is made even more evident by ritual chaos going on all around her. The city is filled to capacity with exuberant festivalgoers, many of them fueled by the drinking of ceremonial alcohol, who engage in raucous games of tug of war involving her sacred chariot and the chariots of other deities.

When there are signs that a reigning Kumārī is human rather than divine, signs such as the loss of blood, the child is replaced by another girl. Any serious illness could be an indication that a girl is no longer a goddess. But the most watched-for sign is the loss of blood. Most girls are installed at a very young age. By the age of five or six years, some show signs of mortal status by the loss of blood associated with "baby teeth" falling out. Others are disqualified by first menstruation or a wound that brings blood loss. When such signs occur, they indicate that Durgā-Taleju is about to make herself present in another child.

On leaving office, a royal Kumārī receives a small stipend from the state in recognition of the services she rendered as a child goddess, and she is henceforth required to be present at certain festivals where rituals that maintain the welfare of the Nepalese people are performed. Other Kumārīs also continue to play ritual and political roles. Chanira Bajracharya, a former Kumārī of Patan (a former city-state near Kathmandu), was asked about her experience in an interview with Julie McCarthy (2018). Chanira Bajracharya described the transition to ordinary mortal as "tough" (McCarthy 2018). She had to work very hard to reach the level of education that she sought, due to the fact that she had only had tutoring sessions for an hour or so per day. Retired Kumārī Rashmila Shakya says that she was several years behind when she joined her classmates in ninth grade (Tree 2015: 148). Not only was she underprepared but she was treated differently from other students and not required to participate in class activities due to her prior life, making the transition more difficult. This retired Kumārī suggests that instead of giving retired Kumārīs a stipend, they should receive scholarships that would allow them to obtain higher educations (Shakya and Berry 2007: 144). Rashmila Shakya also voiced complaints about some of the physical difficulties she experienced in transitioning from a divine being to a human being. After going without shoes for eight years and never walking on the ground outside her home, Rashmila found wearing shoes uncomfortable. She had problems walking on uneven ground, found potholes perilous, and was terribly self-conscious walking in crowds or in traffic (Tree 2015: 147). Her sisters teased her, saying that she clomped around like a horse (Tree 2015: 147).

Another factor that affects the happiness of retired Kumārīs is the prospect of finding a life partner. According to Nepalese anecdotal tradition, former Kumārīs often remain single. Many men are said to be afraid to take former goddesses as wives. They are said to emit *shakti* energy long after the goddess has departed. That energy can take the form of an electrical charge that could be dangerous to potential husbands. There is plenty of evidence, however, suggesting that these allegations are greatly exaggerated. Former Kumārī Rashlima Shakya insists that this narrative is simply untrue. She told ABC reporters Terry Moran and Jackie Jesco (2016) that all the former Kumārīs she knows are married. When Isabella Tree met with a group of over a half dozen retired Kumārīs, all were married (2015: 185). So it would seem that the idea of the unmarriable retired Kumārī is part of the fabric of legends that people tell to exoticize the Kumārī lifestyle.

The Tricolor Symbolism of the Kumārīs

Through the vivid colors that they wear, royal Kumārīs convey information about state power, information that is available at a glance on major festival days. On such days, the people of Nepal gather along with the residents of the Kathmandu valley to take in the sight of the living goddess in the form of the state Kumārī riding in a large decorated cart. Pulled by a gang of boisterous youth, the cart containing the Kumārī offers a visual opportunity for darshan: the act of seeing and being seen by a divine being. Taking darshan of the Kumārī is a highlight of such annual religious processions as the fall festival of Indra Jatra, celebrating the god Indra's visit to earth that brings the assurance of plentiful rain. Seeing the beautifully dressed young woman who embodies the warrior goddess on such an occasion is a powerful moment, as I can attest. The people who stood near me at that time spoke in hushed tones about their good fortune in being able to stand so close to a Kumārī. The goddess, meanwhile, sits quietly in the midst of utter chaos. She sits calmly as young men shout vociferously, sing loudly, attempt to ram other carts, and fling colored powders everywhere in the hope that they will cover peoples' bodies with garish colors. Sitting serenely in her cart, the royal Kumārī protects it from chaos just as she protects the Nepalese people from legendary enemies, such as the buffalo demon that she vanquished after the ambitious demon took over the realm of the gods and sent all the male deities crying for help.

Such discipline enables these young women to embody the divine power needed to protect the people of Nepal. The highly disciplined lifestyle these young women lead is visually communicated by their clothing, makeup, and ornamentation. The presentation of self that is associated with state Kumārīs gives visual proof of their exalted position. The rich clothing, jewelry, and makeup that these young women wear convey the possibilities of life organized into a pattern of forces that work in a complementary way. Unpacking the rich symbolism of the colors that Kumārīs present, one can see the importance of three cosmic forces in the visual package that the Kumārīs communicate. Their clothes, jewelry, and makeup present a combination of three colors: red, black, and gold. These three colors correspond to the three *guṇa*s of Hindu philosophy. The term "guṇa" means "strand" or "thread," referring to the constituent elements that make up everything in an embodied existence. Each of the three guṇas has its characteristics. The interplay of all three guṇas creates the world as we know it. The three guṇas are evident in nature: some things are clearly dominated by a particular guṇa. The guṇas also manifest in personalities: some people are dominated by one guṇa or another, and one can see that their temperaments are strongly oriented in particular ways.

What are the color associations of the three guṇas? The colors are, to start with the most dramatic, a bright red that signals activity and fertility. The Sanskrit term for this red strand of existence is *rajas*. This active color combines naturally with its inactive opposite color, black. Black signals inactivity, de-animation, depression, and recovery. The term for the dark strand of existence is *tamasa*. These two colors, red and black, form a duality that is transcended by a third color: white, yellow, or gold. This third luminous color represents a transcendent third to the duality of action and inaction. It represents the wisdom that links activity with its opposite, inactivity. It represents that awareness that one cannot always be active: recovery time is necessary. White/yellow/gold symbolizes the superior guṇa, *sattva*. One needs to have the transcendent vantage point of wisdom to appreciate the possibilities and limits of embodied life.

The three guṇas are discussed in a variety of Indian philosophical texts. Their earliest articulation is in the ancient philosophical system of Samkhya, a system that contributed to the development of yogic practice in India (Larson 2005). According to Samkhya thought, the three guṇas explain why things and people are the way they are. It is the interplay of the three guṇas that determines the physical and psychological characteristics of all things. Another locus classicus for the three guṇa system is a Hindu scripture called the *Bhagavad Gita* ("Song of God"), a much loved text that many Hindus keep as bedside reading and refer to with great affection as "the Gita." Chapter Fourteen of the Gita (Lombardo 2019: 80ff) describes the creation of the world, an action that results when the balance of the three guṇas is disrupted. Everything in the created world contains the three guṇas in different proportions. In this way, the Gita describes the three strands as encompassing all of embodied life. Thus the Gita elaborates on the concept of the three guṇas, explaining that they constitute who we are in our current goals of life and customary mode of being in the world. It is by seeing beyond the disequilibrium of unbalanced guṇas that liberation can be found:

> When the seer perceives the doers
> as none other than the gunas
> and also knows what is higher
> he comes to attain My being
>
> Going beyond these three gunas
> which produce the body, freed from
> the pain of birth, old age, and death
> Atman (the soul) achieves immortality. (Lombardo 2019: 82)

So the vision of the Gita is that once one sees beyond the imbalances of the guṇas typical of the world we know, one can achieve liberation. The Atman, the soul, is immortal from the beginning, but one needs to go beyond the guṇas in order to realize this freedom. The Kumārīs exist for the liberation of others: by seeing the Kumārīs one can observe the guṇas in a state of balance and equilibrium. Interestingly, the viewer can cease to identify with his or her surface and instead come to appreciate his or her own inner essence, the Atman, by apprehending the surface, the decorated skin and attire, of the Kumārīs.

Kumārīs Today

What is life like for these young women today? No doubt there are many difficulties. Given all that has been said here about the many forms of discipline that govern the lives of the Kumārīs, it is no surprise that they are a subject of concern on the part of those who want to ensure that everyone enjoys unencumbered human rights. In recent decades, the Kumārī tradition has been scrutinized by human rights activists who worry about the potential of abuse in a life that limits girls' freedom and restricts their education. As we have seen, former living goddesses complain about the difficulties they experienced in transitioning from a divine to a human sphere of activity. They must overcome physical difficulties (like walking on uneven ground and walking in shoes), social difficulties in adjusting to being treated as an ordinary person, emotional difficulties in accepting criticism, teasing, and ridicule, and professional difficulties in achieving educational goals commensurate with career ambitions. Then there are the sad ironies of getting reacquainted with a family with whom one has never spent any intimate time. Former Kumārī Rashmila Shakya describes being terribly confused when brought to her natal home to live there after eight years as a living goddess. She thought she was visiting the place to do some sort of ritual and, when left there, was confused. She missed her caregivers, whom she regarded as her family (Tree 2015: 149). Sapana Pradhan-Malla, one of Nepal's leading human rights lawyers, told *The Guardian*'s Luke Harding (2001) that she believes that it is a violation of human rights to take away the childhoods of these girls. The girls need more of an education, they need to be able to play outside and leave the house more frequently, and they need psychological counseling when their reign is over to help them integrate with communities of people who have never lived segregated lives and don't understand the toll that isolation takes on a young girl. The Kumārīs need to be told from a very young age that there is a bigger world outside that they will be a part of one day. They need to develop skills to help them navigate this larger world once their reigns are over. Subin Mulmi, a lawyer for the Forum of Women, Law, and Development, points out that medical care can be an issue for the living goddesses (Zand 2018). Their ritual purity carries such weight that a high value is placed on staying indoors for all but ritual occasions. Hence, they may not be taken to the hospital if a serious illness occurs.

However, such worries about abuses of the Kumārīs' human rights did not convince Nepal's supreme court (Letizia 2013). In 2008, the court rejected a petition against the tradition, citing its cultural and religious significance. Although the court suggested that some reforms were needed, including increased schooling, increased medical care, more time spent with parents, decreased visiting hours by devotees, and enhanced financial support for retired Kumārīs, it found that the Kumārīs play an important religious role in Nepal and that to eliminate the institution would curtail the free exercise of religion. Others defend the institution from claims that it curtails the human rights of girls by pointing out all of the abuses that ordinary girls and women suffer in Nepal. Razen Manandhar lists the following widespread practices to suggest the absurdity of focusing on the sequestration of a few little girls:

> being [the] victim of infanticide, discriminated at early childhood as [a] girl, deprived of education, forced to sleep in hazardous cowsheds during menstruation, being sent to work as child laborer, forced to fast in the name of husbands or would-be-husbands, marrying at early age, forced to be married off with elderly groom, being rejected by groom's family (or even being burned) for not bringing sufficient dowry, and forced to live life of widows. (Manandhar 2018)

Clearly, it is difficult to draw the line and say exactly what constitutes abuse in a society where many aspects of life differ based on one's gender.

It will certainly be interesting to see how the institution of the royal living goddess changes with the many political transformations that have occurred in Nepal in recent years. The government is now controlled by socialist parties who have at least a theoretical commitment to freeing the populace from the ideological mystifications of religion. Maoists, however, have continued to invest in many of the traditional rituals that supported the monarchy, regarding them as "cultural practices." In *Demoting Vishnu: Ritual, Politics, and the Unraveling of Nepal's Hindu Monarchy*, Anne Mocko has documented some of the ways that socialist leaders of the new government have approached rituals that used to uphold the monarchy. The most important ceremony of all is the king's *tika* ceremony in which the Kumārī puts a forehead mark of red powder on the king. If she does so without hesitation and with proper ceremonial form, this action is thought to indicate that the king will reign unchallenged in the coming year. If she refuses to offer the tika or does so in a careless way, this is thought to indicate future vulnerability to interlopers and other threats to the king's power. Mocko shows how, in 2007, both the prime minister and the no-longer-powerful king sought the blessings of the Kumārī during the festival of Indra Jatra. The prime minister went for the blessing at the traditional time. The king went much later, around 11:00 p.m. The Kumārī gave her blessing to both men, but she showed favoritism to the king. She did this in a subtle way, not noticed by many. She put the traditional forehead mark on the king with the traditional left hand (i.e., a Tantric context, hence the left hand is considered auspicious, contrary to typical South Asian patterns). But she used the right hand for the prime minister (Mocko 2015: 140–1). Rashmila Shakya explains in her autobiography (2008: 53) that the right hand is used for commoners. The prime minister, it seems, didn't garner the respect that his office would suggest on account of his lack of royal blood.

One suspects that an institution as strongly woven into the life of the citizenry as the cult of the royal Kumārī will stand the challenges that such new circumstances pose. The recent Supreme Court ruling is probably a pretty good indication of the resilience of the Kumārī institution. Time will tell. Meanwhile, for the girls and women themselves, the prevailing sentiment is that, despite the sacrifices, the institution of the living goddess should be maintained. Former Kumārī Chanira Bajracharya commented to a BBC correspondent that she was sorry to see a very small slate of candidates recently put forward to be selected as a living goddess (Zand, 2018). When she herself was chosen, there were six other girls being considered. There were only two little girls put forward by their families on the occasion Bajracharya commented on. Bajracharya illustrates the attitude expressed by many former goddesses: she sees some problems with the institution but thinks it should be continued. Bajracharya wants to help current Kumārīs by providing them with basic training on the larger world long before they need to enter that world; she hopes to start a support group for current Kumārīs that would help them to prepare for the future (Zand 2018). There are many ways that the institution could be improved. If the reforms being considered are successful, the beings who embody the goddess capable of protecting the nation from harm will themselves be protected from harm and allowed to flourish.

References

Allen, M. (1996), *The Cult of Kumārī: Virgin Worship in Nepal*, Kantipath: Mandala Book Point.
Anderson, B., *Imagined Communities: Reflection of the Origin and Spread of Nationalism*, rev. ed., London: Verso.
Eck, D. L. (1996), *Darśan: Seeing the Divine Image in India*, 2nd ed., New York: Columbia University Press.
Fuller, C. (1992), *The Camphor Flame: Popular Hinduism and Society in India*, Princeton, NJ: Princeton University Press.
Glowski, J. M. (1995), "Living Goddess as Incarnate Image: The Kumārī Cult of Nepal," Thesis, Ohio State University, Columbus, OH.

Hume, L. (2013), *The Religious Life Of Dress: Global Fashion And Faith*, New York: Bloomsbury Academic (Dress, Body, Culture).

Kaiser, S. (2012), *Fashion and Cultural Studies*. London and New York: Berg.

Kinsley, D. R. (1988), *Hindu Goddesses : Visions of the Divine Feminine in the Hindu Religious Tradition*, Berkeley, CA: University of California Press.

Larson, G. J. and Īśvarakrsṇa (2005), *Classical Sāṃkhya: An Interpretation Of Its History And Meaning*. 2d rev. ed., New Delhi: Motilal Banarsidass.

Letizia, C. (2013), "The Goddess Kumari at the Supreme Court: Divine Kinship and Secularism in Nepal," *Focaal—Journal of Global and Historical Anthropology*, 67: 32–46.

Lombardo, S. and R. H. Davis (2019), *Bhagavad Gita*. Hackett Publishing Company, Inc.

Majupuria, I. and P. Roberts. (2007), *Living Virgin Goddess Kumārī: Her Worship, Fate of Ex-Kumārīs & Sceptical Views; Most Authentic and Exhaustive*, Saharanpur: Gupta.

Manandhar, R. (2018), "Living Goddess Kumari and Human Rights Issues," *Medium*, September 29.

McCarthy, J. (2018), "The Very Strange Life of Nepal's Child Goddess," *National Public Radio*, May 28, 2015. https://www.npr.org/sections/parallels/2015/05/28/410074105/the-very-strange-life-of-nepals-child-goddess (accessed August 15, 2018).

Mocko, Anne (2015), *Demoting Vishnu: Ritual, Politics, and the Unraveling of Nepal's Hindu Monarchy*. London, New York: Oxford University Press.

Moran, T. and J. Jesco (2016), "This 7-Year-Old Nepali Girl Is Worshipped as a Living Goddess on Earth," *ABC News*, September 8.

Śākya, D. (2013), *The Goddess Tulaja and Kumāri in Nepali Culture: A Collection of Research Articles About Istadevi Tulaja Bhawani and Aradhyadevi Kumāri*. Kumari Prakashan, Kathmandu; Sole distributor, Vajra Books.

Shakya, R. and S. Berry. (2007), *From Goddess to Mortal: The True-Life Story of a Former Royal Kumari*. 2nd ed. Kathmandu: Vajra Publications, 2012.

Tree, Isabella. (2015), *The Living Goddess: A Journey into the Heart of Kathmandu*, New York: Eland Publishing.

Zand, S. (2018), *BBC Our World: Nepal's Living Child Goddess*, December 15.

CHAPTER 4
INTERVIEW WITH KODO NISHIMURA
Otto von Busch and Mark Larrimore

Kodo Nishimura *is a Buddhist monk and a makeup artist born in Tokyo in 1989. He graduated from the Parsons School of Design in New York. After graduating, he started to thrive as a makeup artist, working behind the scenes of events including Miss Universe and NY Fashion Week. In 2015, Kodo trained to be a monk and was certified by the Pure Land school. He rose to fame following his appearance in Queer Eye: We're in Japan. He has spoken at the United Nations Population Fund, Yale University, and Stanford University as an LGBTQ activist, which attracted wide coverage on the likes of CNN and the BBC. His book "This Monk Wears Heels" is available in February 2022. His mission is to empower all people sharing Buddhist wisdom with a touch of makeup.*

KODO: When I was eighteen years old, I entered a two-year college in Boston. I used to feel inferior there, because most of the students were either dance majors or football players, and they looked physically attractive. At that time I had eczema and my body structure was much smaller than most of them, so I blamed my ethnicity for feeling bad for myself. But in 2007 Miss Universe Japan won Miss Universe amongst all types of beauties from around the world. I doubted, "How can a Japanese woman be so excelling in terms of beauty?" I started to read a book about her, and it said she was able to highlight her Japanese charms and her originality. She was a dancer and she performed vivaciously on the stage. Also that Japanese people have black eyes that can create a great contrast with smoky eye makeup, and many have silky black hair. I really loved the makeup she had on.

That's how I started applying makeup on myself because I felt I could amplify my almond eyes. It was easier to buy makeup products in the US because at drugstores, the clerks did not seem to care about what I was buying unlike Japanese cosmetic counter ladies. They asked me if I was looking for a gift for my mother or girlfriend. At Sephora in Boston, Drag queens and men were selling makeup and they have so much glitter on.

In Boston, I was living with my best friend. She was really careless about makeup, applying blue shimmery eyeshadow without looking at a mirror. So there was a gap between the eye shadow and the lash line. One time she said was having some personal difficulties. I had my eyeliner and mascara that I recently acquired, so I wanted to help her by applying makeup, because she was one of the few people who befriended me. I did her makeup and she completely transformed and we couldn't believe it, we never imagined that she could look like that. She was a new person with makeup. She started putting accessories on, and we started taking photos with my little digital camera until late at night.

Since then I noticed that some part of her soul was lit up. She became more radiant and more outspoken. Soon after she started putting makeup carefully: foundation, eyeliner, eye shadow, and mascara. She became jovial and I could clearly feel the power of makeup because she was my closest friend. I started to want to learn more than just eyeliner and mascara so that I can help my friends to feel even more beautiful. That's when I started to want to be a makeup artist. After graduation from the school in Boston, I entered Parsons the School of Design and studied Fine Arts. During junior year, I started assisting a makeup artist who did makeup for my idol: Riyo Mori who won Miss Universe in 2007. It was my dream to work with that artist. The job was extremely tough, but I was extremely passionate. I was eager to learn everything that I could absorb so that I can do makeup that can make my friends look like Miss Universe.

At that time, at school, I was concerned about my artistic expressions. Since Parsons is filled with students from all around the world, I was always thinking, "How can I make my art stand out amongst other students?" I was looking for something that is original that I could highlight and to express in my art pieces. Just like how I was learning about highlighting Japanese attributes just like how Miss Universe Japan won at the international pageant.

I wasn't really sure of who I was or where I came from; what my originality was. When I was growing up in the temple in Japan, I loved Disney princesses and I didn't really care about Buddhist statues. I didn't know why we had to believe and how we could be liberated and be taken to the pristine pure land after we die. I was very skeptical about Buddhism. But I always had an option to inherit the temple. I thought if I were to study Buddhism and understand what it is about, maybe I could find my originality and become a bright person in a global setting. Also, I wanted to understand the job of monks so that I can make a valid judgment to inherit the temple or not.

So I joined the training to be a monk. Training in Kyoto in February was extremely cold. In August, it was scorching hot. I even sweat from my ankles. By praying and chanting with our legs crossed for about five hours a day, my legs were bruised. Due to fatigue, I had a fever, I lost my voice and I was drained. "Oh my goodness, this is not what I expected it to be." But I could not give up to find the answer.

For me to join the training as a homosexual was nerve-wracking. Especially because I was in the closet in Japan. During the training sessions the trainees bath together, around eighty male trainees. It was so awkward and kind of ironic because men were separated from women to avoid temptations. I didn't want other men to feel uncomfortable because of my sexuality. So I kept quiet. When I was changing in the bathroom, some loud guy from a rural area talked to me, "The first time I saw you, I thought you were a fag." And I thought, "OH NO! Why are you asking me that question, here and now?" It was the worst possible topic. But I thought twice. I have spent over seven years in the US and I have gotten more comfortable with my sexuality, and what's wrong about me being a part of the LGBTQ community? If I don't speak up, nothing will change.

So I said, "Yes, I am" to him. The guy was so surprised and he started asking me about sexual conducts between men. I thought it was too much to answer. Another trainee interrupted the conversation, "Oh, do you know Kodo? He is a makeup artist who lives in New York." And for this loud guy, even coming to Tokyo was a big deal. And learning that somebody came from New York, was just too overwhelming for him, and he became speechless. So I put on the clothes and I was walking back to the dormitory, the loud guy walked past me and told me, "Good luck in New York." *Wait, what did he just say?! Now he is encouraging me?* I was very proud of myself that I could stand up for myself and change his perspective about me. I am glad that I spoke the truth confidently, so that Japan is able to change for the better.

At the end of the training, because the trainees are divided into men and women, I wasn't really sure if I would be welcomed to become a monk as a homosexual who feel both male and female. Also, I love to wear makeup and heels. What was bothering me was the fact that some ceremonial choreographies during the Buddhist ceremonies are different depending on your sex. For example, there is an urn with incense in it, with smoke coming out. As we walk into the temple, we have to walk over the incense urn to purify our bodies with the smoke, men with the left foot, women with the right foot. So when it comes to these choreographies, I didn't know whether to walk over with my left or right leg. I also have transgender friends too, so how do I teach them to join the ceremony once I become a monk?

I was not sure if I should become a Buddhist monk, because I might degrade the impression of other monks by not following the rules, or I might offend some people by wearing makeup. If so, I wouldn't want to be a monk.

During the training, we were not supposed to ask questions to the teachers. The traditions were to be solely endowed. But I consulted one assisting teacher because he seemed open minded. I had opened up about my concerns and he talked to the master monk who was extremely renowned and respected; and he invited me to his office. It was the day before the conclusion of the whole training. I was very nervous to ask my questions.

The master told me that Buddhist teaching says everybody can be equally liberated, even if you are a criminal or prostitute. As long as you are faithful, anybody can be liberated. That is the most important purpose of our Buddhism, and it is not the choreography that was determined after the teaching. So you can perform whichever you feel comfortable with, and you can tell others to do so as well.

Also, in Japan, monks can get married and have different jobs; they can earn money and have children. Monks wear various clothes such as suits or watches depending on their occupation. So what would be the difference if you wear something shiny? I don't think wearing something shiny is a problem. I was amazed by the master's answer. He was so logical, flexible, and forward-thinking. He showed me that our school is adopting and evolving with the time, while maintaining the core teachings.

Through this experience, I realized that I can give a message to people who are suffering from limiting religious values in the world. There I found my mission that was unique to me. Later I was interviewed by variety of media, about being a monk, a makeup artist, and a homosexual. As I talked about my stories, I received many messages from all around the world. Some Brazilian boy on Instagram told me stories such as "my Catholic mother tells me that gay is unacceptable, even though she says 'Treat others as God treats you' she denies my sexuality." I knew the boy was feeling lost and trying to find some solution or escape. I wanted him to know that in Buddhism his sexuality is celebrated, his sexuality is nothing wrong. And after messaging with him for a few months, he told me, "I got it, thank you." And he started wearing makeup and skirts. He sounded happier. Recently he sent me a photo of him at the school music festival. He was wearing makeup and a skirt standing next to his smiling mother. He said his mother now accepts him.

Later, I also lived in Los Angeles for a year, I was living with a roommate who was dating a Mexican boyfriend. He was an Italian Catholic and he told me that he was told that being gay is against God's will since he was young. He told me that he feels guilty that he can't fight the temptation. I told him, "Well, I'm not willing to change your belief and I'm not criticizing your religion, but in Buddhism, it accepts who you are. Personally, I want you to be happy and I don't see anything wrong with your sexuality." And he told me, "Thank you." I hope that he was inspired by the existence of another perspective, that he feels a little lighter. So that's my mission now, to tell people to talk about my experience with Buddhism and give them a broader view. A person can be a Buddhist monk, a makeup artist, and a homosexual and be proud and happy. I recently collaborated with Japan Buddhist Federation and created "The Rainbow Sticker" to demonstrate Buddhist message that everybody is welcomed without discrimination, and we can all be liberated equally regardless of any differences to people. I designed the sticker design with rainbow flag and a shadow of palms together in the middle. The sticker is pasted on bulletin boards and entrances of many Buddhist temples in Japan, and I also mailed to my supporters in over 40 counties. I am happy that we are making visible progress to welcome people of all gender and sexuality.

OTTO: It sounds like, with makeup, you helped your friend experience a sense of growth, a sense of transcendence. Is there an overlap between your practice as a makeup artist and your service as a monk?

KODO: Yes. My reason to do makeup and to share Buddhist teachings to others is that I want to encourage them to feel confident and worthy of themselves. I might be using trendy makeup products and ancient Buddhist wisdom, but I am using them with the same spirit.

MARK: I know that some of your work also involves makeup seminars with LGBTQ people. Can you say something about those?

KODO: When I went back to Japan, I participated in a photoshoot campaign to promote LGBTQ rights. Some of the participants were transgender women, but their makeup jobs were not great. I mean, it was melting; they did not have a source to learn makeup techniques from because the makeup books and magazines were mostly meant for biological women.

So, I organized an LGBTQ-friendly makeup seminars where I teach makeup for all genders. They were really happy to learn about the possibilities of makeup. Some of the participants told me that they felt like a princess and they could finally walk on the street confidently, with their heads high.

In March of 2019, I was doing a three-week makeup session, at a studio, and in my temple. In the studio, I did lectures where I talked about basic makeup skills and also how to cover beard shades, etc. And in the temple guest room, they practiced on themselves. It was a group of twelve students. Some of them are cancer survivors, some of them are transgender people, some of them wanted to be a professional makeup artist. I taught them what they could do to look how they wanted to look. And coming to the temple, I think the participants felt relaxed and peaceful. It's not only about the physical makeup skills but also updating how we perceive ourselves and feeling confident in being authentic.

MARK: In contrast to Shinto shrines, many Japanese people associate Buddhist temples with death and funerals. But they are not just about remembering the dead and taking care of the dead.

KODO: Right, Japanese people are not very religious in my opinion. Buddhism is closely related to funerals when it was originally intended to give wisdom and balance to lives. I think religions prosper when times are harder, after the wars, or in poverty. So I think people are happy enough not to strongly depend on religions for emotional stability today. So that's why they go to the temples mainly for funerals and ceremonies.

In my opinion, if the religion doesn't survive, it is ok. If people do not need it, then nobody can force it. It's like providing food when people are full. It might not be what the people are looking for right now, but I am sure it will come back when people need it again, like a circulation.

MARK: The Pure Land Churches of America is one of the leading Buddhist organizations in America supporting gay marriage. So it seems there may be something in the Pure Land tradition itself that makes it especially open and inclusive. What are your thoughts on this?

KODO: There is no clear mentioning about LGBTQ people in Buddhism, but in one of the Buddhist sutra called "Amida Sutra," which depicts the scenery of the pristine pure land, it says there are many colorful lotus flowers. It says, "Blue lotus flower should shine in blue, yellow lotus flower should shine in yellow, red lotus flower should shine in red, and white lotus flower should shine in white. They are all radiant and beautiful and in each way." The master says that it can be interpreted as a celebration of diversity. Recently Japanese Buddhism is rigorously learning to accept diversity and equality.

Buddhism is not the same depending on where you find it. In Japan, LGBTQ events are held, and also women have been able to be monks since the year 584. On the other hand, when I visited Thailand, the customs looked different. In Theravada Buddhism, they have their rules. The nuns are called Meachi, and they wear white robes and they cannot be on the same level as male monks. Most of them pray in the back of the male monks, on a lower level of the floor. I interviewed a nun and she told me that she would prefer to be a monk but there are not enough female monks who can perform a ceremony to ordain women as female monks, so there are few ordained nuns, so their status is not as equal. Also, I learned that gay people are not openly out at temples and transgender women do not usually ordain because it is expected to be for straight men. I would like to introduce that Pure Land Buddhism can be a hope for many people in the world.

OTTO: I'm curious how you think about the outer change of appearances and an inner change. Fashion, and of course makeup, we are told is shallow and doesn't matter. And then, on the other hand, we think religion is really deep and matters a lot. You manage to put these together, and really highlight the profoundness of change and that appearances echo so deep inside of us? How does that transformation happen?

KODO: I know that fashion and makeup are not shallow for sure. When I put makeup on, I feel more beautiful, powerful, and capable. This sentiment lasts even after I take off the makeup; makeup has an effect on my soul that lasts forever. Buddhism is very similar in a way that it is a wisdom that protects me that I am equally valuable to anybody. Both of them teach me that I can feel worthy and be confident in who I am. That is when I felt a change in me.

OTTO: It's interesting how you highlighted the makeup is on you forever. The seasons change and we change clothes, it's ephemeral, but once you've had this experience of being seen or being recognized or just seeing yourself in front of the mirror as who you could be, there seems to be something more to it more to it.

KODO: Yes, it stays. It's very powerful, people often feel that they can do something more. One female student from my makeup seminar told me, "Recovering from illness was my goal for years. But now I know I can feel glamorous and energetic. I have a new goal that I want to study different languages and help other people." She was able to go beyond what she expected. She also told me, "I was in bed sick for five years, but because I was glammed by you, I was given a dream that will change my future." Just like her case, I have seen many sparks of hope by experiencing makeup.

OTTO: Do people treat you differently as a makeup artist because of your other role as a monk? When you go to the hairdresser, it creates a sort of intimate relationship where people can talk about intimate things, and they'll confess things that they otherwise may not say. Is this sort of pampering opening up a certain kind of spiritual space between people?

KODO: Maybe people have an unusual experience with me knowing that I am both a makeup artist and a Buddhist monk. When people are showing me their bare faces, they often open up their hearts. Some start to share their secrets and concerns with me. And by sharing it, they feel much lighter, and I might say something Buddhist here and there to help them. As the makeup application continues, their faces and spirits start to glow. It is a synergic effect; maybe they are evolving into a better version of themselves. It is an effect of not only makeup on your face but a makeup on your mind.

SECTION TWO
PRACTICES OF EMULATION
AND TRANSFORMATION
Otto von Busch and Jeanine Viau

The notion of dressing deeply points toward dress as a practice, more a process and discipline than a commodity. Fashion runs deep involving the soul in processes of feeling and discernment, emulation and transgression. The concept of soul must not signify something readymade or finished, but a divine connection in a continuous becoming; it can decay and be corrupted as much as to be refined and reborn. Or, moving away from the normative regime of betterment and corruption, the soul may be a site of endless speculation, the point of diffraction for a host of possibilities.

From the perspective of Sloterdijk's notion of anthropotechnics, or the "practicing life," the journey within is a struggle against the distraction and corruption of life, and it is a struggle against life itself toward perfection, the higher possibilities of human being. "The perfect thing is that which articulates an entire principle of being" (Sloterdijk 2013: 21). The process of improvement does not strive for social goods, of success, wealth, or even health, but overcoming inner obstacles toward betterment. For example, Joseph Walser's study in this section of ascetic nudity and dress in Ancient Indian religion reveals monastic aspirations to overcome worldliness. Sloterdijk suggests framing these efforts at betterment as the "deep play" of self-transgression. In the practicing life, deep play is the exercise toward spiritual heights (Sloterdijk 2013: 14). The practice of life is an inner gesture, more than the daily chatter of the self, of becoming whole and worthy, becoming perfect, a self beyond expectations.

However, the language of perfection and betterment becomes troubling when established social or spiritual norms do not suit the evolving soul, or the means of realizing one's ideal self are restricted by oppressive forces. Donna Haraway's (1992) concept of diffraction attunes to alternative strategies that open to endless possibilities, continuous destinies rather than perfection, and messier processes of self-generation. Hassanah El-Yacoubi's chapter, for example, details the intersections of hijab practices, cultural difference, and entrepreneurial tactics as women of Muslim faith meet hostilities with innovation and make themselves known in American markets. Similarly, Benae Beamon refracts the singular form by turning to the transgressive collective becoming of black and brown queer boihood, where an ethic of honor replaces the imperative of perfection.

The quest for the soul may break through the daily chatter of inner voices, as the soul is sometimes found in the silence within. Other times, the soul finds its voice in public through collective disclosure and movement making. As Sara Ahmed observes, emotions are not a private matter belonging to individuals: "emotions are not simply 'within' or 'without' . . . they create the very effect of the surfaces or boundaries of bodies and worlds" (2004: 117). In a similar vein, we must not think the soul is strictly a private matter. It is made through the process of mediating between the subjective and objective aspects of experience, as William James explains ([1902] 1994: 542). Subject-object interactions invite new methods for examining and materializing feelings, such as the textile and image meditations that Tanya White brings forth in her chapter to disclose the power and danger of sublime compulsion, even when, perhaps especially when, under the duress of extreme religious discipline. Also, re-territorializing affect as a public matter opens up unexpected sites for soul excavation, such as the public university classroom, as examined in Jeanine Viau and Shekinah Morrison's dialogue for this section. Bringing fashion to the soul or the soul to fashion makes both public artifacts.

Dressing deeply is a walk on a tightrope, a performance of ascending heights, using psychotechnical artistry to reach perfection, integrating spiritual and capitalist aims, crafting the fine line between discipline and deterioration, managing private and public feelings, and affecting change. As Elizabeth Wilson (2004: 383) suggests, it is the triviality of dress that allows this special relationship. As we denigrate it, or even *because* we denigrate it, we can indulge in our shallow fascination with it, while simultaneously letting it be "the vehicle for deeply significant ideas, aspirations, and feelings." Calling such practice merely being a "follower" of fashion, or a religious drone for that matter, does not do justice to the inner and outer transformations that it affects. The fashion of ascetic discipleship is not merely a matter of mimetics but a process of materializing the ideal life. Corporeal emulation, such as the imitation of Christ, affords the closest possible proximity and affiliation with the divine for the devotee, a mutually constructed intimacy. Then there are the makings of new visibilities, wearing down animosities and binaries with the entrepreneurial spirit, and spelling different affective possibilities through public discernment, putting one's soul out there so to speak.

The chapters in this section offer examples of these practices and transformations. Joseph Walser examines the threadbare religious regalia in India as the concretization of aspirational ideals, positioning the wearer as a serious ascetic practitioner. It is the barely dressed or unclothed combat of the flesh, while simultaneously letting minimal robes be a vehicle of spiritual practice itself, exposing the body to the elements and the world that needs to be overcome to reach spiritual perfection. Although also concerned with garments that are not too revealing, according to Hassanah El-Yacoubi, the women of the Modest Fashion Movement in America are more worldly in their approach. Among women of Muslim faith in the United States, modest fashion is a mode of agency powerful enough to answer anti-Muslim sensibilities and reshape mainstream silhouettes. El-Yacoubi shows how this struggle is driven by young entrepreneurs and influencers creating their own fashion events and online content that celebrates the beauty and ingenuity of women of Muslim faith and leverages their new visibility to resist multiple forms of injustice.

Benae Beamon also honors the transformational potential of emergent subjectivities to draw fresh contours of visibility. She professes the self-affection of such collectives as bklyn boihood "to be fly as shit" despite the occlusion and limits placed on black queerness. Here, self-revelation and determination diffract normative aesthetics and illuminate the form of black transness. It is a process imbued with a co-creative affective spirituality interweaving sacred and secular dimensions of Afro-diasporic experience.

Chapters in this section also attend to mixed mediums and methods as processes for attending to the intersections of religion and fashion. Tanya White uses original textile and image collages to evoke a sublime feeling in the viewer as she develops a parallel reading between the bodies of Christian iconography and contemporary supermodels. Sublime emulation of discipleship is embodied in the process of imitation and devotion, as in the process of making art. In these settings, the emaciated flesh becomes a mark of devotional process toward an ideal for living, if in spiritual practice or in the ideal of a sublime aesthetic body. The sublime, terrifying while alluring, is the tightrope between life and death in ascetic practices for supreme perfection over body and soul.

Jeanine Viau and Shekinah Morrison's dialogue examines fashion as a complex of methods and materials suited to soul-making in a public university classroom. Taking an autoethnographic approach in the style of the chapter and in the pedagogical strategies used in the classroom, they deploy fashion as a catalyst for self-revelation, a form of articulation that invites teachers and students to examine their most deeply held values and struggles. They discuss how fashion reinvigorates concern for the soul in public education and reenergizes learning sites that are increasingly depersonalized for the sake of capitalist efficiency.

Neither the silhouette nor the soul is ever finished, whether striving for the ideal aims of discipleship, maintaining communion through emulation, or evolving new visibilities and shapes of justice. In analysis and practice, emphasis is on process, on methods of inner working, sorting feelings, and becoming seen. Deep dress is just such an endeavor, sometimes disclosing ascetic aspirations, sometimes making lives more livable in the world.

References

Ahmed, Sara (2004), "Affective Economies," *Social Text*, 79 (22, 2): 117–39.
Haraway, Donna (1992), 'The Promises of Monsters: A Regenerative Politics for Inappropriate/d Others', in L. Grossberg, C. Nelson and P. Treichler (eds), *Cultural Studies*, 295–337, New York: Routledge.
James, William ([1902] 1994), *The Varieties of Religious Experience: A Study in Human Nature*, New York: The Modern Library.
Sloterdijk, Peter (2013), *You must change your life*, Cambridge: Polity.
Wilson, Elizabeth (2004), "Magic fashion," *Fashion Theory*, 8(4): 375–86.

CHAPTER 5
NAKED OR NUDE?
READING THE THREADS, THE BARE, AND THE THREADBARE IN ANCIENT INDIAN RELIGION
Joseph Walser

Introduction

When I was in high school, one of the teachers whom I remember fondly was my creative writing teacher, Ms. Mary Jane Kooiman. Not that I ever had a knack for writing fiction, but what I loved about her class was her way of sensitizing us to the subtle nuances of language. In one of her particularly apt illustrations of word connotation, she told us, "Nude is what you are when you are under the smiling gaze of your lover. Naked is what you are when you step out of the shower and realize that the only towel is at the other end of the house." So why bring up nudity in a book on religion and fashion? Isn't the body au naturale the opposite of both? I suspect that even the most self-confident reader of this chapter would prefer to avoid attending religious services in the buff. Furthermore, while religions have spawned recent fashions (e.g., Kosher Casual lines, Burkini swimwear for the pool, and Snoga outfits for the mat), what is religious about such fashions is precisely their reference to the nudity that they cover up.

Here, I will begin with the simple observation that none of us see either clothes or the unclothed body shorn of significance. And our reading of that significance and indeed its ability to force itself into our awareness hangs on the contrast, manifest or implied, to the unclothed body. As Roland Barthes points out,

> Is not the most erotic portion of the body where the garment gapes? . . . it is intermittence . . . which is erotic: the intermittence of skin flashing between two articles of clothing (trousers and sweater), between two edges (the open necked shirt, the glove and the sleeve); it is this flash itself which seduces or rather: the staging of an appearance as disappearance. (Barthes 1975: 9–10)

Hence, the body can be erotically nude (in Ms. Kooiman's sense) only through the juxtaposition with nudity that clothing allows. Even artistic representations of nudes in which there is not a stitch of clothing in sight were painted or sculpted with reference to the clothing that is not there. As Anne Hollander observes, "An image of the nude body that is absolutely free of any counterimage of clothing is virtually impossible. Thus, all nudes in art since modern fashion began are wearing the ghosts of absent clothes—sometimes highly visible ghosts" (Hollander 1993: 85–6). She points out that often, for instance, the breasts of painted nudes defy gravity in ways that are only possible in a corset or bra, and that the position of the legs suggests the natural position assumed by women wearing the fashion of skirt at the time.

But while the differential between skin and clothing can be erotically charged, this is certainly not the only potential significance. Again, encountering nudity devoid of significance is impossible: we find it always embedded and debated within a discursive tradition. And within this broader discourse, it is power that is refracted through the sign of absence. For instance, the thematic nudity of Adam and Eve that we find in European artists such as Hugo Van der Goes and Albrecht Dürer indexes a state of Edenic naturalness and innocence if only to highlight the subsequent clothing and corruption of the viewer. The nudity of the first pair is erotic (they are, after all, the parents of all humanity), but for one steeped in the Christian tradition of the fifteenth to sixteenth century, the force of that eroticism would only highlight the profound sense of loss of the Fall into clothing—a Fall that in turn provides the justification for Christianity itself. But, of course, traditions do not remain static, and secular translations of the Christian project render the Edenic "state of nature" into the "state of freedom" that undergirds the dreams of liberty of the modern secular state (Asad 2018: 13–16). It is not surprising that we find nudity indexing this pristine state of liberal freedom in eighteenth-century paintings such as Delacroix's "Liberty Leading the People" celebrating the birth of a new political order in France.

Ancient India

The significance of nudity is not, however, universal. Leaving the specifically Euro-American context, we find nudity thematized in South Asia as well, although its significance is quite different in this context. In contemporary India, Nag Sadhu yogis (nag from naga which is a Prakritization of Sanskrit, nagna = "naked") and Digambara Jain (ambara = "clad in" dik = "space" or "skyclad"[1]) monks do not wear clothing, in contrast to the Buddhist monks and nuns who do.

Here, I wish to argue that it is useful to think of both the religious garb and the nudity it contrasts with as fashion. In doing so, I want to get away from simplistic interpretations that make robes or the lack thereof into forms of communication or symbols (despite the fact that traditional codifications of such interpretations are not hard to find). Religious regalia, as well as the lack thereof, in the Indian context are less silhouettes of the existing soul than a concretization of the aspirational ideals of the office the mendicant/ascetic would like to embody. That said, while not an explicit communication, religious fashion is nevertheless interpreted by those with the cultural capital to do so. Religious garb distinguishes the bearer or the bare (as the case may be) from and more importantly above others. But perhaps more than other fashion, religious fashion conveys normative force—not necessarily to conform or to adopt—but to acknowledge and to participate in its tacit division between the tasteful and distasteful.

If in the remainder of this chapter, I would like to discuss both the religious fashions around nudity in ancient India. The reason I begin so far back is that it is in the early writings on nudity that we find not some single "meaning of nudity" for any tradition but, rather, a set of debates about its meaning. It is the debate and the potential of its rhetoric about the body to empower or undermine that is carried forward in traditions down to the present.

Naked Asceticism

Greek authors such as Ptolemy (c second century CE) refer to naked ascetics among brahmins whom he refers to as *gymnosophistai* or "naked philosophers" (McCrindle 1885: 130). While Ptolemy does not give us the rationale behind this nakedness,[2] we do have an explanation of ascetic nakedness from the early Jains in the "Shaking It Off" (*dhuta*) chapter of the *Acaranga Sutra* (fourth to sixth centuries BCE[3]).

> The naked (*acela*—"unclothed"), fasting (monk), who combats the flesh, will be abused, or struck, or hurt; he will be upbraided with his former trade, or reviled with untrue reproaches. Accounting (for this treatment) by his former sins, knowing pleasant and unpleasant occurrences, he should patiently wander about. Quitting all worldliness, one should bear all (disagreeable) feelings, being possessed of the right view.
>
> Those are called naked (*nagina*) who in this world, never returning (to a worldly state), (follow) my religion according to the commandment. This highest doctrine has here been declared for men. (Jacobi 2002: 55–6. Cp *Acaranga Sutra* p. 184)

Most of these naked ascetics are referred to by the epithet "unclothed" (*acela*), both in Jain and in early Buddhist texts. There are two points of interest in the previous passage. The first is that we have, in the second paragraph, the word "naked" (*nagina*) used as a kind of honorific form of address, indicating a release from returning to the temporal world. But the honorific value of the epithet has to be read in the context of enduring the suffering brought on by being unclothed. Thus nakedness, far from being a reference to some primordial state, marks a kind of masculine silent endurance of suffering. As such, I suggest we read the bare body of the sage here as "naked" in the sense of being fully vulnerable to the physical injury of cold nights, hot days, sunburn, and insect bites. But walking around naked also subjects the ascetic to the ridicule and reproach of those who see his exposed body with all of its flaws and imperfections. Public nakedness thus renders the ascetic vulnerable to violence that might stem from social approbation. The Jain hero is thus one, like Mahavira in the *Acaranga Sutra*, who endures both scorn and the hardships of being exposed to the environment.

> "I shall not cover myself with that robe," only in the winter (he used it). . . . More than four months many sorts of living beings gathered on his body, crawled about it, and caused pain there.

> For a year and a month he did not leave off his robe. Since that time the Venerable One, giving up his robe, was a naked, world-relinquishing, houseless (sage).
>
> Then he meditated (walking) with his eye fixed on a square space before him of the length of a man. Many people assembled, shocked at the sight; they struck him and cried. (Jacobi: 79–80)

The key to understanding this practice, at least in early Jain texts, is that by embracing the vulnerability of nakedness, the ascetic is inviting the physical and emotional suffering in order to burn off karma. We find a similar, if slightly more complicated, logic among the early Pasupatas—an ascetic order of brahmin worshipers of Siva. According to Alexis Sanderson, the Pasupata ascetic,

> [t]hrowing off all the outward signs of his observance . . . moved about in public pretending to be crippled, deranged, mentally deficient or indecent. Passers-by being unaware that these defects were feigned spoke ill of him. By this means the Pasupata provoked an exchange in which his demerits passed to his detractors and their merits to him. By acting in this way, he was simply making unorthodox use of a thoroughly orthodox principle. He was exploiting his ritual status as one who had undergone a rite of consecration (*diksa*) to initiate an observance (*vrata*); for in the *srauta* system one bound by the observance (*vrata*) consequent on consecration (*diksa*) for the Soma sacrifice was similarly dangerous to anyone who might speak ill of him. (Sanderson 1988: 665)

Sanderson doesn't tell us that these Pasupatas were naked, but it would certainly fit the pattern given the shock with which Mahavira's nakedness was greeted. And while not all Jain renunciates were brahmins (and thus would not have undergone the consecration that would allow for the karmic transfer), simply the idea of burning off karma through enduring the hardship that nakedness entails makes nakedness as an ascetic practice a common tool for getting rid of karma.

Buddhist Monastic Robes

Buddhist monks and nuns could be equally enthusiastic about getting rid of karma but were distinctive among ascetics of their day due to the robes they wore. But how shall we read these robes? In India and in Southeast Asia, monks wear a robe consisting of three rectangular pieces of cloth: one worn around the waist covering the legs, the second covering the left shoulder and the uppermost covering the whole upper body. By contrast, in East Asia, the two inner robes have been replaced by a garment with sleeves and leggings. The outer garment (the samghati), however, is still worn.[4] The construction of these garments (or at least the outer one) is supposed to be constructed from a number of panels of cut cloth sewn together. In Buddhist monastic regulations, the construction of the Buddhist robe from seven panels being sewn together is authorized by a story in which the Buddha looks out onto the fields of Magadha and asks Ananda if he could provide the monks with robes that looked like that.[5] A less benign fashion in monastic wear would interpret the robe as a form of ascetic hardship insofar as monks may adopt the voluntary ascetic practice (dhutanga) of sewing discarded pieces of cloth or rages into a robe (the practice of pamsukula). In this practice, the marker of heroic asceticism is shifted from the naked body to the clothed one, such as the example we find in the Lalitavistara which rather famously has the Buddha making his robe out of the funeral shroud of a dead woman.[6]

However, when we look at relief sculptures from Pakistan (Gandhara), North India (Mathura), or South India (Amaravati) which have the earliest representations of the Buddha, we notice that none of the monastic robes displays the seven sewn panels (or any other indication of assemblage for that matter) that we find in monastic literature.[7] Anna Filigenzi has argued that the lack of sewn panels in Gandharan reliefs is due to the fact that the Magadha story was not the origin story for these monks. Pointing to a relief in which the Buddha is shown exchanging robes with a hunter,[8] she argues that monks in this region took this story to be the origin of Buddhist monastic robes—hence no panels. In fact, as a distinctive form of dress, what sets Buddhist monastic apparel apart from non-monastics is simply how much of the body is covered. In reliefs from Mathura and Amaravati, it is the laymen who are depicted as going shirtless adorned primarily with jewelry around their necks while courtesans are often depicted topless and wearing clothing low around their hips. The Buddha and his monks and nuns stand out in this regard insofar as the only ones in sculpted reliefs who cover their upper torso. This distinction is less apparent in Pakistan than it is in the south for the simple reason that the climate was colder, and the laity covered up accordingly.

Whatever the origin story of the Buddhist monastic robes, the monastic robe along with other items such as the begging bowl serve as insignia establishing a distinctive Buddhist identity. On its simplest level, the robe and bowl distinguish the Buddhist monk or nun from their counterparts in other groups. For example, in the section of the Buddhist monastic code governing monastic dress, there is a group of rules such as the following:

> At that time the Bhikkhus conferred the *upasampada* [full] ordination on persons that had no alms-bowl, they received alms with their hands. People were annoyed, murmured, and became angry, saying, "Like the Titthiyas." . . . [The Buddha said,] Let no one, O Bhikkhus, receive the *upasampada* ordination without having an alms-bowl, He who confers the *upasampada* ordination (on a person that has not), commits a *dukkata* offence. (Rhys Davids: 223)

The story is repeated with "robe" being substituted for "bowl," stating that the new ordinands then went out on alms rounds naked. As in the former case, not surprisingly, "people were annoyed." Here, the reason for the annoyance is that receiving food in an alms-bowl instead of in the hands and dressing in robes in lieu of going around naked is what marks off Buddhist identity from that of the "Titthiyas" (a difficult term, but here denoting non-Buddhist religious professionals). But beyond the confusion of sectarian identity, the Buddhist monastic codes tell us repeatedly that nakedness is "impure . . . disgusting, loathsome" (in Pali: *asuci, jeguccam* and *patikukam*[9]—the same three adjectives are used to describe a sewer into which a man is lowered in the Digha Nikaya's "Payasi Sutra" [Digha Nikaya, 2.325]). But where the Jain monks endured the scorn and disgust brought on by their nakedness, the Buddhist authors wanted monks and nuns to cover it up. In the chapter of the monastic regulations on robes, we find a monk trying to convince the Buddha that going naked is a great form of asceticism, presenting the Jain argument to the Buddha.

> The Blessed One, Lord, has praised in many ways the moderate man and the contented who has eradicated (evil), who has shaken off (*dhuta*) his passions, who is gracious, reverent, energetic. Now this nakedness, Lord, is in many ways effectual to moderation and content, to the eradication of evil, to the suppression of the passions. . . . It were well, Lord, if the Blessed One would enjoin nakedness upon the Bhikkhus.
>
> The Blessed Buddha rebuked him saying, "This would be improper, O foolish one, crooked, unsuitable, unworthy of a samana, unbecoming, and it ought not to be done. How can you, O foolish one, adopt nakedness as the Tithhiyas do? This will not conduce . . . to the conversion of the unconverted."
>
> He addressed the bhikkhus and said, You are not, O Bhikkhus, to adopt nakedness as the Tithhiyas do. Whosoever does so, shall be guilty of a grave offence. (Rhys Davids 1899: 245–6)

The Buddhist monastic robe as it is discussed in monastic regulations is only half of the story. If the authors of these texts want us to see the unclothed body as *naked* (as opposed to nude) and its nakedness as offensive, it does so partly to cast competing mendicant groups—and more importantly their bodies—as offensive. In doing so, we should also keep an eye on representations of the Buddhist body in the early Buddhist sculptural tradition.

Representations of clothing are simultaneously representations of the bodies they (partially) conceal. Just as Hollander has shown that nudes in Western art are usually depicted with reference to the clothed body, so too, we should understand Buddhist monastic fashion in reference to the unclothed or semi-unclothed body and the *bodily fashions* of the day. On the one hand, we can see the significance of the Buddhist monastic robe with its large folds in early Gandharan art to lie primarily in the amount of the body that it covers up. The robe is to be read both in contrast to the monk's Jain and Ajivaka counterparts, who are not only depicted as naked but depicted as unpleasantly so. Pia Brancaccio has discussed several representations of the naked ascetic, Patika in Gandharan art. She notes that in each representation of Patika, his naked body is a fat one. In the two reliefs she examines, one cannot help but compare Patika's chest with the bare chests of the laymen who are trying to help him stand up (the Buddha has miraculously stuck him to his stool). While the latter appear muscular and well apportioned, Patika's chest, in contrast to the Buddha's own, is decidedly flabby (Brancaccio 1991: 122). The fact that naked ascetics in Gandharan art are depicted as corpulent visually calls into question the degree of their commitment to asceticism. And here, it should also be remembered that it is particularly in the Northwest that Buddhists especially revered extreme acts of fasting. As Juhyung Rhi has shown, it is only in the Gandhara area that we find artistic and literary representations of the Buddha's own heroic fasting with no indication that this was a practice that he abandoned as unworthy (See Rhi 2006). The fat ascetics of other groups would have been held up (unfavorably) to the hyperbolic example of the Buddha's own fasting.

Unflattering representations of naked ascetics stand in contrast not only to the emaciated body of the true sage but also to the pleasingly (i.e., "nude") masculine body concealed by the drapery of the Buddha's robes when he is not fasting (see Figure 5.1). And here we should pay close attention to the way the Buddhist sculptors conceived of the nudity underneath the robes because there we find a subtle distinction between the nakedness of their ascetic competition and the presumed nudity concealed by the Buddhist robe.

There are two important points to consider when looking at the sculpted stone. First, an artist can make stone "cloth" do things that real cloth will never do. Second, an artist can render the body in ways that defy human biology in order for the clothes to perform in the way the artist wants. Hollander gives us the example of Ceres from the Vatican Sala Rotunda, whose breasts are set unnaturally wide on her chest in order to support the drapery of her robe in such a way that it doesn't look in danger of slipping off. We

Figure 5.1 Sculpture showing drapery of the Buddha. Photograph by Shoshin Kuwayama.

find a similar distortion of the body in representations of the Buddha but to different ends. Kushan-era Buddhas from Mathura have unnaturally gauzy robes covering them—such that they tend to look more like sculptures of naked Jain saints until, upon closer inspection, we can see the diaphanous folds of a robe lightly sketched on the left shoulder. Even when the folds are more prominent, the cling of the robes shows us every contour of the Buddha's torso even as it claims to cover it.

What we end up seeing before we notice that the Buddha has a robe is a torso that is often depicted with unnaturally wide shoulders. Here too, we should keep in mind that clothes are not the only things that have fashion. Bodies have their fashions too. When I was a teenager, many of my friends wanted to have biceps like Lou Ferrigno. Today, my students are far more likely to refer to the ideal masculine body as having "six-pack" abs than having large biceps. So too, in the first few centuries of the Common Era, the ideal masculine body around Mathura had broad shoulders, whereas torsos of the Buddha from the Gandhara region (probably in a nod to images of Heracles that were being repackaged as Vajrapani in the Gandhara area) tended to have more prominent pectorals than those farther south. Artists used stone drapery to full advantage to reveal the Buddha's body as simultaneously modest and at the same time pleasingly masculine, all according to local tastes.

But, whereas the drapery of the Buddhist robes allowed artists to display the Buddha's manly torso (as regionally inflected) to full advantage, the same technique of rendering the cloth as diaphanous (the "wet drapery" look) presented artists with quite a different problem of the nudity being covered up: his penis.[10] While the artists wanted to present the Buddha's body as pleasing and—more importantly—masculine in every way, they also wanted to preserve his modesty. This grew increasingly difficult for standing Buddhas as his robe became increasingly gauzy. Early depictions of the Buddha do show the genitalia under his robe, but by the fifth century, artists began to depict the standing Buddha sans genitalia.[11] Serenity Young notes:

> It will be recalled that during [the Kusan Dynasty, ca. first to third century CE] Buddhist iconography briefly celebrated male powers of fertility, . . . standing male figures from this period display penises under the folds of their garments, even statues of the Buddha. These statues have a distinct articulation of muscle and strength that express male power. As noted, this articulation of the male form disappeared rather quickly; indeed, male forms become somewhat feminized, or at least lost any suggestion of overt masculinity. (2004: 71)

For our purposes, what is significant about the later depictions of the Buddha's body is not so much that they are "feminized"[12] but that the penis is no longer depicted under even the clingiest of robes. Brown argues that the Buddha's lack of visible penis under his revealing robes can be explained by one of the thirty-two major "marks of the Buddha" in which the Buddha's penis is traditionally said to be "sheathed" or "concealed" "as in the case of a noble thoroughbred elephant or horse."[13] Young, following Dehija, argues that the sheathed penis actually becomes one of the thirty-two major marks of the

Buddha's body in the wake of the artistic tradition—marks that reflect the virtues that he has perfected over the span of innumerable lifetimes. Brown's argument assumes the sculptural innovation to precede the textual tradition, but this is clearly not the case.[14] Rather, it would appear that in the fifth-century artisans and their patrons merely decided to render the literary device of the sheathed penis "visible," in plastic art. While other marks, such as cranial protuberance and *usnisa* had always been represented, the sheathed penis was somewhat awkward. The Buddha's marks are usually thought to render his hyperbolic virtue visible or, better yet, "legible." But not this one. The mark of the sheathed penis makes what is noticeable among normal men, invisible for the Buddha—paradoxically rendering modesty and restraint visible through a visible absence. But why is that important? Just as a vow of poverty is meaningless when taken by the destitute, a vow of celibacy is hollow for the undesirable troglodyte or the impotent. For this reason, early Buddhist authors and artists found it necessary to maintain the Buddha's body not only as hyper-masculine but as sexually pleasing—even if he no longer uses it to please others sexually.

Thus, it is not just the fashion of the Buddhist robe that contrasts with the layperson, on the one hand, and with the naked ascetic on the other. The Buddhist body is itself contrasted with ascetics—either by way of a heroic ascetic masculinity or by way of the hyper-masculine strength of a healthy male torso with its "horse-like" potency sheathed beneath.

Brahmins and the Thread

Buddhist monastics and their robes are not only depicted in contrast to naked ascetics. Monastic insignia are also to be understood in light of what was (or was becoming) the paragon of religiosity in ancient India: the brahmin. Brahmins are a caste, usually referred to as the highest caste (at least when the author is himself a brahmin), and are credited with transmitting knowledge of sacred things. Visually, brahmins are rather uniformly depicted with their torsos either fully exposed or with one shoulder exposed to show their sacred thread, a string worn from left shoulder across the chest to mark initiation into Vedic learning. A good test case from the first and second centuries can be found in labeled sculptures of the future Buddha, Maitreya, who by all accounts is a brahmin by birth. Whether in Gandhara or in Mathura, Maitreya is always depicted as having at least one shoulder bared and as sporting a noticeable sacred thread during the Kushan Era.

Some have claimed that the category of "Buddhist" was opposed to that of "brahmin" from very early on. Regarding their clothing, Gregory Schopen has argued that we should look at the Buddhist robe as counterposed to the brahmin sacred thread. He notes a passage from the Mulasarvastivadin monastic code in which the Buddha declares to the monks: "They must not resort to wearing the sacred thread" (na brahmasutra-pravrtim bhajeta). Schopen surmises that the robe and the thread form markers of contrasting social identity, stating, "the focus here is on the issue of confusion or the clouding of identity and, as in previous cases, the response is unequivocal: a rule is made that Buddhist monks must not wear what blurs their social identity" (Schopen 2007: 73). This makes good sense if you assume that "Buddhist" was understood to be a different category from "brahmin." If this were the case, then it would be plausible for the difference between the two social identities to be marked by the different insignia they wore.

This rule Schopen translates is certainly remarkable, and at the very least it calls into question the assertion, now commonplace, that the Buddha somehow "redefined" or "reinterpreted" what it means to be a brahmin, so that any good Buddhist monk (regardless of caste) could then be considered a brahmin. The idea of Buddha as the redefiner-in-chief was first put forth by Kenneth James Saunders in 1915. Saunders, the literary secretary of the YMCA of India, Burma, and Ceylon, was quite an enthusiast of early Buddhism and saw in Buddhism all the reforming spirit of Protestant Christianity. In the introduction to his translation of the Brahmana chapter of the *Dhammapada*, he writes, "Like other social reformers, Gautama set himself to redefine current terms. Very much as Saint Paul redefined the term 'Jew', he gave to the proud title brahman a new meaning and showed that he is the true noble who acts nobly" (Saunders 1915: 51). A few years later, he would write,

> Brahma and Brahman, the Vedas, the Brahmins, Nirvana, the Dharma, the Atman, Karma itself he redefined them all. Early Buddhism, like early Christianity, consisted in a revaluation of values, a transformation of ritual rightness into moral righteousness, a bringing of an other-worldly joy and peace into the midst of a sorrowful world. Gotama like Jesus towers above our vindication of his originality (Saunders 1924: 26)

This idea that Buddha redefined brahmanical terms so that they somehow attain a very different value has, of course, been repeated ad nauseam by scholars such as Steven Collins,[15] Richard Gombrich,[16] Patrik Olivelle,[17] Brian Black,[18] and Nathan McGovern,[19] to mention but a few. The only thing that has changed from 1915 is that the explicit comparisons with the Protestant Reformation have been dropped. But if Buddhists actually did believe that they (or at least the most accomplished among them) had attained that status of brahmin, why this rule against dressing the part?

Elsewhere in the Chinese translation of the Mulasarvastivadin monastic code,[20] we find another story in which Mahamaudgalyayana (one of the Buddha's chief disciples and a brahmin by birth) goes to his uncle who is practicing in a hermitage. His uncle tells him to leave since only brahmins are allowed at the retreat. Maudgalyayana protests that he is a brahmin, to which his uncle replies that no one who does not wear the sacred thread, hold the sacrificial ladle, perform the fire sacrifice, or who is bald can be called a brahmin. To this Maudgalyayana replies that shame is his sacred thread, true kindness is his ladle, and that speaking truth is his fire. Maudgalyayana here is echoing the so-called "redefinition of the brahmin" passages such as we find in the Dhammapada passages Saunders translates. What is fascinating about this story is that this is the only story I am aware of in which this "redefinition" of brahminhood is actually applied to a named person.[21] Most passages discussing what a "real" brahmin is are taught to somebody or are spoken by the Buddha while teaching to brahmins. Nowhere else in Buddhist literature does a monk claim that his accomplishments qualify him to be referred to as a brahmin. And the fact that the story repeatedly emphasizes that Maudgalyayana already is a brahmin by birth[22] means that the only instance of the so-called redefinition of brahmin status in early Buddhist literature is applied to none other than a brahmin by birth. Nobody who is not born a brahmin is ever referred to as "brahmin" by the Buddha or anyone else.

So, why does Maudgalyayana not wear a sacred thread here? It isn't clear. He has taken it off at some point, but there is really no indication that he was ever asked or expected to take it off. The same question can be raised about the 500 Jatilas under Uruvela Kassapa who throw their hair and ritual implements in the water in order to follow the Buddha (see Rhys Davids: 152). While it is tempting to see this as a repudiation of Vedic learning in favor of Buddhist learning, I think this interpretation is doubtful. While later than our monastic regulations sources, we do find accounts in brahmanical texts of brahmins discarding their sacred thread and other ritual paraphernalia in water or on the ground. This was simply one of the ways that brahmins renounced the world. For example, the Aruni Upanisad states:

> A householder or a Vedic student or a forest hermit should discard his sacrificial string on the ground or in water. He should deposit his external fires in the fire of his stomach and the *gayatri* in the fire of his speech . . . [saying:] I am truly Brahman. . . . Brahman is the string; and assuredly I, who know it, am the string. Let a wise man who knows thus discard the external string. . . . A man who knows the import of the Veda may indeed abandon these either before or after his Vedic initiation: father, son, fire, sacrificial string, rites, wife and everything elsewhere below. (Olivelle, 116–17)

It is, therefore, not at all clear from Schopen's rule that we should read the monastic robe as somehow signifying the absence of the brahmanical string. Brahmins could wear a thread or not wear one and retain their caste status. Looking at the broad range of Buddhist literature, distinguishing Buddhist dress and insignia from that of brahmins is simply not a concern at any time period. Indeed, the Mulasarvastivada vinaya passage may well be the exception that proves the rule. Among the monastic codes of the early Buddhist sects, only the Mulasarvastivada code[23] has this rule. It is absent from the codes of the Mahasamghikas, Mahisasakas, Dharmaguptakas, and the Theravadins. We can only assume, then, that if a brahmin were to ordain in any of these other monastic orders, there would have been no need to take off the sacred thread—probably most brahmins simply continued to wear it beneath their robes. More to the point, none of these monastic codes (including the Mulasarvastivada account that Schopen translates) stipulates that a brahmin must remove his sacred thread upon ordination to the monkhood. So how to interpret the rule? Readers in ancient India would have been familiar with these six unruly monks; their misbehavior appears in numerous origin stories for monastic rules. Any Buddhist listener would have been aware that they were not born brahmins. The unruly six decide to put on sacred threads so that they can get more alms like a brahmin they saw receiving food. The Sanskrit "pravrtim" here can also be translated as "to don" or "to put on," instead of simply "to wear." Read that way, I would have to agree with Schopen that "Buddhist monks must not wear what blurs their social identity." But, I differ insofar as I see the concern here as not the blurring of a brahmin and a Buddhist identity but of a brahmin and a non-brahmin identity. Brahmins could wear a thread or not wear one, but non-brahmins could not choose to wear one. Monks are forbidden from wearing a sacred thread if they were not born in the proper caste to wear one. In this sense, the robe marks the difference of the brahmin Buddhist monk from the brahmin Buddhist layperson insofar as the former covers his thread with the robe while the latter does not.

In the early centuries of the Common Era, there was no contrast between Buddhists and brahmins any more than there is a contrast between "women" and, say, "Minnesotans." Many brahmins were Buddhists.[24] The case of Maitreya is illustrative. No one (or at least no Buddhist that I am aware of) would suggest that Maitreya is currently a heretic or that he will somehow cease to be a brahmin when he becomes a Buddha. Assuming his brahmanical status to be something he overcomes would be about as anachronistic as expecting Christians to assume that Jesus renounces his Judaism at the crucifixion—interesting idea, but it simply isn't a thing among Christians. The sacred thread that Maitreya wears is not, therefore, a mark of alterity but rather a mark of high Buddhist birth.

Conclusion

The main theme of this book is that religious apparel should be considered as a kind of "Silhouette of the Soul." For Indian asceticism, however, it was always the body itself, with its major and minor marks, with its insignia of emaciation or masculinity that was an index to the unseen inner state of the sage. To understand religious garb or lack thereof in a South Asian context, then requires us to be aware of the *interplay* between the body and the cloth, being careful not to reduce even this interplay to a set "meaning" but being open to debates among not only the laity but the ascetic groups themselves.

Notes

1. This term is also used in later Upanisads such as the *Turyatitavadhuta Upanisad* with synonyms such as *asambara* ("wearing space") used in the *Paramahamsa Upanisad*.
2. Two centuries later, Pseudo-Origen (fourth century CE) tells us that sages dwelling around the Tungabhadra River in Andhra Pradesh, "Throughout life they go about naked, saying that the body has been given by the Deity as a covering for the soul" (McCrindle 1877: 120).
3. See Ohira (1994: 9).
4. Much has been written on the symbolism and uses of monastic garments, and I will not go into depth here. One particularly helpful article is that of Kieschnick 1999.
5. See, for example, Vin. I.126. Msv II. 50–1.

6. This topic has been treated at length by Gregory Schopen (2007).
7. The earliest depiction of the Buddha dressed in a robe made of sewn panels (in this case, of rags) is from fifth-century Ajanta. My thanks to Pia Brancaccio for this reference.
8. Filigenzi 2005: 105–6. Pia Brancaccio tells me that the patchwork robe can be found in a few paintings at Ajanta.
9. For example, Vinaya 1.291, 293.
10. This was first pointed out in Brown 2002: 166ff.
11. Brown (p. 166) dates the first Buddha image to be lacking genitalia to 434 CE at Govindnagar.
12. Brown argues, I think rightly, that it is not at all clear that these Buddhas were coded as "feminine" by the standards of the day.
13. Brown 167. Brown quotes Conze's translation of the Large Sutra on Perfection of Wisdom. For what it is worth, this passage is not in the earliest translation of the large Perfection of Wisdom, translated by Moksala in the first half of the third century CE.
14. If the first Buddha to be depicted without noticeable genitalia beneath his robe was carved in 434 CE, then we have discussions of the Buddha's penis being hidden like a horse at least two centuries earlier in the translations of Kang Mengxiang (T. 184, p. 464c15, translated between 196–220 CE.) and Zhi Qian (T. 76, p. 883c6, translated sometime between 222 and 253 CE). If the *Da fangbian fu bao'en jing* is indeed a Han dynasty translation, then it mentions (at 156, p. 164c17) that the Buddha's penis is sheathed, "like an elephant, horse or king."
15. See Collins 1982: 32–3.
16. See, for example, Gombrich 2006: 20.
17. Olivelle 2011: 60.
18. Black 2011: 152.
19. See McGovern (2018).
20. This story does not appear in the Gilgit manuscript but can be found in Yijing's seventh-century translation at T. 1451 p. 208c7ff.
21. Gombrich 2006: 20, rather, carelessly states that the *Catusparisat Sutra* opens with "a set of three verses (Vin I,2) in which [the Buddha] repeatedly refers to himself as a brahmin." He does no such thing, nor does the "snooty brahmin" who comes afterward say that he does. The verses *may be read* (as Gombrich does) to imply that the Buddha identifies himself as a brahmin, but the grammar of the verses speak about the brahmin in the third person. The Buddha never says that he is a brahmin.
22. The listener would have already known this, and lest they forget, the story tells us that the objecting Brahmin is his uncle.
23. The rule can be found in the Ksudrakavastu that Schopen translates from Tibetan (and also in Yijing's seventh-century Chinese translation of the same at T. 1451, p. 208c7ff.).
24. For a lengthier discussion of Buddhist brahmins in early Buddhism, see Walser (2018).

References

Acaranga Sutra: Part I, Original Text with Variant Readings, Hindi Version Notes, Annotations and Appendix, ed. Shobhacandra Bharilla, Beawar: Shri Agam Prakashan Samiti, 1944.

Asad, Talal (2018), *Secular Translations: Nation-State, Modern Self, and Calculative Reason*. New York: Columbia University Press.
Barthes, Roland, Richard Miller and Richard Howard (1975), *The Pleasure of the Text*, New York: Hill and Wang.
Black, Brian (2011), "Ambattha and Svetaketu: Literary Connections between the Upanisads and Early Buddhist Narratives," *Journal of the American Academy of Religion*, 79(1): 136–61.
Brancaccio, Pia (1991), "The Buddha and the Naked Ascetics in Gandharan Art a New Interpretation," *East and West*, 41(1/4): 121–31.
Brown, Robert (2002), "The Feminization of the Sarnath Gupta-Period Buddha Images," *Bulletin of the Asia Institute*, 16: 165–79.
Collins, Steven (1982), *Selfless Persons: Imagery and Thought in Theravada Buddhism*, Cambridge: Cambridge University Press.
Filigenzi, Anna (2005), "Gestures and Things: The Buddha's Robe in Gandharan Art," *East and West*, 55(1/4): 103–16.
Gombrich, Richard F. (2006), *How Buddhism Began: The Conditioned Genesis of the Early Teachings*, London: Routledge.
Hollander, Anne (1993), *Seeing through Clothes*, Berkeley, CA: University of California Press.
Jacobi, Hermann (2002), *Jaina Sutras Part I: The Akaranga Sutra, the Kalpa Sutra*, Delhi: Motilal Banarsidass.
Kieschnick, John (1999), "The Symbolism of the Monk's Robe in China," *Asia Major*, 12(1): 9–32.
McCrindle, John Watson (1885), *Ancient India as Described by Ptolemy*, New Delhi: Today and Tomorrows Publishers.
McCrindle, John Watson (1877), *McCrindle's Ancient India, as Described by Megasthenes and Arrian*, London: Trubner & Co.
McGovern, Nathan (2018), *The Snake and the Mongoose: The Emergence of Identity in Early Indian Religion*, New York: Oxford University Press.
Ohira, Suzuko and Pariṣad Prakrta Grantha (1994), *A Study of the Bhagavatisutra: A Chronological Analysis*, Prakrit Text Series; No. 28, Ahmedabad: Prakrit Text Society.
Olivelle, Patrick (2011), *Ascetics and Brahmins: Studies in Ideologies and Institutions*, London: Anthem Press.
Rhi, Juhyung (2006), "Fasting Buddhas, Lalitavistara, and Karunapundarika," *Journal of the International Association of Buddhist Studies*, 29(1): 125–53.
Rhys Davids, T. W. and Hermann Oldenberg (1899), *Vinaya Texts Part I*, New York: Charles Scribner's Sons.
Sanderson, Alexis (1988) "Saivism and the Tantric Traditions," in Stewart R. Sutherland (ed.), *The World's Religions*, 660–704, Boston: G.K. Hall.
Saunders, Kenneth James (1924), *Epochs in Buddhist History: Buddhism in India, Nepal, Tibet, Ceylon, Burma, Siam, China, Japan, Korea*. The Haskell Lectures; 1921, Chicago, IL: University of Chicago.
Saunders, Kenneth James (1915), *The Heart of Buddhism: Being an Anthology of Buddhist Verse*, trans. and ed. K. J. Saunders. London; Toronto: H. Mildord, Oxford University Press.
Schopen, Gregory (2007), "Cross-Dressing with the Dead: Asceticism, Ambivalence, and Institutional Values in an Indian Monastic Code," in Jacqueline Stone (ed.), *The Buddhist Dead: Practices, Discourses, Representations*, Honolulu: University of Hawaii Press.
Walser, Joseph (2018), "When Did Buddhism Become Anti-Brahmanical? The Case of the Missing Soul," *Journal of the American Academy of Religion*, 86(1): 94–125.
Young, Serinity (2004), *Courtesans and Tantric Consorts: Sexualities in Buddhist Narrative, Iconography and Ritual*, New York: Routledge.

CHAPTER 6
EMPOWERED ENTREPRENEURS
WOMEN OF MUSLIM FAITH AND THE MODEST FASHION MOVEMENT IN THE UNITED STATES
Hassanah El-Yacoubi

Setting the Stage

"Muslim New York Fashion Week"

Lights, camera, and tears—the stage was set, the audience in awe. Attendees told me they felt like they just attended "the Muslim New York Fashion Week." Afterward, Instagram coverage of the event was full of comments like "modest is hottest!" and "one of, if not the, best Muslim-run events I've ever been to." The PFH Modest Fashion Convention came alive for the fifth year in a row in Irvine, California. The largest of its kind in the United States it was surely an experience to be remembered. Models were runway-ready, all clad in various sartorial styles ranging from a myriad of modest activewear, swimwear, casual and formalwear, and even bridal wear. I noted the sunny hues, the stylish silhouettes, the statement gowns, the flowy fabrics, Muslim models in flawless makeup, donning hairdos or hijab-done ensembles, all appearing unique yet converging on one main element: pride in being a woman of Muslim faith. Attendees came from all over the country to witness and participate. The crowds were bustling with excitement as the seats were filled with grandmothers, mothers, and daughters. I had the pleasure of meeting three generations of women from daughters to their mothers and their grandmothers, all sharing one common goal of supporting their community of Muslim sisters. It was a sight to see but more so a moment to be cherished and remembered for the mark it would leave on the hearts and minds of hundreds of attendees that left some in tears. Tears of joy, as it was not merely the fashions that awed the audience, nor the glamorous runway, theatrical stage lights, or even the aesthetics of the show, but rather the symbolic meaning its presentation conveyed and embodied. Finally, women who are Muslim are being portrayed in a positive light, in control of their image, in a setting that has historically been exclusionary to them and their religious values. It was a nationally recognized fashion show and convention with a twist: it was dedicated solely to Muslim modest fashion.

The 5th Annual PFH Modest Fashion Convention held on August 5, 2018, in Irvine, California, was one of the largest modest fashion expositions in the country (Kandil, 2017). It gathered nearly a thousand women from around the nation for a day's worth of connection and collaboration through networking, shopping, entrepreneurship, and fellowship among local and national Muslim brands, influencers, and women seeking support and a sense of community. Attendees explained to me that for a community that is often silenced and scrutinized, witnessing their Muslim sisters being represented in a way that reflected the diversity of their subjectivities was momentous. Western assumptions, that of Europe and the United States, deeming Muslim women as drab and unfashionable were quickly put to rest as the vibrant Modest Fashion Movement traverses fashion scenes around the globe, with Muslim-majority countries at the helm of it. The annual PFH Conventions are an extension of this movement. It was a production female Muslims, and particularly Muslim fashion enthusiasts, have only dreamed of seeing. Something had forever been changed. Not only were these women giving new meaning to Muslim embodiment through sartorial practices, but their subjectivities were shaped by their roles as entrepreneurs catering to various aspects of Muslim lifestyle.

Introduction

This chapter seeks to illuminate the ways by which the social institution of veiling practices was transformed by the advent of the Modest Fashion Movement (MFM) in the United States, a movement I have been part of since 2009. It was then that I realized many members of my own community desired to wear the hijab and dress modestly but did not feel confident in taking on that visibility. Culturally, at that time there were barely any modest clothing options across the mainstream marketplace making being modest and fashionable a mutually exclusive endeavor. However, in 2015 this would all change with the advent of the MFM when the Muslim modest sector proved to be a highly lucrative yet underserved market and big fashion brands began to cater to Muslim sartorial needs. I explore how outcomes of this phenomenon rendered Islam more legible within the Western cultural fabric and imagination. I argue that the MFM has reformed the popular perspective on veiling within the United States by restoring the heterogeneity, complexity, and historicity of such practices whereby new opportunities have been created for women of Muslim faith.

Following the attacks of 9/11, the US American Muslim community has actively demanded new social and political possibilities to fight for an equal space within religious and public establishments. This was particularly true for women of Muslim faith as it relates to conflicts surrounding women and gender, which led to a growing presence of the veil in the United States. The hijab began to reemerge during what Leila Ahmed (2011: 213) called a "new cycle of history" as a result of the growing presence of Islamism within the United States and around the world. The veil took on new cultural meanings within the post 9/11 era that would eventually pave the way for new acceptance of the practice within mainstream North America. There are plenty of other ways to understand the reasons for veiling, as Ahmed suggests, such as the hijab as a form of identity formation as well as a fashion statement, which is the focal point of this chapter. It is within this cultural context that the MFM burgeoned.

It is the purpose of my work to show Muslim subjectivities as a cultural construction of Muslim identity that actively rejects the passivity and docility ascribed to Muslim womanhood. Additionally, as a feminist intervention, I see it as my mission to diversify and disaggregate the static impressions of the monolithic "Muslim woman" seemingly sealed within Western imaginations, and I intentionally seek to engender new nomenclature that provides a fresh conceptual framework for understanding female Muslims in a way that portrays their subjectivities as mobile, stylish, and boundless. This new wave of visibility reifies the intricacies of veiling practices as it operates on a continuum of cultural changes throughout history and specifically within this contemporary moment. I should note that while the focus of this chapter is on veiled women and veiling practices in the United States, it should be noted that despite the MFM's attempt of an inclusive representation of Muslim womanhood, this new visibility has a propensity to highlight predominantly white hijab-donning women though 40 percent of US Muslim women do not wear the hijab, which presents a false equivalency of modest attire with hijab-wearing women (Pew 2017). Muslim womanhood is manifested through multiple modes, and modest fashion being a very powerful one, and the one I am a participant within, but it is not the only avenue. By moving beyond the veil as a mere marker of religious identity and, instead, as an expression of individualized Muslim personhood, this chapter highlights the diversity of not only Muslim sartorial practices but also Muslim lifestyle.

"Muslim Women" versus "Women of Muslim Faith"

In this chapter, I adopt the identifier "women of Muslim faith" in order to subvert the reductive stereotypes associated with the term "Muslim woman." As Miriam Cooke explains,

> The Muslimwoman is both a noun and an adjective that refers to an imposed identification that the individual may or may not choose for herself. The Muslimwoman is not a description of a reality; it is the ascription of a label that reduces all diversity to a single image. (2007: 140)

Hence, by extension, the plurality of the term "Muslim women" also collapses complex identities into a homogenous entity as a result of the violent aftermath of colonial and Oriental depictions whereby female adherents of Islam were stripped of their diverse makeup and cast with a broad stroke (Kandiyoti 1991). "Muslim women" is usually deployed as an ahistorical term that freezes female adherents to Islam in time and space. It conjures an impression of an imagined group of women who have no independent existence, are inept, incomplete, and lack power. While the term may allude to brown women, it certainly does not account for white and Black female Muslims.

The plurality of this diverse group of women is not captured by the term "Muslim women" and instead connotes a collective formation of an already constituted and conflated group of women, which has its roots in a colonial process that wiped away their diversity and ascribed singularity across Muslim subjects and Islamic culture. Instead of perpetually referring to this group as "Muslim women," I propose using the phrase "women of Muslim faith" particularly in the present tense, since "Muslim women" can unintentionally conjure an imagined singular woman that is antiquated. "Women of Muslim faith" places the emphasis on their gender before their religious orientation, rendering them as active human agents in the present first and foremost, fully capable of choosing their religious identity and sartorial presentations. "Women of Muslim faith" offers a fresh framework that is not totalizing and does not start from a point of reference that assumes commonality among this group of women, and instead intentionally searches for harmonious dynamism through difference and variability.

This new phraseology offers a fresh theoretical lens that enjoins an epistemological shift toward Muslim identity formation that is anti-essentialist by expanding the scope of womanhood, irrespective of the strictures of language, and posits women as active subjects and not the objects of study. It is a point of reference that pushes back against grand narratives prevalent throughout the media and Western academy to include new horizons that successfully capture and reclaim the distinct ethos of female Muslims in all its states of flux and fluidity. As Sylvia Chan-Malik (2018) argues, centering women as subjects and not objects is essential in examining how they have shaped Islam and its cultural meaning throughout the United States. This chapter applies a similar theoretical lens in understanding how women yield to modest fashion as a form of female Muslim subject formation.

Diversifying Islamic Veiling Practices

Donning the hijab, or what I call *hijab practices*, manifests through a multitude of head dresses from scarves to turbans and even hats worn with various sartorial styles rendered with individuated and personal meaning. Fadwa El Guindi posits the veil as a "complex cultural phenomenon" that is deeply rich and nuanced, which at its core is "a language that communicates social and cultural messages" (1999: xii). Such a definition allows for the emphasis to be placed on the cultural forms veiling takes on across different regions, such as the Middle East and the UK, or even subregions like the Levant and West Africa. The hijab specifically takes on various forms across the globe especially within non-Muslim countries like the United States (a country which has seen its longest wars situated in Iraq and Afghanistan). Instead of fixating on a specific version of hijab practices that merely meets the Islamic dress code based on the Quranic interpretations of modern scholars of religion and Islamic studies, it also allows the individual import imbued within such performances to flourish.

While scholarly interpretations of the specific requirements for modest dress may vary between traditionalists and modernists, hijab is typically understood to be the covering of the entire body with the exception of the hands and face. This translates into a dress code that embraces hijabs and various forms of head coverings, high necklines, long sleeves, flowy silhouettes, and to the floor hems. Through understanding the veil as an alive and adaptable practice, female Muslim subjectivities can thrive and equally exist in a space that encourages the complexity and creativity of subject formation instead of inhibiting and limiting it to the confines of inevitably varying textual interpretations.

The primary symbol of the monolithic Muslim woman has been and continues to be the hijab, or headcover, which has also been deemed as an "oppressive" and static Islamic practice through the European colonial encounter, despite the fact that historically veiling has never meant one thing nor has it been performed uni-dimensionally. In fact, it is important to establish that Islam did not invent the practice of veiling; instead, it modified an already existing custom that was prevalent during seventh-century Arabia and prior to dating back to ancient near Eastern communities from Greeks to Romans, Jews, and Assyrians (El Guindi 1999: 3). Hijab practices have adapted across time and place according to each unique cultural interpretation. In fact, it was not solely a female practice either, as male veiling, though different, was quite common in pre- and post-Islamic Arabia and takes on various cultural forms throughout the Middle East until today. Hence, it is no surprise that veiling practices are taking on new meanings and cultural permutations within a contemporary US context. The exhausted emphasis on veiling as a gendered female practice was part of the Orientalist discourse on female Muslim subjectivities created in order to justify colonialism and colonial rule over Muslim societies. Muslim women, and more generally the Oriental woman, were depicted in a way where "she never spoke of herself, she never represented her emotions, presence, or history. *He* spoke for and represented her" (Said 1978: 6). Orientalism's greatest feat, as Edward Said argues, was not merely engendering a successful campaign geared toward a collective discourse on the Orient but rather is manifested in its demonstration of Eurocentric power over the Orient that is deeply embedded across academic and cultural formations to this very day. As such, the Muslim subject, and in particular women, has been in a constant state of dismantling deep-seated Orientalist systems of power that have shaped Muslim identity and culture for generations. Many women are attempting to distinguish themselves beyond the confines of a "secular" or "traditional" dialectic and in so doing have creatively fashioned an identity through sartorial practices that seek to disrupt the Western trope of the "oppressed Muslim woman" (Abu-Lughod 2013).

Historically, the Western gaze was exhibited through dress and the body, as it was for European colonialists of the eighteenth and nineteenth centuries. The emphasis on dress and female bodily comportment has always been a point of fixation where cultural value systems and social principles were manifested through clothing and corporeal appearance (Foster 2004: 11). To dress in a way that marked visible difference between the locals and the natives was the basis for the "us" and "them" dichotomy, them being the veiled Muslim other, which still holds true in Western societies today. Diverse groups of women of Muslim faith who reclaim Islam as a cultural and social identity through individuated expressions of contemporary Muslim womanhood are directly affected by such biased depictions. It is against this historical backdrop that Muslim women within this modern moment, and throughout history, have sought to pushback against the grossly inaccurate depictions of Muslim womanhood prevalent within Western consciousness. Paradoxically, what was once deemed a symbol of oppression is now taking on new symbolic meaning in the quest for cultural identity, as new deployments of the hijab become reflective of the individual realities experienced by women of Muslim faith.

Modest Fashion Movement (MFM)

Just a decade ago, modest fashion was deemed unattractive and traditional throughout European and American consumer markets. Now modest fashion is considered a way of dress that is fashionable and desirable by women who are not only Muslim but from other faith groups as well. I propose the term "Modest Fashion Movement"[1] to articulate this "transitional moment" as Elizabeth Bucar (2017) calls it, whereby women of Muslim faith are experiencing heightened levels of representation and visibility within Western culture. In 2017 modest fashion became one of the most prominent fashion styles around the world evidenced across coveted runways, international magazines and malls, and numerous fashion media outlets proclaiming that "modesty has gone mainstream" (Gonzalez 2019). This movement has been referred to as a "trend" across many publications, but such typology connotes ephemerality which does an injustice to this phenomenon as modest fashion is here to stay. The potential of this visibility was recognized through a myriad of media coverage of not only the fashions but the women involved in this movement in the capacity of consumer, entrepreneur, influencer, designer, model, and stylist. I refer to it as a *movement* because like other social movements many women all around the world, be it activists or non-activists, are participating in various forms of intervention, acts of individual agency and creativity loosely related but not necessarily tied to an organized collective. As one of the PFH Convention's influencers Syrian-American activist Isra Chaker (2018) put it, "this is not just a movement, this is setting the Muslim women narrative straight with what it's true intention should always be: love love and more love." The MFM has no formal organization nor does it advocate for one specific goal, and instead represents very distinct personal initiatives as well as an imagined collective that simultaneously cross and contradict.

My understanding of the modest fashion phenomenon employs a definition of modesty that is "polysemic" as Reina Lewis (2013) describes it, which enables adherents of that aesthetic to embody multiple manifestations of modest fashion according to their own interpretation. Certainly, many women dress that way out of religious conviction, but it is important to note that motivations for modest wear are not solely based upon religiosity. For some women, dressing modestly is more about being a part of a community and indicative of cultural norms that are subject to change. For others it is more of a personal preference for bodily comportment, and for some it is a creative way to gain social mobility. Thus, it is my intention to broaden the scope of modest dress in a way that is reflective of how modest dressers perceive themselves to be operating within a cultural context. Defining a proper form of Muslim womanhood and visibility has been the task of Muslims both traditionalists and progressivists, fundamentalists,

Western feminists, Muslim countries, and non-Muslim states. As such, I find it analytically unproductive to make any pronouncements as to which types of modesty are considered proper form and instead employ an understanding of modest fashion that is reflective of an ever-evolving and shifting form of female Muslim subjectivities, all while recognizing the norms and practices that bind this group together. Helpful is Jill D'alessandro's characterization of modest fashion in Western Muslim circles as a preference for hyper-stylish garments across various levels of bodily coverage (2018: 48). This variety extends to diverse concerns for cultural aesthetic expression and how clothing reveals or conceals the shape of the body.

Social media has been a powerful mode of networking and an outlet for movement makers seeking to showcase their version of modest fashion with Instagram being the preferred platform for up-and-coming and established fashion influencers. A quick search on Instagram for "modest fashion" garners nearly three million posts not to mention the thousands of profiles dedicated to modest fashion inspiration. Many Muslim fashionistas or "Muslim style arbiters," as associate curator of costume and textiles arts at the Fine Arts Museums of San Francisco Laura Camerlengo describes, turn to Instagram to foster fresh dialogue and visibility surrounding Muslim fashion and faith in twenty-first-century America. This is done through a plethora of styles that coincide and or conflict with normative understandings of veiling practices. For example, many US American Muslim women have adopted a turban-style head covering such as rapper and modest fashion influencer Neelam Hakeem of @neelam_ who wears various styles of turbans and hoodies instead of a headscarf. This type of style leaves the neck bear which is considered questionable within more conservative Muslim circles. This style of head garb is a popular type of head dress among Black and Sikh women and has been adapted by many Arab women. I should note that turbans are not worn solely by women and are a common head wrap for men throughout the Arab region (El Guindi 1999: 105). Modest fashion influencer Mona Shams of @garbsandcarbs usually wears hats instead of a traditional scarf to cover her hair, which is always paired with turtle necks to ensure her neck is covered. Influencer and cofounder of Wise Systems Layla Shaikley of @laylool wears a hijab that is loosely wrapped around her head leaving a visible amount of her hair uncovered. Modest fashion influencer and content creator Zahraa Berro of @zahraa_hberro also likes to wear her hijab loosely but pairs it with an under-piece that provides full coverage of her hair and neck. All four of these women express a unique yet similar style of head dress manifested through hijab practices which are rooted in their own personal convictions of how hijab should be perceived and performed.

As the number and popularity of these influencers reveal, modest fashion now permeates mainstream fashion media and markets in the United States. Where not long ago modest dressers struggled to simply find apparel companies that cater to their religious requirements of long sleeves, high necklines, and maxi length silhouettes, this niche market segment has now opened a window of opportunities for Muslims in the capacity of designers, stylists, spokeswomen, models, and beauty experts. In 2015 H&M featured UK-based Muslim model Mariah Idrissi in their international campaign ad that went viral for its push toward inclusivity and diversity (Matera 2017). American Eagle, an American lifestyle brand, became one of the first brands to release a hijab collection featuring a Muslim model named Halima Aden, who shortly thereafter became the first hijab-donning model to be signed to IMG, a coveted global management agency. Not only has modest dress become a viable market segment, but Muslim lifestyle needs are now being taken seriously. The "big business" of the modest fashion market has repeatedly been recognized by journalists, scholars, and bloggers. Modest fashion purchases by women who are Muslim is estimated to be $44 billion in 2016 and 2017, which amounts to almost 18 percent of the total estimated $243 billion spent by Muslims on apparel (Loveluck 2018). While the majority of modest fashion buyers are based in the Middle East, there has been a growing demand for modest wear in the United States and United Kingdom.

The Making of a New Visibility

Modest fashion as a trend has been presented as a recent phenomenon over the past two decades, despite the fact that it is tied to a long history of Islamic dress that varies across communities and geographies. In fact, historically clothing has always served as a powerful medium between the East and West dating back to the Ottoman period during the late nineteenth century (El Guindi 1999). Yet, there is something different about how modest fashion, or "the new modesty," as founder of popular luxury fashion e-commerce site the Modist Ghizlan Guenez called it (D'Alessandro 2018: 51), is being perceived in the twenty-first century throughout the Middle East, United States, and Europe. While modest fashion is generally understood to be dominated by Muslim women, clothing worn by women of Jewish, Sikh, and Christian faiths has also been characterized as modest fashion (Singh 2017).

Modest styles are not solely for Muslim desires nor do Muslims have a monopoly on modesty, but it certainly has served as a catalyst in altering the perception of the veil in the United States. It stands in contradistinction to the "imaginary veil" conjured in the Western imaginary as an "awkward black cloak that covers the whole body including the face and is designed to prevent women's mobility" (Hoodfar 2001: 424). In many ways the MFM provides an opportunity for women to destabilize the Western gaze through asserting individuated sartorial expressions of modest fashion that render their positioned selves as impervious to the Western onlooker, both male and female, and to the American Muslim observer as well. It also creates an avenue for women of Muslim faith to assert their consumer power and creative intervention within the mainstream marketplace. This has positioned them as both competitors and participants in the exploitative nature of capitalist market economies that prey on commercializing Muslim identities, but what distinguishes Muslim entrepreneurs from neoliberal consumer culture is intentionality.

Many Muslim companies such as special events company Crown Your Occasions and modern Muslim baby gear company Jasmine and Marigold have expressed their desire to elevate the Muslim experience within the United States by catering to Muslim needs. For them, social mission far outweighs profitability. Yet capitalist domination continues to manifest through the commodification of modest fashion in its various forms across a neoliberal global marketplace. This is the "double face" of fashion that, on the one hand, has long been viewed as a method of subordination and exploitation within feminist theorization and, on the other, offers liberating possibilities. Elizabeth Wilson argues that to solely view fashion through the lens of oppression toward women is to "miss the richness of its cultural and political meaning" (2003: 13). Through modest fashion a counter-hegemonic visualization is offered of an empowered self that deliberately emphasizes the boundaries of difference, instead of diluting it, in ways that destabilize the authority of Western feminist scholarship and cultural practices. The goal for many participants is to visibly assert pride in their religious identity (Janmohamed 2016: 36–7).

The MFM was spearheaded by female Muslim millennials seeking to carve an individuated identity for themselves instead of allowing gendered Orientalist representations of Muslim womanhood, such as the oppressed and silenced Muslim woman who needs saving trope, prevail within mainstream Western culture (Janmohamed 2016: 96, 27–35, 100). The rise of Muslim modest fashion has engendered a new "cultural cool" that birthed a wave of modest influencers who refused to accept the exclusionary tendencies of the mainstream marketplace. Many Muslim curators of style began showcasing their own renditions of modest fashion that are colorful, creative, and daring in an effort to help other women struggling with being both modest and fashionable.

To be clear, this "new visibility" does not imply that it is only in this contemporary moment that women of Muslim faith are talking back through modest sartorial expression. Instead, it is the opportunity of them being "heard,"[2] particularly by Western mainstream markets, that is emphasized as novel. For instance, some mainstream brands such as Nike have seriously engaged female Muslim athletes to understand the specificity of their wardrobe needs to ensure the appropriate fabrics and fits are accounted for. While there are clear capitalist gains for Nike since the Muslim market has proven to be lucrative, this type of public exchange and acknowledgment has created new opportunities for not just Western markets but many Muslim entrepreneurs as well. What is new is the fact that their corporeal and stylistic needs have been augmented to the point of breaking through exclusive marketplaces and spaces that have rarely, if ever, accounted for them.

The efficacy of this varied visibility is manifested through the fact that the sartorial needs of Muslim women have finally penetrated the mainstream Western marketplace through consumer engagement, inclusive marketing campaigns, and an overall amiability toward veiling practices irrespective of the presumed market value. I believe this "new visibility" manifested through the MFM has created a net positive toward female Muslim subjectivities in the United States and has afforded women new prominence that erodes Orientalist and neo-Orientalist depictions of Muslim womanhood by denaturalizing the male and female gaze that deemed their subjectivities as historically invisible in both Western and Muslim consciousness. But is increased visibility adequate enough in eroding nineteenth- and twentieth-century literary, linguistic, and cultural misrepresentations?

Dr. Shenila Khoja-Moolji (2017) argues that heightened visibility does not necessarily materialize through "emancipatory possibilities." She contends that this new visibility is "limiting and oppressive" because it presents a bifurcated notion of Muslim womanhood where on one front they are viewed as "savvy consumers and empowered fashionistas" and on another as "suspect, jihadi, and threatening." In her view, such representations are instead "simply new modalities through which state and capitalist forces can advance the surveillance of Muslim women or make profits off of them." But such framing of this new prominence is in and of itself limiting and laden with presumptions of Muslim womanhood that further perpetuate the neo-colonialist framework that binds female Muslims to the shackles of the Western gaze. What Khoja-Moolji fails to account for is the interconnectedness between the dichotomous representations. The notion of Muslim women as suspect that she invokes is precisely what the MFM works to dismantle by carving a new type of Muslim visibility into public consciousness. It is one that embodies the complexities of their religion and culture while simultaneously blurring the lines between theology and praxis (Janmohamed 2016: 37). Many scholars who theorize about the veil (Ahmed 1992; Abu-Lughod 2002) rightfully call for working against reductive interpretations of veiling that render Muslim women as subordinate, but when can we actually start to implement this practice discursively *outside* of our own scholarship? When can we start to instinctively conceive of this group of women without invoking the "oppression" or "backwardness" that haunts their subjectivities? When can we speak about female Muslim subjectivities without alluding to an already constituted group of women embedded within our consciousness? When can we randomly stumble upon a cable news show and not see headlines that ask if Islam oppresses women or not? Such assumptions were evident when Donald Trump criticized Gold Star mother Ghazala Khan's silence during her husband Khizr Khan's speech at the Democratic National Convention in 2016 regarding their fallen son soldier Army Caption Humayun Khan. Commenting on Ghazala's silence, Trump said that she may not have been allowed to speak, alluding to the fact that she is controlled by her husband, thereby furthering stereotypes of the oppressed Muslim woman by Muslim men (BBC News 2016). Trump's remarks reflect the growing level of Islamophobia that is rampant within the United States. When experts are invited to news outlets to defend Islam and clarify misconceptions, they are almost always asked if Islam oppresses women. The framing of that question assumes women's oppression before their liberation, which is at the root of anti-Muslim sentiment. When will representations of Muslim women across mass media outlets reflect a point of departure from hackneyed and essentialist constructions of this gendered group of people and highlight the immense progress being made toward creating an understanding that reflects the actual realities of these women? I argue that the MFM is one of the most profound articulations of this departure from marginal subjecthood into mainstream Muslim modes of being. The MFM demonstrates new ways of conceptualizing Muslim womanhood through sartorial creativity that shatters the monolithic images of Muslim women as clad in all black, faceless, and draped in cloak-like garments further promoting their invisibility as portrayed across media outlets (Goldman 2016). It is an effective way of integrating female Muslim subjects into US mainstream culture through various corporeal renditions that reflect the realities of these women.

Intersectional Trends in the American MFM

As I said earlier, social media influencers and entrepreneurs are key creators of the MFM, and many American Muslim influencers offer important intersectional perspectives to this new visibility and empowerment for women of Muslim faith. Los Angeles-based beauty guru of Ethiopian descent Aysha Harun reaches an audience of nearly 400k subscribers on YouTube and 227k followers on Instagram where she shares beauty tips, home décor, vlogs, and more. In the wake of the deaths of George Floyd, Breonna Taylor, Ahmaud Arbery, and many other Black people who have been killed by police, she released a video titled "Life update + why I stopped supporting a certain brand," uploaded to YouTube on June 10, 2020, describing what it is like to be a Black Muslim influencer and content creator in North America. She admitted that she has to work "ten times harder than non-Black women; it's a hard pill to swallow but it is the facts." As a businesswoman and influencer, Harun has repeatedly been put in situations where she has had to prove that her "blackness isn't going to bring down this corporation." Harun outed luxury French skincare company Caudalie for their lack of representation across their campaign ads and for not compensating her for all the content she created for their brand. After multiple attempts with Caudalie's representatives to prove that she is worth the investment, especially since the content she created for them generated nearly $20,000 in converted sales, they still would not pay her using the excuse that they simply did not have the budget to do so when in fact white influencers had paid partnerships with them. In Harun's view, this is how Black women are constantly "manipulated" in the industry which has led to stark racial disparities within the world of influencers and content creators. Surely, Harun is one of many Black influencers who are not given the level of gravitas that white or white-passing influencers receive across multiple industries but particularly within the fashion and beauty sectors.

In an Instagram-Live discussion entitled "White Supremacy in Modest Fashion," stylist Hakeemah Cummings (2020) pointed out that many of the mainstream fashion media outlets such as *Harper's Bazaar*, *POPSUGAR*, *Vogue*, *WhoWhatWear*, and *Allure* all published articles between 2017 and 2020 ranking the top modest fashion and hijab influencers featuring an overwhelming majority of white influencers and barely any Black influencers. The lack of racial representation within the modest fashion industry is viewed as a form of "silencing," to quote Cummings, to nonwhite influencers whom usually have to work even harder for less return on their investment. It is a slap in the face of sorts, thereby sending the message that Black bodies are less desirable and thus less appealing for big brands to work with. The MFM in conjunction with the Black Lives Matter Movement has encouraged multiple brands to be more inclusive toward people of color by ensuring their campaign ads are more visually diverse across race and religions, as well as implementing more structural changes such as diversifying company leadership, despite the fact that many other companies are still being taken to task for perpetuating practices that underrepresent minority communities. As three critical categories of race, religion, and gender strategically intersect on some of the world's most visual and powerful platforms, a shifting display of Muslim womanhood from nonnormative marginal embodiment to a mainstream articulation of normativity is challenging biased Western constructions of Muslim lifestyle and Islamic practices.

It is clear that one of the main functions of the MFM is a need for visible religious and ethnic diversity within the global Muslim community that shatters stereotypes surrounding what it means to be and look like a female Muslim. The MFM marks the birth of a robust wave of female Muslim entrepreneurship where women on the grounds have started businesses offering consumer goods unique to various aspects of Muslim lifestyle from clothing to specialty cuisines, jewelry, skincare, services, and more. It is imperative that these women's efforts are not eclipsed by mainstream neoliberal market players seeking to claim their piece of the multibillion-dollar Muslim fashion market. Take, for example, modest womenswear brand Veiled Collection which has nearly 200k followers on Instagram. Founded by young Syrian-American Muslim entrepreneur Nora Chamaa, with a motto of "quality you can see and feel at prices you can't believe" Veiled Collection quickly stood out among other modest brands for its clear dedication to high-quality modest styles that are affordable. A bird's-eye view of their Instagram page portrays a diverse array of modern modest formations including plus-size models, hijab-donning women, and models with beautifully styled manes, turban-wearing women, loose silhouettes and more fitted styles, Black women, brown women, multiracial women, all with one thing in common: a desire to mainstream various modes of modesty and reclaim female Muslim corporeality from neocolonial perceptions of Muslim subjectivities.

Infinite Abaya is another modest brand founded by Palestinian American Muslim entrepreneur Dr. Anwar Hijaz, who launched her brand by designing elegant and modern abayas[3] that are suitable for all body types and quickly began offering scarves, long-sleeve maxi dresses, kimonos, accessories, and more. Both Veiled Collection and Infinite Abaya have become among the go-to brands in the United States for the American Muslim community seeking modest attire. The "explosion of creativity" inspired by the constraints of Muslim modest requirements is now a global multibillion-dollar industry with many non-Muslim and even more Muslim brands claiming their stake in the game. Participants of the MFM be it through consumers or producers of this niche market are reclaiming and reorienting the terms of the veil through their own feminist renditions of veiling practices against the exploitative influence of neoliberalism which has ventured into the world of Muslim fashion and lifestyle. The MFM sparked a cornucopia of entrepreneurial opportunities for not just Western markets but many female Muslim entrepreneurs seeking to be top influencers within this movement in various capacities, which refutes the notion that women of Muslim faith are being exploited and dominated by market calculations since these women are at the forefront of this movement.

Ultimately, modest fashion has diversified hijab practices throughout the United States and created a cultural shift that is inclusive toward women of Muslim faith. The MFM in particular has altered the social institution of veiling within the United States and serves as a powerful disaggregation of the monolithic and Orientalist impressions imposed onto women of Muslim faith by visually showcasing multiple ways of performing Muslim womanhood even when some representations, arguably, are antithetical to the textual basis for modest dress in Islam, which stipulates the female body to be entirely covered with the exception of the face and hands. In many ways the MFM offers an epistemological corrective that challenges Orientalist and neocolonial depictions of Muslim womanhood as "oppressed and or mute victim" (Webb 2000) and instead depicts women as active agents of change through new corporeal visibility. Participants of the MFM reclaim the hijab through localized expressions of modesty that express a deeply individuated Muslim identity with a shared adherence to multiple manifestations of modesty, relocating Muslim corporeal expression from the margins of Western culture into the mainstream.

Notes

1. While this phenomenon has been referenced differently by various authors and scholars, I have not seen it coined as the Modest Fashion Movement. Others have referred to the "modest movement," such as Jill D'alessandro (2018: 49) and Balbir K. Singh (2017: 161).

2. I am elaborating on Miriam Cooke's (2007) discussion on Muslim women talking back in a way that asserts their identities against the gross misrepresentations of Muslims post 9/11. She argues that their desire to talk back is not new but the chance of them being "heard" is. I take this notion a step further by arguing that Muslim women are being heard in a way that we haven't seen before and it is propelled by the MFM.

3. An abaya is a flowy outer garment that has long sleeves with floor-length silhouettes.

References

Abu Lughod, Lila (2002), "Do Muslim Women Really Need Saving? Anthropological Reflections on Cultural Relativism and Its Others," *American Anthropologist*, 104(3): 783–90.

Abu Lughod, Lila (2006), "The Muslim Woman: The Power of Images and the Danger of Pity," in Lettre Internationale, Denmark. https://www.eurozine.com/the-muslim-woman.

Ahmed, Leila (1992), *Women and Gender in Islam: Historical Roots of a Modern Debate*, New Haven, CT: Yale University Press.

Ahmed, Leila (2011), *A Quiet Revolution: The Veil's Resurgence, from the Middle East to America*, New Haven, CT: Yale University Press.

Amer, Sahar (2014), *What Is Veiling?* Chapel Hill, NC: The University of North Carolina Press.

"American Muslims' Religious Beliefs and Practices," (2017), Pew Research Center's Religion & Public Life Project. July 26. https://www.pewforum.org/2017/07/26/religious-beliefs-and-practices/.

BBC News (2016), "Fury over Trump Soldier's Mother Remarks," *BBC*, July 31. https://www.bbc.com/news/election-us-2016-36935175.

Bobley, Georgia (2017), "A Tween Fashion Brand Just Featured a Hijabi Model For The First Time," *POPSUGAR Middle East Love*, February 20. https://me.popsugar.com/love/Justice-Features-First-Hijabi-Model-43197063.

Bucar, Elizabeth (2017), *Pious Fashion How Muslim Women Dress*, Cambridge, MA: Harvard University Press.

Chaker, Isra (@hassanah_PFH) (2018), "So It Begins," *Instagram Photo*, August 5, https://bit.ly/2WaUOwA

Chan-Malik, Sylvia, (2018), *Being Muslim: A Cultural History of Women of Color in American Islam*, New York: New York University Press.

Cooke, Miriam (2007), "The Muslimwoman," Springer Science + Business Media B.V, 144–9. https://bit.ly/38cE2kr (accessed February 20, 2020).

Cummings, Hakeemah (@hakeemahcmb) (2020), "White Supremacy in Modest Fashion," *Instagram Video*, June 13. https://www.instagram.com/p/CBUArHKDJCm/ (accessed June 13, 2020).

D'alessandro, Jill (2018), "Global Style Muslim Modest Fashion Today," in Jill D'alessandro and Reina Lewis (ed.), *Contemporary Muslim Fashions*, Munich: Delmonico Books, 48–63. https://amzn.to/2IaE5CO

D'alessandro, Jill, Reina Lewis, and Laura Camerlengo (2018), *Contemporary Muslim Fashion*, Munich: Delmonico Books. https://amzn.to/2IaE5CO

El Guindi, Fadwa (1999), *Veil: Modesty, Privacy, and Resistance*, Oxford: Berg Publishers.

Foster, Shirley (2004), "Colonialism and Gender in the East: Representations of the Harem in the Writings of Women Travelers," *The Yearbook of English Studies*, 34. https://www.jstor.org/stable/3509480

Goldman, Russel (2016), "What's That You're Wearing? A Guide to Muslim Veils," *The New York Times*, February 20. https://nyti.ms/2vubfuo

Gonzalez, Victoria (2019), "Instagram Stars Have Turned Modest Fashion into a Movement," *Lamag*, June 5. https://www.lamag.com/lalifeandstyle/modest-fashion/

Hoodfar, H. (2001), "The Veil in Their Minds and on Our Heads: Veiling Practices and Muslim Women," in E. A. Castelli (ed.), *Women, Gender, Religion: A Reader*, 425. New York: Palgrave Macmillan.

Janmohamed, Shelina (2016), *Generation M Young Muslims Changing the World*, London: I.B. Tauris.

Kandil, Caitlin Yoshiko (2017), "Muslim Women Find On-Trend Apparel at This Modest Fashion Convention," *La Times*, August 17. https://lat.ms/376Tpxv

Kandiyoti, Deniz (ed.) (1991), *Women, Islam and the state*, (Vol. 105). Philadelphia: Temple University Press.

Khoja-Moolji, Shenila (2017), "The "New" Muslim Woman: A Fashionista and a Suspect," *LARB*, February 20. https://bit.ly/2vmMCQq

Lewis, Reina (2013), *Modest Fashion: Styling Bodies, Mediating Faith*, New York: I.B. Tauris & Co Ltd.

Loveluck, Louisa (2018), "The Big Business of Modest Fashion," *The Washington Post*, October 4. https://wapo.st/3me2QiW

Matera, Avery (2017), "American Eagle's Denim Hijab Is ALREADY Sold Out," *Teen Vogue*, July 21. http://www.teenvogue.com/story/american-eagle-denim-hijabs.

Pew, Research (2017), "American Muslims' Religious Beliefs and Practices," *Pew Research Center's Religion & Public Life Project*, July 26. https://www.pewforum.org/2017/07/26/religious-beliefs-and-practices/

"Religious Beliefs and Practices," Pew Research Center. https://pewrsr.ch/2vmaZ0F

Said, Edward W. (1978), *Orientalism*, New York: Pantheon Books.

State of the Global Islamic Economy Report (2016/17), Toronto: Thomson Reuters. https://bit.ly/32F7GO8

Singh, Balbir K. (2017), "The Commodity Fetish of Modest Fashion," *QED: A Journal in GLBTQ Worldmaking*, 4(3): 161–4. www.jstor.org/stable/10.14321/qed.4.3.0161 (accessed June 9, 2020).

Webb, Gisela (2000), *Windows of Faith: Muslim Women Scholar-Activists of North America*, Syracuse University Press.

Wilson, Elizabeth (2003), *Adorned in Dreams: Fashion and Modernity*, New Brunswick, NJ: Rutgers University Press.

Young, Sarah (2018), "L'Oréal Makes History with Hijab-Wearing Model in Hair Campaign," *The Independent*, January 19. http://www.independent.co.uk/life-style/fashion/loreal-hijab-hair-advert-model-amena-khan-muslim-beauty-blogger-ardere-cosmetics-a8167331.html.

CHAPTER 7
FASHIONING THE SUBJECT
BLACK QUEERNESS, IDENTITY, AND AN ETHIC OF HONOR
Benae Beamon

My grandmother died when I was twenty-three, though she started to experience the onset of Alzheimer's when I was fourteen. She was a strong-willed, older black woman, thin, hardworking, and dedicated to routine. She was always on the move, cared deeply about her family, and loved her husband profoundly. As a black woman who was impacted by the Jim Crow South and the reverberating effects of racism in the United States afterward, she didn't have much education and knew the bonds of labor in ways that I never will. Her seven children are proof that she knew the intensity of labor and birth, and her life supporting my grandfather on the farm, picking blueberries, collecting pecans, gathering eggs from and caring for the chickens, showcases her understanding of the unrelenting call of early mornings and consistency. Both meant that she must have known the toll that labor takes on the body, though she never seemed bothered by it. That small-statured, pragmatic, feminine, God-fearing woman is nothing like the queer, artistic, masculine of center woman that wrote this chapter, but when she passed, I was desperate to connect with her materiality, her reality, and the things that kept her. The items that held her body, inspired her, or spoke to who she was. I was thirsty for the material ripples that would carry her into the present and that would manifest an intimacy with her because the items that we hold close and connect with often take on a kind of intimacy in relation to our skins and ourselves. While I took many things, one that comes to mind is a jacket—a brown bomber jacket that is fairly light and has a detachable hood. When I wear it, it is oversized and an intentional instantiation of a feminized masculine expression. I style it with scarves and heavy outdoor work boots, and when I first wrapped myself in it, I found a pecan in the pocket. That nut reminds me of the beautifully paradoxical relationship between our realities. The pecan reminds me of the labor, choices, and, at times, limitations imposed upon her in ways that I may never fully grasp, and in return, I have taken that jacket, and by connection, my grandmother, with me to Ivy League institutions and queer gatherings that would have always been beyond her scope.

This paradox undergirds a reality, a constant connection between the visible and the invisible, both of which together constitute a singular reality. I am reminded of the many ways in which black life is relegated to invisibility, encaged, and discarded—the ways in which black life necessarily requires a balancing of these two seemingly incongruous realities. From the black bodies stashed away in the townships of Soweto and Langa to the "criminal" bodies hidden from public view, invisibility is a proven investment in the disposability of certain bodies. The removal of persons from homes, neighborhoods, and city centers speaks to true hegemonic interests, the desire to erase blackness. These attempts at invisibilization are unsustainable, not because of narratives of resilience but, rather, out of social and hierarchical necessity. There is a natural balance between invisibility and visibility (imposed or otherwise) because those castigated are at times made hypervisible solely for the reinscription of their oppression. Furthermore, daring and brazen proclamations arise despite such hegemonic encroachments. Resisting hegemonic tendencies can make space for more capacious understandings of humanity and relational possibilities. As Ralph Ellison so eloquently claims, "I myself, after existing some twenty years, did not become alive until I discovered my invisibility."[1] This chapter argues that black queer and trans individuals actively resist incessant hegemonic attempts to invisibilize black queerness by inscribing their subjectivities on their persons through style. Put differently, black queer and trans individuals write themselves into existence every day through fashion. Moreover, I claim that this fusion of self and style is situated in a moral frame of honor that is actualized through an ethic of self-revelation and self-affection.

This chapter defines black queerness as that which is socio-politically and socio-culturally nonnormative. While this will occasionally refer to particular identities that are sexual and gender minorities, especially when stated as black queer, but black queerness broadly speaks to an Afrocentric bent toward said non-normativity in such a way that it leans into a communal ethic, lifts experiential realities, and rests on a restructuring of common, neoliberal timelines/commitments. This is all to say that black queerness, here, is not relying solely on a concept of identity but rather a way of approaching life that steps outside of hegemonic forces, defying/subverting them. This subversion, then, privileges blackness, and while I believe this is a moral frame that black queer and trans individuals embody, I think it encompasses more than just black queer and trans identity itself. Along with defining black queerness, I also want to make a distinction between fashion and style. As Otto von Busch notes, a distinction is often made between "'clothing' and 'fashion,' in which the former denotes the functional, technical, and protective aspects of dress, while the second is seen as symbolic, signifying, and communicative."[2] Von Busch continues claiming that "clothing is part of the Hellenic time concept of *chromos*, the duration, while fashion resides in *kairos*, the propitious moment or opportunity. Clothing can . . . be chronic and everlasting, but never fashion."[3] While clothing is an enduring constant, fashion is constantly changing and intrinsically linked to the present moment, meaning that it is always in flux. Von Busch affirms this noting that "from this perspective of kairos, fashion is indeed like passion, a sudden burst of energy, a firing of ephemeral intensity[;] . . . [it is] a phenomenon in a constant dynamic flow of becoming, that never stands still or is subordinated to permanent substance."[4] With these definitions in mind, this chapter is primarily interested in the concept of style, which is deeply connected to that of fashion. This chapter defines style as a consistent navigation of the ephemeral nature of fashion.[5] Ralph Ellison's thoughts on light and its value to the invisible man help to sharpen my understanding of navigation, particularly in relation to visibility. Ellison writes that "light confirms [his] reality, gives birth to [his] form."[6] Ellison describes the way that light gives shapes to the form. Light is central to self-realization, to making the form clear and readable. This understanding of light, as doing the work of revealing the form, sheds light on the way that clothing, like light, outlines the impressionable skin, the material reality of the form. By revealing the form, clothing marks the contours of the self-determined body, setting the stage for the possibility of cultural intelligibility on the subject's terms (Butler 2004: 57). Nikki Giovanni writes, "style has a profound meaning to Black Americans. If we can't drive, we will invent walks and the world will envy the dexterity of our feet . . . if given scraps, we will make quilts. . . . We will take what we have to make what we need."[7] Giovanni's if, then chorus affirms that style is finding, identifying, and relishing in the form that belies the circumstances without obscuring them. This is to say, that style is constantly in process, being generated and regenerated, and finds clarity, vision, or possibility despite that which seems limiting.

This chapter will put style and honor in conversation though disavows the notion of honor as merit-based concept of honor that is to be militaristic and capitalist. Rather, honor denotes respect or esteem and is tied to a notion of integrity, that is, purpose or value in that which extends beyond itself. This understanding of honor as a moral frame can be enacted in many ways and, for my purposes, specifically through an ethic of self-revelation and self-affection. Self-revelation, here, refers simply to the revealing of the self to the other. While seemingly simplistic such an ethic requires vulnerability and a desire for connection. Moreover, self-revelation assumes self-knowledge and a sense of self-worth. Self-revelation, therefore, implicitly stands on a recognition of the self and an understanding that it *ought* to be shared with others and one's moral agency in doing so. This idea of self-revelation is implied in a theory of self-expression, which is a common theoretical frame in fashion studies. For example, Joanne Finkelstein, a fashion studies scholar, claims that "in everyday life, fashion appearances are interpreted as literalization of the wearer's character."[8] Finkelstein asserts that subjectivity is not fixed but constantly invented and that fashion is a social interface through which said invention occurs.[9] Although Finkelstein offers one perspective, the self-revelation point to which I am laying claim in relationship to black queerness is a moral one and witnesses an agential capacity within the individual to self-determine. Catrina Jones, founder and designer of Nicole Wilson, claims that "fashion is . . . a way to showcase our identity [and] our tool to educate. It's our opportunity to say 'I'm here. I matter. I exist. I am.'"[10] Jones alludes to the ways in which style creates space for expressive irruption that comes from determining and then lifting one's subjectivity. However, these claims around subjectivity are both declarative and proclamatory; that is to say not only does one exist, but one is worthy of recognition/acknowledgment *because* one exists.

This point echoes that of Toni Branson, fashion designer and CEO of Style Is Freedom (SIF), who asserts that style is like "freeing yourself every time you get dressed."[11] Branson notes that style has a distinctive function highlighting and laying claim to a particular social subjectivity, noting that people "creat[e] the persona [that they] want the world to see and embrace it through [their] choice of clothing." While she uses the term "create,"

Branson seems to be thinking through it as a determining way of taking agential power over one's subjectivity; Branson's language also equates style not only with a particular subjectivity for social interface but also affirmation of said subjectivity. Branson's comment parallels the words of Boka Maroba, a South African trans man and activist at the Other Foundation, who believes/uses style "to make clear to others" his identity. This interest in clarity is partially a pragmatic one, offering safety and an external reflection of a sense of subjectivity, which assumes some self-understanding.[12] However, as Che Gossett claims, this is also about the complications of blackness in relation to transness, since "blackness ruptures trans representability, respectability, and visibility."[13] In light of Gossett's theorization, Maroba's claims about clarity also speak to the ways in which black transness, uniquely, denies its hegemonically imposed obfuscation in afterlife of colonial violence through the illumination of the form, thereby rewriting the notion that to be black and trans is to "assum[e] a body" and consequently the right to dignity and integrity.[14] Jones, Branson, and Maroba uncover the ways in which self-understanding allows for consistent presentation of a clear vision through style. Such clarity lays bare the form in all of its nuance and intricacy and makes a statement evincing the individual's existence and worth. The subjectivity presented through black queer and trans style is life-giving and revolutionary, especially for black queer and trans people.

During New York Fashion Week (NYFW) in 2017, DapperQ, a popular queer fashion blog, held its annual fashion show entitled R/Evolution, which was rooted in this understanding of black queer and trans style as radical. DapperQ owner, Anita Dolce Vita, claimed that the show, R/Evolution, honored "'the constant evolution of queer style as its own aesthetic, its revolutionary roots, and its power to be leveraged as a tool for resistance.'"[15] Dolce Vita went on noting,

> R/Evolution is an act of defiance. It is our space to stay visible in the face of attempts at erasure . . . in honor of all efforts of resisting, [from] the activists being arrested in protest to the individual whose impactful act of resisting is smashing the binary by getting up, getting dressed, and just existing.[16]

Dolce Vita lays claim to three very important things, (1) the unique aesthetic of queer style, that is, its independence from other notably gendered/normative fashion aesthetics, (2) the ancestral understanding of this aesthetic that necessarily grounds its contribution to individual self-understanding, and (3) the recognition that dress, and consequently style, functions as a pertinent aspect of existence, an active "smashing of the binary," ultimately speaking to self-determination despite hegemonic constraints. Dolce Vita highlights the intimate connection between queer aesthetic and queer subjectivity as demonstrative of queer self-determination and, thereby, revelation, simultaneously marking an undoing of gender, or at least binarist expectations.

The gender normative aesthetic promoted in fashion, which is necessarily a raced aesthetic, feeds the white supremacist, heteropatriarchal, and consequently binarist, hegemonic machine.[17] This means that it lends itself to the "processes by which Blackness loses its human form, as well as to the processes that enable the human to take on a Black form," that is, the very systems that determined the limitations within which black humanity was possible.[18] This relegation was less a consigning of humanity to blackness or black bodies as much as it was a restructuring of humanity with new circumscriptions that determined blackness just legible enough for social death, thereby maintaining the enterprise of whiteness. Christina Sharpe affirms this point in her acknowledgment of "'the quotidian unmaking of being that is everyday blackness [and] the ease with which fungibility and killability mark black life forms.'"[19] In an essay on queer form and blackness, Andre Carrington asserts that "becoming human, for [black people, and I would say black queer and trans people, in particular] has involved redressing this [systemic] dispossession rather than relying on it."[20] Style is the light that gives shape to the form. It draws black queerness into a kind of cultural legibility, while simultaneously disrupting hegemonic claims of intelligibility that constitute normative senses of order.[21] The clarity and outlining of the form that style calls forth is somewhat akin to Brittney Cooper's embodied discourse, wherein black queer and trans aesthetic "disrupt the smooth function of the culture of dissemblance and the politics of respectability as the paradigmatic frames through which to engage" black queerness.[22] While Cooper references this notion of radical inclusion in relation to textual resources, my argument is that it is also relevant for material resources and realities. The material reality and brazenness of style function as a valuable social interface and medium through which black queer and trans individuals express and reveal their subjectivity. However, simultaneously black queer and trans individuals lay claim to their worth, asserting their humanity by issuing the Levinasian moral imperative: "do not kill."[23] I am arguing, here, that the revelatory function of black queer and trans style/aesthetic is a radical, material activist posture that subverts hegemonic forces, "redressing dispossession" through its claims of humanity, agency, and worth that honors black queer and trans subjectivity.

Understanding the clarity of form and that it is the expression of subjectivity undergirds an ethic of self-affection. The notion of self-affection that I am establishing, here, is rooted partially in the idea of self-care and an acknowledgment of the gestural realities intensified through the co-creational reality of our clothing, specifically our style. Lucia Ruggerone wrote about the "two-way creation of affect between bodies and clothes."[24] Ruggerone asserts that the practice of wearing clothes as an *embodied* experience is rooted in a "body-clothes *assemblage*" that "conceptualizes practices not as bounded events, but as fluxes or becomings."[25] The affective, then, is understood as the body's capacity.[26] Ruggerone claims that the affective, or extra cognitive, is mediated through the senses, emotions/emotional discourse, etc., and intensified through the "encounter between a human body and objects that initiate a process of mutual becoming with either a positive or a negative outcome."[27] Self-affection refers to body and clothes as participating in their own mutual interface and co-constituting the resultant subjectivity of one's style. Self-affection is also concerned with the way in which subjectivity is cultivated through the exposure of the form, using clothing, which literally outlines one's impressionable skin, making it part of the consciousness (and thereby the becoming) that comprises the gestural realities of one's affect.

Such gestural realities allow for an array of gender expressions, embracing black queerness. The brazen and intentional guiding principles of bklyn boihood, a collective for black and brown queer and trans people that honors a multiplicity of masculine expression, offer a great example of self-affection and the ways in which it overlaps with self-revelation. The organization, bklyn boihood, presents itself as a collective, offering workshops, etc. and producing materials that visibilize the many queer black and brown masculine expressions. However, as the collective has grown, so too has its interest in fashion and style. In an interview on the Gender Blender podcast, bklyn boihood collective members note that along with Van Bailey's involvement came a "celebration of aesthetic and adornment and fashion as visibility." Style became so central that not only has the collective since uncovered its own particular aesthetic but also invested in a collective moral commitment to style, including it in their articulated guiding principles. These guiding principles function essentially as an ethical statement, fully articulating the collective's intentions and commitments, including their distinct devotion to style, which is as follows:

> *We believe in our inalienable right to be fly as shit.* Since the beginning of time black and brown folks—especially those of us not accepting/living on the conventional spectrums for gender and identity have been fly. We believe in that. We invest in it. It is a core part of how we show ourselves love and provide personal affirmation. Fashion, for us, is part-politic, part-storytelling and part-survival.[28]

This statement affirms the ongoing importance of lineage, which queers the temporality of fashion itself. While fashion is ephemeral and definitive of the present moment, this present discourse about the past and the ancestral context draws both into conversation, allowing them to inhabit a single space concurrently. While this principle already speaks to a moral commitment and themes of affirmation and cultural disruption, it also acknowledges the communal functionality of fashion. This communality in relation to affect is reminiscent of L. H. Stallings's thoughts. Stallings asserts that the beauty of the flesh is that "flesh has no ego. It can be collective and communal, a thing that feels, or an encasement [because] . . . Black flesh is illusive."[29] This reference to flesh is an acknowledgment of black embodiment as a thing of value in itself and speaks to the innumerable qualities of black flesh, such that the notion of deception is replaced by a kind of inexplicable maneuvering of space and embodiment as adapted for the sake of survival. The flesh is the form, and Stallings calls our attention to a unique kind of capaciousness and possibility that has always proven central to black life. Moreover, Stallings notes that the illusiveness of black flesh prescribes "a black diasporic styling of identity and subjectivity . . . [that] substitutes aesthetics as formative guideposts for dealing with the confines of Western embodiment."[30] Stallings speaks to the ways in which this self-determined engagement with flesh is also a way of constituting identity and subjectivity via aesthetics, making them foundational to black individuality/self-understanding and black communality. This capturing of aesthetic through black queer style, then, brings to bear an Afrocentric recognition of the ways in which the self and the community are co-constituting. As Monica Miller writes in her work *Slaves to Fashion*, in practice style "is both personal and political, about individual image and group regard, and begs to be read from both an intraracial and interrracial perspective."[31] Miller reaffirms the co-constituting nature of the self and community, which I'm arguing breaks open hegemonic systems of dispossession, allowing for greater possibility within an intentional, or imperative-driven, social interface.

Ruggerone argues that "clothes choose us as much as we choose them . . . [and that this] productive relation is one that affords us an enabling encounter—i.e., allows us to increase our power of acting or our force of existing."[32] This particular relationality through style empowers and allows for malleability; each encounter and relation between the individual is different, making the gender nonconformity and the multiplicity of gender expressions that constitute it possible. Moreover, the outlining of the impressionable body means that it makes the spatial, embodied materiality of black life legible and acknowledges the possibilities of blackness and comfort along with the ability to gauge the affective capaciousness of black experiences of belonging. I argue here that such a capaciousness and sense of belonging lends itself to an affective turn allowing the agential nature of style to transition to a Lordean eroticism that produces power, possibly inciting a black queer and trans reorienting of space. That is to say that the individual is an active agent with an "expanded" capacity and power to shift, or queer, space just as it intrinsically queers time. Queer Latinx writer Gabby Rivera alludes to this in her opening comments at Dapper Q's R/Evolution. Rivera said,

> now we wear our chose clothes . . . that is the theme of this show: your chose clothes. They cannot save you from deportation. Your chose clothes cannot save you from white supremacy. Your chose clothes cannot save you from DACA ending or from a President that's a white supremacist. But your chose clothes can help you put that armor on and blossom.[33]

The intimate relationship between an individual and their style functions to create new horizons, or more generative possibilities in regular spaces of becoming. Sara Ahmed in Queer Phenomenology explains that "if we know where we are when we turn this way or that way, then we are orientated." "Orientation involves aligning body and space," and sometimes imposes and impresses itself upon bodies, explaining why this proves to be such an intimate connection. One's orientation binds an individual and establishes a particular "gaze that turns to an object, bring[ing] other objects into view," meaning that it determines the horizons visible; it dictates our moral imaginary, or that which one believes to be possible. The way that we orient and order ourselves in space is a question of comprehensibility, movement, agency, and capacity; at its core, it is a moral question of opportunity and possibility. Primarily though, it is part of an ongoing search to "mak[e] a place feel like home, or becoming at home in a space." There are systemic factors that impact this, specifically for bodies of color; Ahmed calls upon Fanon to assert that racism "'disorients' black bodies such that they cease to know where to find things." This lack of direction stems from the fact that in a hegemonic society whiteness and masculinity heteronormativity/heterosexuality are at home in a world that privileges them; however, Ahmed is sure to engage and make plain that "histories . . . surface on the body, or even shape how bodies surface." Self-affection, then, in individual black queer and trans style outlines the form and the impressionable borders of the individual, thereby humanizing but also honoring the subjectivity that constitutes the individual. Meaning that the impressions, scars, and gestures of black queer and trans ancestral realities which are bound to and constitute the individual and their forms are made clear; these impressions are erotic and irruptive as intraracial interface and generously confrontational as interracial interface. Such irruptions are disidentifications, or a "way of dealing with dominant ideology . . . that neither opts to assimilate within such a structure nor strictly oppos[e] it"; rather, it "works on and against dominant ideology . . . tr[ying] to transform a cultural logic from within, always laboring [toward] permanent structural change while at the same time valuing the importance of local or everyday struggles of resistance." Self-affection is an everyday form of resistance, and black queer and trans style as an undoing of the obfuscation of the black form and thereby inherently a proclamation of the value and worth of blackness, black queerness, and the flesh embodies a working on the hegemonic ideology. The turn to think about the co-creational function of style privileges "movement, emergence, and potentiality in relationship to the body often returned to the subject, the subject of emotion, as a surplus of freedom." There is a new capacity identified when acknowledging this co-creative affective reality that expands the potential and possibility of reorienting the space in such a way that venerates black queerness as a subversion of hegemony.

At its core, this ethical rewriting and reconstituting taps into the sacrality of dignity and worth, both of which are moral values out of which black people are commonly siphoned. Moreover, it is a demonstration of the distinctive way that spirituality functions in Afro-diasporic communities, specifically the interwoven and symbiotic relationship between the spiritual and the secular. The beauty of self-affection in this chapter plays with notions of care simultaneously witnessing black embodiment and sensation and prescribing responsive methods in the afterlife of slavery. Christina Sharpe's *In the Wake: On Blackness and Being* asserts that "care in the wake [is] a problem for thinking[, thinking] of and for black non/being in the world." Self-revelation and self-affection, then, arise out of the same moral system that reaffirms the values of black bodies, particularly black queer and trans bodies, and the sensations that make them. To seek to bring clarity to the form and to show it boldly is to see value, power, and hope in both the form itself and the doing of its exposure as well. Stallings also talks about the value and sacrality of light in the process of visibilizing, and in relationship to affect, through the work of African American poet, Robert Hayden. Hayden writes, "here space and time exist in light/the eye like the eye of faith believes./the seen, the known/dissolve in iridescence, become/illusive flesh of light/that was not, was, forever is." Stallings picks up this poetic text noting that the "illusive flesh of light acts as both perception and haptic metaphor for a transaesthetic experience." Stallings points out that within the work, "light [is referenced] as spiritual energy and [an] aesthetic element capable of touching and feeling, as well as changing perceptions of any form." The spiritual energy that

Stallings uncovers comes from the vulnerability and the capaciousness of unveiling the form and submitting to the realities and potentialities of the elements/individuals that one encounters (as well as the gifts that such encounters can become) because "we have a sacred connection to one another." The sacrality of black life and the self-revelation and self-affection of black queerness represents a moral conviction entrenched in black flesh. The brazen decision to own and delve into the beauty and glory, the divinity, of black queer and trans bodies is powerful and is a recognition of the need for black queer and trans people in the world. The establishment of black queer and trans style as well as the privileging of black queerness is a way of imbuing black queer and trans bodies with the honor they inspire and creating an aesthetic that does the same.

The proclamation and investment in black queer and trans aesthetic honor the black body acknowledging the reorientation and self-determination made possible in the becoming and the histories that are carried on the surfaces of those bodies. The reorientation of space centers black queer and transness in a way that is not only subversive but also restructures the moral frame visibilizing the possibilities of black bodies, honoring black queer and trans existence but moreover black queer and trans humanity. Recalling Nikki Giovanni's words, "we take what we have to make what we need." With this chorus in mind, we can see how black queer and trans style reflects this indomitable capacity for innovation and hope within black life. Black queer and trans style boldly proclaims: if we are not considered human, we will acknowledge one another's humanity. If fashion does not speak to us, we will give birth to our own clothing and aesthetic. And if we are made invisible, we will create a new vocabulary that writes our ancestors over the historical muting of their glory.

Notes

1. Ellison (1947: 10).
2. von Busch (2008).
3. von Busch (2008: 34).
4. von Busch (2008: 34).
5. I want to note that this consistency does not negate the possibility of evolution or change in this vision or image. (If anything, it is regularly open to malleability.)
6. Ellison (1947: 10).
7. Giovanni (1994: 154–5).
8. Finkelstein (1996: 396).
9. Ruggerone (2016: 573–93, 576).
10. Taken from an Instagram post at @bynicolewilson.
11. From email questions sent to named designer.
12. Trans people are subjected to unusually high rates of violence, some of the highest among anti-LGBT violence.
13. Gossett (2017: 185).

14. Gossett (2017: 184).
15. Berg (2017).
16. Berg (2017).
17. It should be noted that this goal/idyllic understanding is not separate and apart from the androgyny that is celebrated in fashion as it is an allowance made primarily for white ciswomen or white nonbinary folks, meaning that it is made permissible by a foundation of whiteness.
18. Carrington (2017: 278).
19. Carrington (2017: 280).
20. Carrington (2017: 280).
21. Butler (2004: 34).
22. Cooper (2017: 10).
23. Levinas and Nemo (1985: 97).
24. Ruggerone (2016: 573–93, 586).
25. Ruggerone (2016: 577–8).
26. Ruggerone (2016: 579, 580.
27. Ruggerone (2016: 580).
28. Ruggerone (2016: 580).
29. Stallings (2015: 213).
30. Stallings (2015: 213).
31. Miller (2009: 3.
32. Ruggerone (2016: 582).
33. DapperQ Team (2017).

References

Ahmed, Sara (2006), *Queer Phenomenology: Orientations, Objects, Others*, Durham, NC: Duke University Press.
Alexander, M. Jacqui (2005), *Pedagogies of Crossing: Meditations on Feminism, Sexual Politics, Memory, and the Sacred*, Durham, NC: Duke University Press.
Berg, Alex (2017), "New York Fashion Week's 'Largest LGBTQ Runway Show' Gets Political," *NBC News*, September 15. https://www.nbcnews.com/feature/nbc-out/new-york-fashion-week-s-largest-lgbtq-runway-show-gets-n801636.
Busch, Otto von (2008), "Fashion-Able: Hacktivism and Engaged Fashion Design," *Goteburg*. https://gupea.ub.gu.se/bitstream/2077/17941/3/gupea_2077_17941_3.pdf.
Butler, Judith (2004), *Undoing Gender*. New York: Routledge.
Carrington, Andre (2017), "Mike Brown's Body: New Materialism and Black Form," *ASAP/Journal*, 2(2): 276–83.
Clough, Patricia T. (n.d.), "The Affective Turn: Political Economy, Biomedia and Bodies," 25(1): 1–22.
Cooper, Brittney C. (2017), *Beyond Respectability: The Intellectual Thought of Race Women*. Urbana: University of Illinois Press.

DapperQ Team (2017), "DapperQ Wraps 4th Annual Brooklyn Museum NYFW Show," *DapperQ*, October. https://www.dapperq.com/2017/10/dapperq-wraps-4th-annual-brooklyn-museum-nyfw-show-exclusive-video/.

Ellison, Ralph (1947), *Invisible Man*, New York: Signet.

Finkelstein, Joanne (1996), *After a Fashion*, Melbourne: Melbourne University Press.

Giovanni, Nikki (1994), *Racism 101*, New York: Quill.

Gossett, Reina, Stanley, Eric A., and Burton, Johanna (eds.) (2017), *Trap Door: Trans Cultural Production and the Politics of Visibility*, Cambridge: The MIT Press, 185.

Miller, Monica L. (2009), *Slaves to Fashion: Black Dandyism and the Styling of Black Diasporic Identity*, Durham: Duke University Press, 3.

Levinas, Emmanuel and Philippe Nemo (1985), *Ethics and Infinity*. Pittsburgh: Duquesne University Press.

Munoz, Jose Esteban (1999), *Disidentifications: Queers of Color and the Performance of Politics*, Minneapolis, MN: University of Minnesota Press.

"Our Guiding Principles," *Bklyn Boihood (blog)*, May 6, 2016. http://bklynboihood.com/our-guiding-principles/.

Ruggerone, Lucia (2016), "The Feeling of Being Dressed: Affect Studies and the Clothed Body," *Fashion Theory: The Journal of Dress, Body and Culture*, 21(5): 573–93.

Sharpe, Christina (2016), *In the Wake: On Blackness and Being*. Durham, NC: Duke University Press.

Stallings, L. H. (2015), *Funk the Erotic: Transaesthetics and Black Sexual Cultures*, Urbana: University of Illinois Press.

CHAPTER 8
FROM THE MEDIEVAL CHRIST TO FASHION'S HEROIN CHIC
THE SUBLIME EMULATION OF THE EMACIATED PARADIGM IN SECULAR AND RELIGIOUS ICONOGRAPHY
Tanya White

Beauty in distress is much the most effecting beauty. (Burke [1757] 1998: 110)

Currently, in fashion academia and some areas of the industry, there is an increased awareness and effort to advance a body image that promotes a more diverse and expansive representation. These efforts aim to speak through visual iconography to previously excluded bodies by including a broader spectrum of shape, size, ethnicity, gender, age, and ability. Body image in visual messaging, especially in fashion platforms, is not a new area of study. The media's thin ideal has long been criticized and villainized for its harmful influence on its faithful audience. To most, as an important issue of social justice and progress, the need to change our models of body and beauty seems intellectually obvious, reasonable, and responsible. However, the predominant icon, emaciated to varying degrees, never seems to permanently leave popularity or collective consciousness as the ultimate embodiment of beauty, discipline, and status.

This inquiry stems from a desire to reveal religious and secular links that form the societal blessing and iconizing of fashion's more severely represented archetypal body. I aim to understand how and why these images still elevate sublime emaciation as a tool of worship and, through analysis and experimental art, dislodge the paradigm's cultural and aesthetic influence on today's body ideals and ascetic ideology. To argue the linkage between body ideal and morality, and across sacred and fashion visual domains, I transpose two iconic figures from different genres, periods, and legend: the medieval crucified Christ and fashion's heroin chic supermodel of the 1990s. In identifying their shared physical traits, I trace the provenance and symbolic associations embedded in the visible codes exhibited in these iconized bodies. The physical mimesis originating in the images of Christ, who embodies supreme goodness, and echoed by fashion's editorial archetype, establishes a plausible explanation for society's collective physical and psychic emulation of the sanctified emaciated body. Through the visual overlay between these icons, I expose their shared affect formed in the stylization and fragility expressed in their most legendary figurative images, as well as the shared affectation in devotees, whether monastics in the Middle Ages or Godly dieters today. The heroin chic body image exemplifies an unsettling trend in fashion's recent history whereby a contemporary version of an emaciated and wounded body image is fashionably sold. This trend likens to the medieval Christian taste for piety ordaining an increased adoration with grotesque stigmata, pronounced by gaping holes that disrupted and gouged the contour of the crucified idol's skeletal body. Catherine Walker Bynum writes, "in medieval hymns, poems, and paintings by the flesh of Christ, ripped open and spilling forth pulsating streams of insistent, scarlet blood, to wash and feed the individual hungry soul" (1987: 31). Emulation and attention to this common affect reveal the powerful role these imaged bodies maintain within societal structures that predicate a harmful ideology, even program a belief that deifies the blatantly emaciated body as sacred, fashionable, and sublime.

Subliminally, this emaciated paradigm could demonize a body that does not reach this ideal, marking nonconforming bodies as imperfect, flawed, or bad. The moral delineation between the good and bad body moves the problem beyond superficial aesthetic ideals. While worshiping the emaciated condition as a measure of strength and goodness, conversely, an undisciplined body can result in a moral judgment of weakness in personal qualities and behaviors. The emaciated visual image is covertly tied to high morality and, therefore, greater human value, and, as I will show, deific status. The thin body is idolized, but moreover, some believe the emaciated body is emblematic of superhuman resolve, even sacred power. Societies' adulation rewards the follower for being more than thin because to be sublimely emaciated takes superior will above bodily appetite. In holding these model bodies up to mass adulation, we as a society seem to sanctify this body as physically good, a visual example of bodily perfection. Historically and currently, the unspoken correlation of body image, asceticism, and morality is what continues to fortify and consecrate the emaciated idol in visual culture.

Methodologically, I combine theoretical inquiry with material and visual exploration. While identifying the aesthetic vocabulary that is expressed in images, I examine sensory qualities through my creative practice making experimental images, textiles, and soft-worn sculpture. My aim is to translate the feeling that emotes from these images in order to disrupt and transgress harmful body image paradigms. The aesthetic concept anchoring this study is "the sublime," which I define in the next subsection of the chapter. Each subsequent section opens with a digital collage integrating images of frail bodies with my experimental textiles. These pieces convey the complex sensory and emotive qualities corresponding to each layer of analysis and the strange allure and iconic stature that the emaciated form enjoys. As the chapter develops and my understanding of the sublime deepens, the emotive quality of the creative work distils and becomes my own affective language. With these images, I simultaneously create and reveal my visual and material interpretation of the research and writing process.

Sublime Visions: Deathly Form, Formlessness, and Precarious Deformity

In *Powers of Horror*, Julia Kristeva observes that we feel the sublime when viewing an external existential crisis (1982: 33). This translation of the sublime describes the sensation of witnessing an event, phenomenon, or image that provokes the simultaneous thrill and fear of mortality. In the following paragraphs, I analyze how the iconic forms of the medieval crucified Christ and the heroin chic fashion model evoke this ambiguous state of existence as an embodied continuum between living/dying/dead and form/deformity/formlessness. These sublime images are considered for their potential to communicate ascetic emulation of deathly form, the seduction of precarious deformity, and the fatal attraction to transcendental human formlessness enacted in our heralded physical idols propagated through religious art and commercial media. I emphasize the shared bodily qualities across these two forms in order to scrutinize the sublime power of these idols to inspire our popular and insatiable taste for ascetic frailty.

Kristeva's sensory description of the sublime at the start of this section is a common principle in theories of this concept. Edmund Burke in *A Philosophical Enquiry into the Beautiful and Sublime* describes an elated response of relief coupled with "self-preservation" when looking at another person at risk of morbid and/or noxious bodily harm (1757: 33). Burke qualifies this sublime feeling as "terror tinged with delight" that occurs when the danger is viewed but not felt or inflicted directly by the witness (1998: 35). Kristeva suggests that the sublime saves us or "restrains" us from unknowable, threatening, and disturbing states of existential abjection (1982: 12). She suggests poetically that "the abject is edged with the sublime" (1982: 11). More specifically for my argument, it is Paul Crowther who, in Critical Aesthetics and Postmodernism, tailors the theory of the sublime specifically to imagery, explaining the feeling as "a deliberate engaging in life-negating imagery to a life-affirming effect" (1996: 115). The emaciated Christ and the supermodel image are bodily symbols that are perfectly defined as sublime as they compose this confusing spectrum of awe. Their bodies entice and disgust as they exhibit both a sickly and saintly vision. This sublime subject matter colludes with fantasizing divinity, dying, and death while forming and fashioning the emaciated paradigm for mass consumption.

In modernism, then increasingly in postmodern fine art, there came a need to qualify the sublime with the development of abstraction and a rejection of romantic and figurative renderings (Shaw 2013, accessed April 16, 2019). Slavoj Zizek's theoretical perspective in *The Sublime Object of Ideology* spoke to this new oeuvre first with discussions of *desublimation* which then evolved to justify the sublime as applicable to awesome negation (1989). It became not only about the Kantian sweeping power of overwhelming presence but devastating barrenness, indefinite, and definite severe absence. Zizek expands the definition to describe the devastating feeling of uncertainty of presence or non-presence, and noticeable and purposeful absence. This is manifested in the theoretical writings and haunting artwork created by scholar, artist, and psychoanalyst Bracha Ettinger. She explains, "Sublimation is a mysterious way to embody a 'hole' in the Real—" (2006: 48.9). Ettinger translates the sublime as an aching lack as she writes and visually expresses the societal trauma and genocide perpetrated by Nazis during the Holocaust (Ettinger 2006:10). The sublime manifests in her painting, copying, and erasing her subjects repeatedly leaving partial visual bodily and psychic remains. This returns to my hypothesis whereby the sublime can be an effable embodied existence and nonexistence within the source imagery to address the disturbing magnetic quality emoting from the emaciated body. I believe this translation of the sublime describes the deathly form, precarious deformity, and formlessness as it visually conjures the impossibility of fleshly emptiness (Zizek 1989: 205).

The surveyed images of the late medieval Christ (Figure 8.1) and the posed fashion model (Figure 8.2) reveal a visually similar body silhouette that defies sensible beauty canons. In *The Female Nude, Art, Obscenity and Sexuality*, author Lynda Nead speaks to the aesthetic conventions that have been used to frame the female body in artistic disciplines whereby "social and cultural representations are central in forming these definitions and giving the configurations of the body" (2002:24–5). As an audience, we might intellectually understand that severely emaciated bodies should not be the standard for a fashionable or beautiful figure because this is not widely attainable for most of society. These emaciated icons are unnaturally void of any excess flesh, fat, and muscle with a prominent skeletal structure. The torsos displayed expose the bony cages of the ribs and hipbones. The skin is stretched thin and taut tenuously connecting and housing the vital internal organs. Although known as female (Figure 8.2) and male (Figure 8.1), the proportions of the emaciated torso are near identical breaking the classical gendered norms and establishing a sublime ascetic

Figure 8.1 Crucifix, seventeenth century, Spanish. Figure: ivory; cross: ebony; scroll: brass (?) 23 1/2 × 11 in. (59.7 × 27.9 cm). The Metropolitan Museum of Art, New York. Gift of Mrs. Francis H. Washburn (1885). Photo: The Metropolitan Museum of Art.

From the Medieval Christ to Fashion's Heroin Chic

Figure 8.2 Model walks Prada's Spring 1997 RTW (pret a porter) collection. Photo: Guy Marineau/Condé Nast via Getty Images.

physique that has been cyclically repeated and iconized in contemporary visual culture (Nead 2002: 23). Susan Bordo states that currently "there is an epidemic of eating disorders" (2004: xxiv). Her writing expresses multiple causes to this growing global phenomenon, one being the marketed fashion body published by popular commercial media (Bordo 2004: xxiv). Using the cited images, I ponder their sublime attributes and the affective power they exhibit over their audience. In stature and spirit, they seem to flirt with deathly form; their collapsed and disjointed carriage suggests precarious deformity, and a dissolving and fleshless body conjures transcendental formlessness. In an attempt to prove these bodies existentially and structurally sublime instead of simply beautiful, I aim to demystify and reduce the harmful seduction, esteem, and emulative potential these imaged bodies have on a receptive audience (Figure 8.3).

> The sublime, which is the cause of the former, always dwells on great objects, and terrible; the latter on small ones, and pleasing; we submit to what we admire, but we love what submits to us. (Burke 1998: 113)

Silhouettes of the Soul

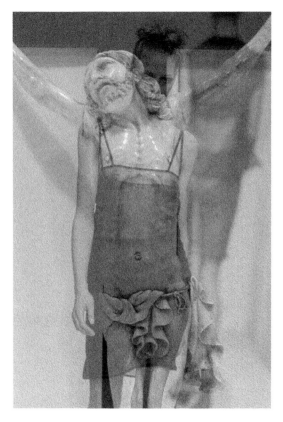

Figure 8.3 Figures 8.1 and 8.2 Digitally superimposed during research process (2020) by Tanya White.

Ascetic Emulation of Deathly Form

Leading into the discussion of deathly form, Figure 8.4 is my visual response to the deadly thin physique. In this the manipulated body framed with texture intentionally perverts the practice of fashion styling to provoke an unsettling editorial statement. Beyond the fleeting impact of beauty or sexual attraction, I deconstruct the ineffable and haunting "hole" imposed by the deathly thin figure and embody this in my visual and cloth recreations. Evocatively, fashion still embraces and contrives this ascetic vision. In high fashion editorials, the appeal is visually capturing the impossibility of this physiological condition. The art direction deliberately lures the viewer toward emulation by celebrating the embodied unreality. As Kristeva says, "the abject is tinged with the sublime," and this occurs when "we are at the limit of otherness" (1982: 11). It is this void or unknowable "otherness" that is powerfully effective in its visual influence on a pliable viewer. Theorist Sara Ahmed describes how cultural impressions are transmitted; some images, objects, text, etc. have a *"stickiness"* that in the act of viewing or experiencing "impresses" and shapes a receptive psyche (2013: 74). Therefore, the widely publicized imaged body of

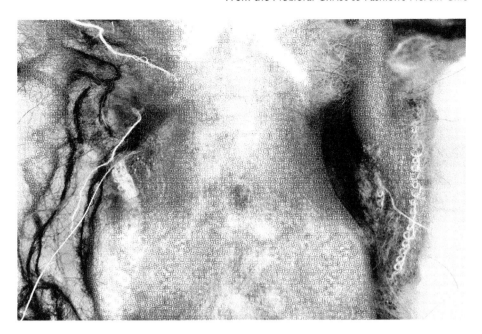

Figure 8.4 Tanya White, *Deathly Form Wearing Textile* (2019). Digital collage, knit with invisible and wool tops. Courtesy of Tanya White.

Christ and the supermodel haunts, causing a psychic stain on a willing congregant. In aiming to channel this transfixing void through my practice-based inquiry, my intention is to critically address the dire nature of this injurious visual patterning.

As I recognize the nefarious fantasy created by the converging points of body shape, proportion, and pose, the figures of the late medieval crucified Christ and the heroin chic supermodel iconography mirror each other respectively in sublime affect The emaciated body ideal is an abjectly sublime figure that has been and is constructed by religious and secular ascetic admiration, promotion, and compulsion. It is a physique that is held as fashionably sublime, and to some, a reverent martyr connoting purity, morality, and superhuman self-discipline (Nead 2002: 20). The ascetic denial of primal drives, needs, and fleshly desires can be received as saintly, salacious, and/or pathological depending on the viewer's ideological persuasion. Whether it is under the powers of god or fashion, the painted and photographed severely emaciated body is documented in an active and suprasensible willful fast. The image captures the subject between a not fully living and near deathly aesthetic state (Bordo 2004: 24). This state is illustrated by the skeletal presence caught within the frame. The subject matter is viewed as tempting death by self-starving. It performs Crowther's theory of the existential sublime whereby images of the crucified Christ and the model bodies are a pictorial staging of purposeful and self-inflicted challenge to health and even life. Thus, this curated body image expresses an overt negation of death that causes sublime delight in their loyal awe-struck followers.

For some onlookers, the reaction to the imaged body does not stir feelings of self-preservation but, rather, a deep pathological admiration of the ascetic control iconized by the emaciated physique. It is this physical image that transfixes and acts as a map of their desired body goal. In the article, "Sublime Hunger: A Consideration of Eating Disorders beyond Beauty," Sheila Lintott uses Emmanuel Kant's theory of the sublime to analyze anorexia writing, "the experience of the sublime shows us that we can transcend our natural inclinations, and if need be, resist them entirely" (2003: 71). In transcending natural inclinations to nourish the body when hungry, the anorexic is actively weakening the vitality of their physical condition. Devout ascetic fasting and mortification practices were/are enacted to mimic the suffering of Christ. This was and is celebrated as saintly behavior (Joseph 2010: 154). In this case, the Burkian self-preservation does not give sense to dangerous self-starving. Instead, its intention is more plausibly explained by Lintott's Kantian theory of sublime hunger whereby there is profound respect for ascetic behavior (Crowther 1991: 116). To the anorexic, and I would add sainted religious zealots, starving/fasting is seen as morally conquering the unruly and evil flesh. This emulation exemplifies the Kantian sublime whereby the affect is deeply contained in the optical reception and subjective feeling of awesome esteem the willing observer feels for the emaciated icon's supreme commitment to asceticism (Lintott 2003: 68).

Furthering the adulation of deathly form is the disturbing use of these images as visual meditations to indoctrinate fundamentalist codes of extreme eating, non-eating, and

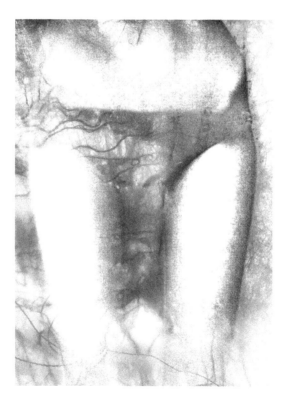

Figure 8.5 Tanya White, *Precarious Deformity Wearing Textile* (2019). Digital collage, knit and embroidery with mohair, horsehair, wool tops, and invisible yarns. Courtesy of Tanya White.

obsessive exercise. With this I mean the continued use of specific heroin chic photographs on *proana and promia* (pro-anorexic, pro-bulimic) platforms and the repetitive worship of the crucifixion as a tool in the attainment of a Godly dieting regime. In the text *Slim for Him*, scripture and religious idols are perverted for the purpose of Christian reducing, purging, and fasting weight loss plans (Kreml 1978). Food is deemed either pure or sinful, and faithful Christians must practice abstinence over junk food and gluttony. Controlling cravings as with other realms of Christian devotion looks to the dying body of Christ as the prominent visual symbol of chastity, martyrdom, and restriction (Griffith 2004: 21). Similarly, the characteristic features of these pro-eating disorder online communities are image galleries that visibly encode an acutely thin body type. This is where they expound wanton starvation by looking at gaunt fashion tropes, diaries of withering physiques, *thinspiration(al)* pictures, and usually a list of ten pseudo-religious proana commandments to live by (2019: 321). These textual affirmations are used like occultist prayer, while the photographs categorized as *thinspiration* project dissolving emaciated bodies. It is Zizek's sublime absence in that it "is an object whose positive body is just an embodiment of nothing" (1989: 205). This reveals deathly form as a heightened visual manifestation of disordered eating that can be admired fervently. These bodies become socially idealized, even revered for their absent bodily presence. The framed body becomes a lethal fixation as it is psychically traced by the viewer leaving evidence of an actively expiring existence. This visualized silhouette is death in progress held as their ultimate reward to strengthen their resolve and observe the sect's deviant codes and even fatal behaviors.

Precarious Deformity

In visually analyzing and making images that connote the severely emaciated body, notably, it is the lack of muscularity revealing a skeletal structure that is precariously held by a thin encasement of skin (Figure 8.5). To me this creates a deformity of physique and body language that is specific to the overly emaciated image. In the source images and my transformation of precarious deformity, the body seems to weakly collapse yet float without tension or gravity. With this, the imaged body expresses a simultaneous physical fragility held in strange concert to a wilfully strong ascetic desire. The tenuous balance of affect is confusing and compelling. It is sublime as it deforms nature and logic. Creating this expiring ratio or deforming the body measurements as in the heroin chic supermodel proportions creates an alternative and subversive visual ideal. The emaciated supermodel is tall yet frail, adult yet not womanly, and this silhouette creates an opportunity for more emphasized, inharmonious, and deformed sublime proportion. The textile frames the impossible and terrible gap between the thighs.

In *Corpus*, theorist Jean Luc Nancy lists "58 Indices of the Body," "22. Different bodies are all somewhat deformed. A perfectly formed body is a disturbing, indiscreet body in the world of bodies, unacceptable. It's a diagram, not a body" (2008: 151). In both Christian paintings and fashion media, the deformation of the body is constructed by the image's creator, in the case of this argument, the artist/painter and the editor/photographer, respectively. The body is manipulated within the frame to have lasting aesthetic impact. The imaged subject, especially their bodily form, affects its audience and becomes a visual icon and idol. The medieval Christ from the passion iconography and the fashion model labeled as heroin chic is conceived by their physical stature and posture. Surveying the specified bodies, they are presented boldly without substance, with no curves or rolls of flesh that would organically pad the waist or hip area. Their stomachs proudly exhibited, so empty they seem distended like victims of famine. These physical attributes that epitomize emaciation are manipulated, affected, and directed to play within the Burkian sublime borders of abject visual deformation. This artifice is lauded without feeling or risk of actual affliction. With this it is the viewer's appreciation of the imaged body that is crafted and curated to create the exoticized "other" in paintings, sculptures, magazines, and even runways. It is this unknowable sensation of being inside that body matter and posture that expands the physically "non-I" fantasy (Ettinger 2006: 86.7). For the witness the impossibly slight figure folds and disassembles, receding from their framed sight. It is sublime in its artfully deformed carriage. For the voyeur there is a pleasure in experiencing the deformed emaciated condition safely without pain, want, or struggle.

This unsettling thinness can be reframed to heighten the Christian or fashion message and excite followers. The severity and difference become the idealized silhouette. Its tenuous deformation can be molded toward significance and elevated to symbolic, even heroic to some devotees. In Christianity the son of God is symbolic of the Eucharist, whereby the body of Christ *is* the bread of communion. It is physically broken in the ceremonial act of devotion (Beckwith 2005: 181). The medieval Christ and the heroin chic supermodel bodies analogize and sanctify beliefs that are formed, deformed, and reformed again in tribute. The model bares her collarbone and shoulder blades to exaggerate the concave and jutting silhouette on the runway. A beloved fashion figure poses aloofly, mugging and slumping in designer campaigns. This bodily attitude exudes coy transgression. The images of the medieval Christ and the waifish supermodel are a visual exploitation of extreme bodily behaviors that are integral to their iconic mythology. With subjective wonder the emaciated figure's pathological state is inherently bonded to the narrative of moral or immoral supremacy. Revisiting secular and religious asceticism, this distressed physical condition proves to the witness the depth of their idol's belief and discipline. The hallowed embodiment of purity—Christian, and impurity—fashion's stylistic assimilation of heroin culture, reveals a twisted association fixing the broken body image to godlike resolve.

In *The Kantian Sublime: From Morality to Art*, Crowther categorizes the artistic sublime into four specialities: cognitive (mathematical, dynamic), artifactual, personalized, and expressive. Crowther's expressive sublime is when the artist's portrayal creates emotive subject matter to an overwhelming affect. As Crowther suggests, "because the subject-matter has been distended by the artist's style, our customary understanding of it, and the associations we form with it, will be challenged and transformed" (1991: 158). This transformation of the sublime is of particular interest with regard to the complex resonance the source bodies inflict with stylized deformation. There is an aesthetic acuteness and plainness sculpted by their physicality that was visually shocking in comparison to what came before and after. The body image, in size and configuration, became more extreme stylistically. Its graphic substance explicitly dissolved and distorted. Additionally, a prominent schematic deformity was the celebration of a wounded body in both genres. During the early 1990s the authenticity of drug culture became fashionably appropriated and fictionalized. In the most incendiary demonstrations, bruises and marked limbs darkly nodded flirtatiously to injecting heroin in editorials and advertisements (Hickman 2002:119). This mimics the medieval aestheticization of a weakened, bloodied, and broken emaciated body suffering and humiliated (1987: 34). The exaggerated, flawed, and violated structure was a guilt-fuelled visual sentiment that was bonded to heavenly selflessness. In both histories, the bodily form is violently flayed. These fashioned or holy flaws are emblematic of terrific fashion rebellion or Godly worship, and they are terribly sublime to mythologically remind and ideologically inspire.

In *Affect Theory, Shame and Christian Formation*, Stephanie Arel explains the physical, emotional, and psychic bodily forming or deforming caused by Christian scripture, counseling, and disciplines. In part, her compelling hypothesis addresses the harmful repercussions of severe religious ideology that processes and confuses Christian feelings of guilt and sin as affective shame (Arel 2016: 9). For my purposes when addressing the imaged emaciated body type and posture imprinted by the medieval crucified Christ, this embodiment of shame provides additional layers of understanding into the origins of this destructive visual patterning. I believe that this body in stature and stance has cyclically modeled the fashioned impression exhibited in the waif archetype (Figure 8.2). Arel does not speak extensively to the imagery as much as the textual theology. As I am attempting to dissect body iconography, I would like to adapt her thoughtful exploration of Christian shame as it relates to the figural humiliation heralded in the act of crucifixion. In the supreme act of sacrifice for human sin, Christ must become human in order to die and be resurrected. In Christian teachings the torture, weakening, breaking, and ultimate humiliation of Christ are essential for this metamorphosis. Christ must become human to die, in order to be resurrected as holy. Described in theological aesthetic theory, this humiliation or mortification is described as "kenosis," "self-emptying" of spirit in the brutal conversion to fully earthly flesh (Evans 2006: 218). This kenosis, an emptying, is especially physicalized in the medieval renditions of Christ on the cross. Returning to the Grunewald Christ (Figure 8.1), the body is caught in spasm, head dropped and turned away, shoulders hunched, the bony torso muscularly depleted and concave, the legs turned inward shamefully. His body droops without strength but seems to actively recoil from onlookers. The deformed physique is a visceral diagram of his kenosis. In the religious or secular understanding this image is law and lore. A body image that has been deified, appropriated, and disseminated. It is sublimely horrific yet to most it symbolizes beauty, martyrdom, and purity.

Transcendental Formlessness

> Fleshy bodies are of the earth and fleshless forms are of the heavens. (Joseph 2010: 155)

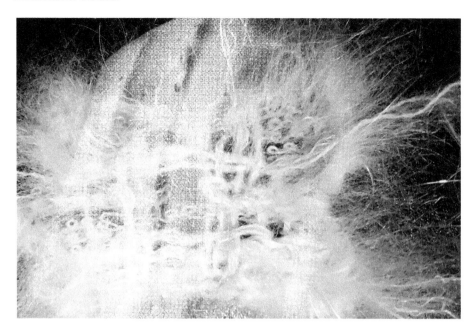

Figure 8.6 Tanya White, *Formlessness Wearing Textile* (2018). Digital collage, knitted, woven, and stained sculpture with invisible and mohair thread. Courtesy of Tanya White.

In interpreting formlessness, I started by weaving, knitting, and stitching with invisible thread, mohair yarns, and wool tops. These textiles were fuzzy, buoyant, and transparent (Figure 8.6). Making formlessness led me to try to define the graceful waif, sylph, fairy, or angel that has long been iconized and worshipped for its frail featherlight presence visually connoting a sublime otherworldly body. It seems to float without the tension of muscle or the earthly weight of gravity. It is ghostly; it is pale, fleshless, and may have a soft halo of downy hair. The sublime formless figure is both seductive and disturbing for its lack of containment; as Kristeva says, the "borders" are "murky" challenging the delineation between internal and external, "I and other" (1982: 11). Jacques Derrida speaks of framing in the sublime, yet to me this specific body in its wispiness, translucency, and omission of any evidence of natural bodily function seems to defy structure and existence. The emaciated unformed body is sublime in its eerie and haunting images expressing an indistinct; I am here nor there, presence. Ettinger speaks of the sublime within the "matrixial borderspace," "The matrix-figure lacks form, image and discourse, even though it inhabits simultaneously these three spaces and even through artwork emerges from it" (2006: 76.7). It is visibly unlimited in the most fragile sense. The sublime can be unlimited with grandness, meaning the object/subject can engulf the viewer/witness, or conversely, it can awesomely underwhelm in its delicacy and feebleness. This body suspends belief in its ability to sustain itself, and this is demonstrated in its lack of substantial form, its disappearing form. It is not human but becoming divine; therefore, it transcends human form into sublime spirit.

The aesthetic comparison between religious art, specifically the passion imagery and heroin chic fashion photography, seems blasphemous and far-fetched, yet the depicted physical abandon transitioning from crucifixion to resurrection and the effects of heroin draw remarkable similarity in written and visual description. In *Junky*, William Burroughs memorializes his first experience injecting morphine, saying, "Morphine hits the back of the legs first, then the back of the neck, a spreading wave of relaxation slackening the muscles away from the bones so that you seem to float without outlines, like lying in warm salt water" (1977: 7). The opiate sensation of morphine is essentially the same as heroin (Hickman 2002: 119). It is this muscular "slackening" and the body "floating without outlines" that I believe is the sublime physicality that has visceral resonance in these iconic somewhat aestheticized cultural depictions. It is again Kristeva's "murky borders" between abject and sublime that create the magnetic visual imprint on our collective psyche of the slack and formless emaciated body. The poetic language aptly composed by Burroughs and Kristeva describes a body that is unhealthy, even obviously tempting an existential threshold. These elegant descriptions seduce and could be the cause of this cultish and morbid fascination in these texts illustrating their behavioral narrative. Scripture and theology can also effectively indoctrinate religious disciples, sometimes sensuously perverting the text toward damaging ends (Arel 2016: 10). Admittedly, my inquiry is to question my own attraction to this subject matter and the artistic renditions. In this, understanding the various cultural sources that poetically idealize these bodies to iconic status, whether famous or infamous.

Slavoj Zizek explains the Kantian theory of the sublime, "the sublime evokes pleasure in a purely negative way: the place of the thing is indicated through the very failure of its representation" (1989: 204). The mental state of sublime emaciation can bring unsettling and pleasurable feelings as the cognitive condition of a prolonged starved brain is flighty, erratic, and euphoric (Bordo [1993] 2003: 55–6). The weakened body becomes a foreshadowed symbol of the not "here" but beyond, not effable but ineffable materiality (2008: 59). Further, Zizek speaks to this tenuous state, "On the other hand, we have the fundamentally precarious status of (symbolic) reality that can, at any moment, dissipate, losing its consistency" (2014: 58). The pictorial bodies of the heroin chic supermodel and the crucified Christ have drastically different repute, but their images are legend, a transcendent religious or fashion vision that is not tethered to "real" experience. Quoting Ettinger again, she speaks of a "Diffuse/sharp vision is not no/yes or *fort/da* opposition (between two places that are equal with regard to their potential focus)" (2006: 76.7). The emaciated posture is edged with diffuse borders that express the idol's real and/or mythic mental, physical, and spiritual personae. The aestheticized body overcome by divine elation or intoxication presents analogous symptoms in visual culture. The lifeless body of Christ in renditions of the pieta seems to glow and drape stylishly like expensive fabric over his mother's lap. His body is glorified in its post suffering and sacrificial luminosity. A fashioned yet sordid drug-induced state becomes an editorial simulation picturing a model mimicking the high, physically glistening with unconscious graceful abandonment. The body and its symbolic condition enthuse the congregate. Witnessing these sublime images as a strange and diffuse mixture of reality and fantasy, conjuring the high and enrapturement expressed in the heroic fragility of the idol's ephemeral form.

Considering the internal functions enacted by a secular or religious ascetic drive or a drug-sick lack of appetite, the sustained denial of nourishment creates an amorphous, dissolving body that is easily comparable to the "hole," "void," or "nothing" that has been discussed previously (Zizek 1989: 58). This compellingly conveys Kristeva's "murky" boundaries and internal/external struggle that is the result of severe anorexia. In anorexic females the bodily function, menstruation, is held in prepubescence. Long-term starving causes a hormonal stunting of natural maturity (Bordo [1993] 2003: xix). The extremely emaciated female body does not menstruate further disturbing the natal processes creating a deficit in estrogen (Nead 2002: 23). This arrests body development, thereby biologically modifying physical, mental, and sexual status. Willingly through fleshly denial, she is not materially, physiologically, or structurally woman or child. Comparatively, the medieval Christ was emaciated to the degree of near skin and bone in renditions of the crucifix purposely to not only show the kenotic process discussed previously but also reduce the corporal sexuality of the iconic figure (Beckwith 2005: 67). This was intended to render a body that was relatable in its gender fluidity and humanity and to dramatically visualize and foreshadow its heavenly transcendence.

To me the concept of sublime as infinite, indefinable, and limitless, something that suspends reason or judgment, could have strikingly positive connotations and liberating consequences toward releasing the need for uniformed bodies and rigid gender paradigms. As gender cues become nonbinary, flexible, and individually owned, there is a feeling of gendered transcendence that could be aptly described as *divine formlessness* in its nonprescribed *masculine* or *feminine* form. Further, when gendering the *son* of God, whether lived, crucified, or resurrected, scholarly opinion is passionately divergent. Christian medievalist Caroline Bynum, for example, argues, "Christ's humanity as bodiliness" (1987: 252). These theories are informed by scriptures, histories, and images that are all culturally mediated interpretations of interpretations. Scholarship must also be tempered by our own growing understanding of how gender has been culturally constructed by projections, assumptions, and biases. In failing health to cadaver, the human body is in process as it becomes unrecognizable, and its earthly presence is abstracted. The formed memory including familiar facial features, feelings, traits, behavior, and the need for differentiation of male/female and man/woman fades with time, life, death, and after death. This is performed and imprinted in art and media's representation of this life and after death continuum (Bronfen 1992: 63).

The image maker/director concocts the subject/object's physicality to cause expressive reaction. In this I would suggest that whether recognized as male or female, masculine or feminine, the specific emaciated idols, the torso of the crucified Christ, and the 1990s image are reverently emulated for their visual structure made up of diffuse visible gender markers. Contemporary theologian Graham Ward argues that if Christ is the embodied icon of the Church, literally his body is said to be the totality of the congregation. He deduces that the Church, therefore Jesus Christ, would be plausibly defined as "a multigendered body" (Ward 2002: 175). Stephanie Arel agrees that Christ cannot be one body if he is symbolic of *all*, of the flock, "a Body which overflows into a community, which unites a *group* of bodies" (2016: 77). Also, a common view from the medieval period is that Christ is the embodied mother of the Church (Ward 2008: 111). During crucifixion, maternal signification has been debated by interpreting the side wounds as "birthing, bleeding and lactating openings" (Bynum 2010). These scholars may not prove the absolute answer of gender assignment pertaining to the *son* of God, but it does allow a diffuse delineation thus a sublimely undefined possibility. I feel this idea of ambiguous or multiple is supported by the referenced images (Figures 8.1 and 8.3). Besides this, these bodies inspire fascination that is not carnal. It is ascetically other and sublime in its credible formlessness as it vehemently transfixes a follower that is agreeable to its emotive power. In its formlessness it allows a broader affective result, religious or fashionable. In the name of God or *Vogue*, the emaciated body speaks to the converted regardless of gender, sex, or sect.

Concluding Reflection

My aesthetic and ethical intent is capturing the sublime quality that I feel is visually imprinted and doubled in worship of the iconic bodies imaged first in the medieval crucified Christ and then in the 1990s heroin chic supermodel. I am aware that certain renditions cause lasting impressions, creating a body image that simultaneously seduces and repulses, is abjectly beautiful, weak and resolute, dying and alive, collapsed and floating. These bodies are described as both miraculous and horrific. A physical condition that is both celebrated and condemned as it is worshipped. Its visual impression is sublime as it is posed to perform deathly form, ghostly formlessness, and precarious deformity of a body that is still exemplified and culturally emulated today. As previously explained, I am not using the theory of the sublime that is easily represented in its grandeur. On the contrary, I am guided by the sublime that is awesome in its ambiguity and feeling that unsettles. The source images contain a similar body ideal that acutely disturbs leaving sensory echoes, traces, and vibrations (Figures 8.1–8.3). This theoretical translation explains a sublime experience where thought and sensation are suspended; it overwhelms creating a purposeful and devastating affective hole, which appears as it disappears.

With grave purpose, I seek to explicitly interpret, through text, images, and cloth, the emaciated body image in an adequately "real" state. In this I am taking into account the effective danger in continually promoting an aestheticized version of this severely unhealthy physical condition. In this writing I do not intend to villainize any particular religious ideology, artist, industry, photographer, or model. I am aware of the temptation to judge and simplify the aims of the image creator or subject matter. Centuries or decades later, it is easy to twist and mischaracterize the affective goal by supplanting these images, with the folklore attached, into our current political and scholarly debate. However, revisiting these images to understand the genesis of the aestheticized emaciated paradigm hopefully brings an awareness to the symbolism—positive, negative, or ambiguous—carried in this visual iconography. Tempering my critique is the need to question my own leanings toward this aesthetic. It is this balance, through textual hypothesis and digital creation, that I feel suitably expresses my admiration, empathy, and discomfort in my own fascination. While searching, I muse, write, and make with sentient rigor to move beyond reductive and overly romanticized mimicry, attempting to yield respectful and thought-provoking results.

References

Ahmed, S. (2013), *The Cultural Politics of Emotion*, Routledge.
Arel, S. N. (2016), *Affect Theory, Shame, and Christian Formation*, Springer International Publishing.
Beckwith, S. (2005), *Christ's Body: Identity, Culture and Society in Late Medieval Writings*, Routledge.
Bordo, S. ([1993] 2003), *Unbearable Weight: Feminism, Western Culture, and the Body*, University of California Press.
Bronfen, E. (1992), *Over Her Dead Body: Death, Femininity, and the Aesthetic*, Manchester University Press.
Burke, E. (1998), *A Philosophical Enquiry into the Sublime and Beautiful*, Penguin UK.
Bynum, C.W. (1987), *Holy Feast and Holy Fast: The Religious Significance of Food to Medieval Women*, University of California Press.
Bynum, C.W. (2010), "Violence Occluded: The Wound in Christ's Side in Late Medieval Devotion," in *Feud, Violence and Practice: Essays in Medieval Studies in Honor of Stephen D. White*, 95–116, Farnham: Ashgate.
Crowther, P. (1991), *The Kantian Sublime: From Morality to Art*, Oxford University Press.
Crowther, P. (1996), *Critical Aesthetics and Postmodernism*, Oxford University Press.
Crowther, P. (2016), *How Pictures Complete us: The Beautiful, the Sublime, and the Divine*, Stanford University Press.
Ettinger, B. (2006), *The Matrixial Borderspace*, Vol. 28, U of Minnesota Press.
Ettinger, B.L. (2006), "Matrixial Trans-Subjectivity," *Theory, Culture & Society*, 23(2–3): 218–22.
Evans, C.S. ed. (2006), *Exploring Kenotic Christology: The Self-Emptying of God*, Oxford University Press.
Griffith, R.M. (2004), *Born Again Bodies: Flesh and Spirit in American Christianity*, Vol. 12, University of California Press.
Hickman, T. A. (2002), "Heroin Chic: The Visual Culture of Narcotic Addiction," *Third Text*, 16(2): 119–36, doi:10.1080/09528820210138272
Johnson, E.A. (1992), *She Who Is: The Mystery of God in Feminist Theological Discourse*, Crossroad.
Johnson, E.A. (2007), *Quest for the Living God: Mapping Frontiers in the Theology of God*, A&C Black.
Joseph, S. (2010), "The Ascetic Jesus," *Journal for the Study of the Historical Jesus*, 8(2): 146–81.
Kristeva J. (1982), *Powers of Horror: An Essay on Abjection*, trans. Leon S. Roudiez, New York: Columbia University Press.
Lintott, S. (2003), "Sublime Hunger: A Consideration of Eating Disorders Beyond Beauty," *Hypatia*, 18(4): 65–86. http://www.jstor.org/stable/3810975.
Nancy, J.L. (2008), *Corpus*, Vol. 4, Fordham University Press.
Nead, L. (2002), *The Female Nude: Art, Obscenity and Sexuality*, Routledge.
Kreml, P. B. (1978), *Slim for Him*. Logos International.

Shaw, P. (2013), "Modernism and the Sublime," in Nigel Llewellyn and Christine Riding (eds.), *The Art of the Sublime*, Tate Research Publication, https://www.tate.org.uk/art/research-publications/the-sublime/philip-shaw-modernism-and-the-sublime-r1109219 (accessed April 16, 2019).

Stapleton, K., S. L. Evans, and C. S. Rhys (2019), "Ana as God: Religion, Interdiscursivity and Identity on Pro-ana Websites," *Discourse & Communication,* 13(3): 320–41.

Ward, G. (2008), *Christ and Culture*, John Wiley & Sons.

Žižek, S. (1989), *The Sublime Object of Ideology*, Verso.

Žižek, S. and T. Scott-Railton (2014), *The Most Sublime Hysteric: Hegel with Lacan*, English ed., Polity Press.

CHAPTER 9
IN AND OUT OF ONE ANOTHER'S CLOSETS
A DIALOGUE
Jeanine Viau with Shekinah Morrison

This dialogue recalls my and Shekinah's experiences as instructor and student in an upper-level undergraduate seminar Form & Fashion. The format follows dialogue chapters included in the work of activist theorists such as bell hooks and Paulo Freire, as well as Carolyn Ellis's *The Ethnographic I* (2004), where she records classroom dialogs with students. The grounding methods of the seminar were Ellis's autoethnography, specifically how it is employed by fashion studies researchers, and serial testimony, a timed, en round practice of sharing experience developed by Peggy McIntosh (Luce-Hitt and Viau, 2019). These approaches reflect bell hooks's call to self-revelation in the classroom. hooks writes, "To hear each other (the sound of different voices), to listen to one another, is an act of recognition. It also ensures that no student remains invisible in the classroom" (1994: 41). For hooks, processes of self-disclosure make democratic learning environments possible, and so "the dream of education as the practice of freedom" (1994: 30). Shekinah and I examine the limits and the possibilities of fashioning new patterns of thought and identity for students and teachers alike. We articulate the disruptive power of hearing difference and the categorical transformations generated through autoethnographic testimony.

> **JV:** As you know, one of our first readings in the course was Toni Morrison's novel, *God Help the Child*, a character study of Bride, an up-and-coming "blue-black" beauty icon. Bride is haunted by the specter of colorism, and its master, white aspiration, manifesting in Morrison's story as respectability, celebrity, ad gloss, and capitalist enfranchisement. Morrison's aesthetic vision is pretty bleak. The reader meets Bride at the height of popular adoration, the pinnacle of beauty, but her fortune is about to turn, as Morrison takes her on an odyssey of violent mishaps and profound self-doubt, manifesting in the biological regression of her body in response to remembering childhood trauma. Morrison seems interested in laying bare the deforming force of white aesthetic aspirations in black life, whether it manifests as the obviously abhorrent colorism disclosed by Sweetness (Bride's mother), or its reconstitution in the dead-end ambition of Bride and Booker's generation. Morrison's novel was an entry point in the course into broader discussions of aesthetic theories and norms active in society, culture, art, and critical theory. In response to *God Help the Child* and some of the other approaches we read in this subsection, you formulated a theory that helped us

synthesize the material and that became central to your group's final project. Would you introduce this concept and talk about how it developed over the course of the semester?

SM: A few of my colleagues and I were grouped together for the seminar's final assignment, and *God Help the Child* was an incredibly pivotal point for the conceptual framework of our project. Throughout the life of the course and the subsection itself, we spent a good amount of time discussing aesthetics and conventional beauty. We also spent an equally hefty time discussing *unconventional* beauty. As it came down to our final projects, my course mates and I came to the conclusion that all of our final papers, and thus the collection of works we had put together to turn into an aesthetic concept, all invoked ideas of *non*-aesthetic.

While working closely with the remainder of the team, I began to have separate conversations with one of the members in specific about the concept that it felt like we isolated while discussing our project at large. Her essay involved the anti-aesthetic properties of tattoos and piercings, or body modifications, as a form of alternate and valid beauty. Mine, on the other hand, was a more autoethnographic exploration of the racial and social navigation of my (conventionally beautiful) white-passing mother. It was then that me and my colleague realized that we were, individually and as a group, dealing with something distinctly different than an anti-aesthetic. Our concepts were a bit beyond the scope of working against conventional aesthetic standards or deliberately going against the grain. Her tattoos and piercings and my mother were both, to us, an example of something new: a *numbing* of aesthetic values. This wasn't being different or navigating as an example of other options of beauty standards. This was a patent example of rejecting typical form and function, rejecting typical standards of aesthetic presentation, numbing this thing down to its pithy but misunderstood reality: every aesthetic, in a vacuum, is individual, and so every individual, in a vacuum, can abstract themselves from an aesthetic presentation and make their own.

This is where *anaesthetic* was born. We found it to be incredibly clever that the word functioned as a pun on medical numbing agents while also incorporating a new take on aesthetic or abstraction from it. Anti-aesthetic already existed and felt more against the grain than away from it. *Anaesthetic*, on the other hand, felt like a better way, to us, to describe taking yourself away from a typical aesthetic and creating your own, even when it feels impossible given the intersectional circumstances at play in any situation. The lack of an aesthetic became an aesthetic in itself and a redefinition of form and fashion. *Anaesthetic* was, as a concept, a call to discourse. Not just "what" is aesthetic, but "*why*." We brought this conceptual idea to the rest of our group, they loved it, and the rest is history.

I would succinctly define *anaesthetic* as the sister concept of aesthetic and anti-aesthetic. The three are interconnected; one cannot exist without the others. It invokes ideas of numbness and disconnectedness from conventional aesthetic standards and could be described as a transcendence beyond the status quo more than a rejection of it. *Anaesthetic* as a concept presents the idea of counterculture as a performance of rejection of normalcy, but the performance itself raises the notion that rather than rejection, some beauty is indeed abstraction.

JV: What I hear in your explanation is that you are adding an affect register to the norms register of aesthetic experience, placing emphasis on the absence of affect as evidence to subvert the givenness or objectivity of aesthetic norms. One question to consider is what about the excess of affect, the opposite of numbness in response to any aesthetic possibility, normative or nonnormative. Similar to the way that aesthetic and anti-aesthetic exist on a continuum, so too excess and numbness occur on an affect continuum. Intersected with aesthetic/anti-aesthetic, anaesthetic would be at one end and perhaps something like empaesthetic (combining empathy, "feeling with" and aesthetic) at the other. Represented in a static model, this intersection might look like a perpendicular plane, where specific affect-aesthetic interactions might be plotted. Experientially, however, the model needs animation so that the registers can spin on multiple axes, perhaps even bend and fold so that the anti-aesthetic becomes the aesthetic norm, and feeling with becomes numbness, constantly redrawing a webbed sphere of anti-an-emp-aesthetic intersections.

Now, "feeling with" does not determine the nature of the affective response. Affective responses might include pleasure, disgust, rage, grief, awe, etc. Also, connections between aesthetics and affect may be liberative as well as nefarious. I am reminded of your reference to Sara Ahmed's work on affect orientations in your final writing assignment for the course. In *Queer Phenomenology*, Ahmed studies habituated lines between feeling and object, and the ways queer affect orientations or disorientations present "different ways of following lines" and "different ways of deviating from them" (2006: 176). For Ahmed, the queer commitment is not compulsory deviation. Rather, queer is a "commitment to an opening up of what counts as a life worth living," what counts as beautiful, an expansion of affective possibilities. This does not preclude following established paths between object, feeling, and future, since "certain straight lines" ensure survival and enfranchisement in cultural political world-making (2006: 178). On the other hand, certain straight lines between aesthetic and affect function to shore up death-dealing supremacist cultures. Ahmed also charts how "feeling with" produces and reproduces white nationalist sensibilities, a shared subjectivity bonded in "love" to defend against "aliens" (2004: 118). Whether open or closed to aesthetic difference, Ahmed shows how emotions are not a private matter belonging to individuals: "emotions are not simply 'within' or 'without' . . . they create the very effect of the surfaces or boundaries of bodies and worlds" (2004: 117).

Speaking of affect orientations, or the ways we are affected by objects, another point of clarity in the course came up with your response to one of the autoethnographic serial testimony exercises. We were discussing Sophie

Woodward's (2016) practice of literally entering into women's closets to interview them about their process of assembling their daily wardrobes and their intimacies with specific articles of clothing. As a way to bring her strategy to life and continue the seminar's autoethnographic examination through the mediums of fashion, style, and dress, I asked everyone to reflect on how they felt standing in front of or inside their closets that morning. I then asked everyone, in serial testimony style, to describe their experience in one sentence to the class. Your answer to this question was immediately instructive and supplied a real-time understanding of how ethnographic methods disrupt expectations and generate new pathways in research. Would you mind recalling your response and your general experience with autoethnographic method in the class?

SM: At the time of this event, I had no closet. The space had been utilized for other things because of the size of my apartment, and I couldn't really afford storage furniture. As a result, my clothing options were limited to a few folded piles on the floor and on a sitting chair in my bedroom. I had clothes, but no closet or drawers to store them in.

It was odd for me to express to my course mates that I didn't have a closet for a myriad of reasons. For one, I knew it was a bit different that these were my circumstances, and that it probably stood out I responded in that manner. Secondarily, I thought it funny that this could be a surprise to people, that someone may not have the physical space to store clothing outside of a dresser or chest of drawers and sometimes not even that. And lastly, biggest of all was embarrassment. I was *so* embarrassed by the collective audible response, as though I had said something weird or disturbing. I understood this as the process of engaged pedagogy, where I knew a level of vulnerability and honesty was expected of me, so my shock didn't last long. It was quickly replaced with excited curiosity: *why* was I embarrassed that I didn't have a closet? Were we not interested in the conversation of how things could be different for others, that some could have closet spaces that were organized, or not, or hung up, or folded, or colorful, or monochromatic, or whatever other possibilities exist? Was my embarrassment actually vulnerability, or was it some feeling of shame or inadequacy? Did we accidentally reveal just how permeating aesthetic-elitism and capitalism-classism are in our collective imagination?

I enjoyed the experiment and the discourse that followed, even if I temporarily felt that my unique situation was worthy of shame. Many questions came to me, and many remain unanswered. Is the clothing the soul of the closet, or instead the clothing *and* closet representative of the soul of the owner? Does a full closet represent you more than an empty one, or not having one? Is the verbal or physical exploration of someone else's closet an exploration of their soul, or do the clothing objects lose their intrinsic nature when abstracted from their owner?

If the closet could arguably be perceived as an outside representation of the physical and mental presentation of the aesthetic self, not having a closet is an *anaesthetic* of sorts. However, I wouldn't say that my clothing catch-all chair was a solid representation of my personal aesthetic or fashion/form presentation. At the same time, I feel that many of my colleagues at the time would have felt the same way about their closets. Does that mean that these collections of fabrics represent us any less? Were we really that different, after all?

JV: Like you, I remember feeling a ripple of anxiety across my heart muscle after you responded to the question, embarrassment over my blind spot in assuming that all of us would have a closet to speak of. This quickly opened to the generative insight of that moment, the way ethnographic methods aim for these kinds of surprises, diffractions that transform stable categories and questions. In hindsight, I wish I had practiced more "feeling with" you, that I had checked in with you after the class to debrief. In the moment, I did not sense your embarrassment. I didn't know you felt embarrassed until we sat down to discuss writing together. I know you processed these feelings fairly quickly; nonetheless, I'm sorry I wasn't more attentive to you. I do take this moment to heart and will ask the question differently in the future.

Two things I want to distill here, first, there are risks in disclosure, as your experience shows, risks that autoethnographic method requires in order to work. Don't we all have closets in the epistemological sense, compartments of knowledge, desire, and experience that can be revealed or hidden from view? Going back to hooks's imperative of self-revelation, of required visibility, this is the power of generating intimacy in the context of teaching and learning. But what about education as the practice of freedom? What if a teacher or a student wants to stay in the closet for any number of reasons, such as saving themselves the embarrassment or for the sake of their professional survival? Baring one's soul, so to speak, literally showing by telling, is more consequential for some than others because, and this is the second point, of disorientations with objects.

Ahmed shows us a similar intervention to your disidentification with having a closet as she examines an assumed object orientation in phenomenological discourse between the philosopher and the table. In taking up Husserl's writing-table as "the very 'place' of philosophy," Ahmed suggests, "we may need to supplement phenomenology with an 'ethnography of things'" (2006: 39). First, she shifts the orientation from the assumed implements of writing to "the unseen portions" of Husserl's room and his extended dwelling, the domestic sphere where work is done by others, work the philosopher depends on in order to have time for contemplation. Considering the gendered dimensions of the relation between kitchen and study in Husserl's milieu, Ahmed asks, "Who faces the writing table? Does the writing table have a face, which points it toward some bodies rather than others?" (2006: 31) In response, Ahmed progressively layers scenarios of relation to the table, and to the objects that inhabit the background, similar to what we did in class with respect to the closet. She arrives, for example, at the table as a supporting device for "queer gatherings" supplying a fully inhabited, multi-oriented phenomenology. Your disclosure that a chair was another place of dwelling for your clothes further disrupts normative object orientations. This is the indispensability and power of ethnographic inquiry.

Something I found interesting in going back to Carolyn Ellis's work is her consistent use of mystical language. She observes, "Something spiritual, emotional—or from my 'gut'—compelled me to write down what happened. . . . In autoethnography, we're usually writing about epiphanies" (2004: 33). You signal this with your analogy between the closet and the soul. Ellis's spiritual language is absent in fashion studies scholars' adoptions of her work, which is perhaps related to the discipline's preference for more externalized, diffuse, and relational theories of subjectivity. Coupling autoethnography and fashion was about showing the relationship between the soul and the social forces that shape it through the interface of style and dress, as Otto von Busch describes (2016: 234). I wanted to encourage you all to tell your stories, and clothing was the catalyst I chose to inspire that introspection, something intimate enough to draw you out, but appropriate for the public university classroom. I know that you took this process very seriously, so I am wondering if you found the experience epiphanic? Should public education be about soul-formation?

SM: Even beyond epiphanic, I found the experience to actually be quite cathartic. There is this idea, especially coming from circumstances in which traditional public education is the only option, that school saps individuality, personality, character, and drive. I know that you and I happened to attend the same high school, and being from different generations, the quality and dynamic of the education system present in that county were quite different. Social systems are typically at play in a swing like this. And to shift the dynamic, the university setting is perceivably enriching to the individual, even if it's hard to accomplish in the absolute finite scale.

I find this to be an interesting question because it feels, often, like the university and public school setting provides an atmosphere of soul *destruction* rather than soul-formation. At least in the traditional and standardized way, public education has functioned to eliminate the individual and develop the corporate drone, although I hate to term it in such a way. Schoolchildren, and even young adults when approaching university and post-secondary education, are taught a basic understanding of productivity, and then asked to go forth and contribute to the market economy in which we exist. Although this isn't the question at hand, it is hard to abstract this from just how difficult I think it would be to shift the dynamic from soul anesthesia to soul-formation in the traditional, public school setting.

I appreciated your courses for precisely this reason. While there were traditional elements, which is par for the course, there were also aspects of dialectical method, autoethnography, Socratic seminar, art exploration, and discursive intro- and extrospection. This provided the opportunity and the passion, for myself and likely a handful of my colleagues, to develop the soul characteristics that we had been conditioned to neglect through the traditional schooling process. Under normal circumstances, I had believed that if education were genuinely about the subject formation of the individual, it would require a distinct shift in the narrative from a relationship between authority figure and their subjects and to a mutual exchange of knowledge, experience, and understanding without the backdrop of malleability and profitability. This, oftentimes, cannot be helped when other intersectional spheres of navigation exist. However, for education to be about soul-formation, which I do think is a distinct possibility with a bit of hard work, education and enrichment itself would have to diverge away from helping to form a soul or a mind, and instead helping an individual to form those elements of themselves *for* themselves through the facilities of your shared discourse in the classroom setting.

To abstract education in the West from capitalism and profitability is where the real work lies. Many things, I think, could be about soul-formation if there didn't have to be some underlying theme of what could be done with or earned from this formation. To digress to my note of catharsis, I found the process of university education to be soul-forming because I myself did the work to make it so. Many of the things I learned and shared with my colleagues and friends throughout the process could readily be turned into something marketable or profitable, and I understand this intimately. With that in mind, I feel enriched, I feel guided, and I feel satisfied with the person that your classroom in specific has helped me to become. That, fortunately, can never be bought.

JV: You remind me of Elizabeth Wilson's observation that "Fashion *speaks* capitalism. Capitalism maims, kills, appropriates, lays waste. It also creates great wealth and beauty, together with a yearning for lives and opportunities that remain just beyond our reach. It manufactures dreams and images as well as things" (1985: 14). Public education in America also speaks capitalism. On the other hand, although fashion, and perhaps education, may seem utterly bound up in the processes and logic of commodity production, there are possibilities for freedom, as you observe. Of fashion, Wilson notes the ways that individuals have managed to make new cultural orders out of the contingent, decorative, and futile. One of the differences that fashion makes is in how its field of objects is intimately tied up with self-examination, expression, and literally, the feeling body. Where Ahmed and Husserl's table belongs as much to the space it inhabits and the other people that surround it, clothing and other materials of self-articulation belong in a closer way to the wearer. This closeness was witnessed in your and other students' ethnographies of things, things aspirational and deeply personal. The power of fashion was also witnessed in the ways these object relations drew you out and into closer intimacies with other people, your mother, for example, me and your classmates, as is evident in this dialogue.

The classroom, then, remains a radical space of possibility as bell hooks articulates. Education is not a destination defined by some triumphant end or epiphanic moment, as you correct. It is consciousness, the existence of possibilities here and now, opportunities and capacities for discernment with others and objects. This does not preclude transformation or epiphanic experiences, but it also does not prescribe those destinations, thereby closing off other generative possibilities. Education exists in consciousness of multiple orientations and, as Ahmed articulates, "a way of inhabiting the world by giving 'support' to those whose lives and loves make them appear oblique, strange, and out of place" (179). Or, as you put it, "helping to form those elements of themselves *for* themselves."

References

Ahmed, Sara (2004), "Affective Economies," *Social Text*, 79 (22, 2): 117–39.
Ahmed, Sara (2006), *Queer Phenomenology: Orientations, Objects, Others*, Durham and London: Duke University Press.
Ellis, Carolyn (2004), *The Ethnographic I: A Methodological Novel about Autoethnography*, Walnut Creek, CA: AltaMira Press.
hooks, bell (1994), *Teaching to Transgress: Education as the Practice of Freedom*, New York: Routledge.
Luce-Hitt, R. and J. Viau (2019), "From Faculty Formation to Student Engagement: Reflections on Serial Testimony," *Faculty Focus, a Publication of the Faculty Center for Teaching and Learning at the University of Central Florida*, 18(1): 8–9.
Morrison, Toni (2015), *God Help the Child*, Alfred A. Knopf.
Von Busch, Otto (2016), "Action! Or, Exploring Diffractive Methods for Fashion Research," in Heike Jenss (ed.), *Fashion Studies: Research Methods, Sites and Practices*, 181–97, London: Bloomsbury.
Wilson, Elizabeth (1985), *Adorned in Dreams: Fashion and Modernity*, London: Virago.
Woodward, Sophie (2016), "'Humble' Blue Jeans: Material Culture Approaches to Understanding the Ordinary, Global, and the Personal," in Heike Jenss (ed.), *Fashion Studies: Research Methods, Sites and Practices*, 42–57, London: Bloomsbury.

SECTION THREE
THE RADIANCE OF THE CONCEALED
Otto von Busch and Jeanine Viau

In *Sartor Resartus*, Thomas Carlyle (1901: 2) claims clothes are the "grand Tissue of all Tissues," as it is that which the human "Soul wears as its outmost wrappage and overall," and it is here, beneath the fabric covers, the person's "whole Self lives, moves, and has its being." We are to ask, what sparks of being glow in the dark depths within? How are we to understand the luminous longings of consciousness? The idea that there is a light, an energy or animating force within, an élan vital, ether, mana, or qi, stitches across a multitude of spiritual belief systems. In some moments in life it glows clear, at other times it is muddled to finally leave the body. This radiance concealed within can become visible, revealing itself through the realm of appearances.

The concealed is something that is present yet masked or hidden. It is not a lack or something missing, but an existence that hints and teases. Here is the soul; enigmatic, mysterious, and arcane; that is, it is closed or shut up, from the Latin *arca*, chest. Like the mask, a common reference in fashion, it speaks of an honesty, unspeakable in the open. "Give [a man] a mask, and he will tell you the truth," as Oscar Wilde famously posits, a statement in agreement with Nietzsche's point that every profound spirit also needs a mask (Whiteley 2017: 26).

The concealed may be something lurking in the depths below, but it cannot be held back. It teases its listener to come closer, to search for it. Like a secret, the arcane asks to be opened; it is the fate of Pandora's box. An emanation, forcing itself outward, it vibrates and lures. It calls for revelation, needs to connect, continuously transgressing its boundaries; both fashion and the soul are something that radiate.

It is the inherent paradox of the soul; it hides, yet it desires to connect and be seen. Fashion wants to be imitated, it needs to replicate, or it is not fashion. Yet, simultaneously, this very same property deflates its value with dissemination: the more it replicates, the less it serves as distinction. But it is its fate to seek companionship. As Rabindranath Tagore puts it, "My soul is alight with your infinitude of stars. Your world has broken upon me like a flood."

But like among the mystical traditions, self-surrender is the process of opening up and letting go of the ego to find ways toward self-realization. The concealed peeks through the folds, revealing itself in the gaps. It marks the soul as something that hungers, desires to connect; it has a striving. It is a radiation that calls and tempts, like mirages, but also the voice of vocation, a dazzling glow that lures the wanderer deeper into the unknown, toward facing oneself. As Elizabeth Wilson (2007: 106) observes, glamour is mystical and untouchable; it is "an *appearance*, including the supernatural, magical sense of that word—as in apparition."

In this section, we follow Michael Muhammad Knight who traces the diverse contours of masculinity within African American Islam and related traditions. Sartorial regimes in these communities "contribute to the intersectional making" of Blackness, masculinity, and religiosity and, in some cases, mark the wearer's own divinity, as with the Five Percenters. Knight casts these dress practices as hermeneutical processes, creative "recodings" of symbols, and sartorial objects through which "these communities materialized technologies of Black Islamic selfhood with their bodies." In the next chapter, Jared Vázquez López examines the performative pursuit of a glamorous selfhood in Holly Woodlawn, a Puerto Rican immigrant, transsexual woman, and actress. Highlighting Woodlawn's queer agency, Vázquez uses Deleuze's notion of the stutter to interpret Woodlawn's more glamorous moments as glossolalic events (the religious experience of speaking in tongues). These events disrupt the failure and ridicule that she experienced through much of her life, offering glimpses of the glamorous woman within. According to Vázquez, Woodlawn's sartorial interruptions are examples of what José Esteban Muñoz calls disidentification, survival strategies by which minoritarian subjects rescript themselves as they negotiate between reception of and resistance to majoritarian public norms, such as white-supremacist-hetero-patriarchal conditions.

Investigating contemporary glamour magicians, Kristen Sollée traces how "fashion alchemists" use rituals, adornment, and appearances to conjure and set free a special form of femininity. Among practitioners of this type of magic, aesthetic power emanates from the depths of the feminine body, summoned and channeled through looks, clothes, and makeup. With these attributes, the witch can unapologetically embody and release fierce feminine energy, altering mood and attention to manifest her will. Damcho, a former Buddhist monastic, also reflects on the relationship between agency and particular materials of self-fashioning. She uses Buddhist terminology to define her journey through latex culture, and how this experience brings a new consciousness to the body as a vehicle for inner awakening. Viewing the body as a temple and mirror, she searches for a special wisdom only accessed through the heightened sensory state of a tight-fitting second skin.

Thorstein Veblen argues in his famous *The Theory of the Leisure Class* (1899), "The need of dress is eminently a 'higher' or spiritual need," that is "not even chiefly a naive propensity for display of expenditure" (1994: 104). Even here, there is a spiritual grounding in the way we shape our appearance before others. Fashion and the soul share a desire to connect, for an aspect of self to break free from the surly bonds of theory. Here, we can dwell on the weave between emotion and meaning, as a "seed of contemplation" (as Thomas Merton might have put it), for those who thirst for that deepened experience of being human.

Underneath the cover, from beneath the dark weight of the everyday, an enchantment echoes. To under the outmost wrappage seek something more and let imaginations wander the arches within. Vault after vaults, that open endlessly.

References

Carlyle, Thomas (1901), *Sartor Resartus*, London: Chapman and Hall.
Veblen, Thornstein (1994), *The Theory of the Leisure* Class, New York: Dover.
Whiteley, Giles (2017), *Oscar Wilde and the Simulacrum: The Truth of Masks*, London: Legenda.
Wilson, Elizabeth (2007), "A Note on Glamour," *Fashion Theory*, 11(1): 95–108.

CHAPTER 10
MAKING ISLAMIC MASCULINITIES

CLOTHING TRADITIONS IN AFRICAN AMERICAN ISLAM
Michael Muhammad Knight

In his famous "The Ballot or the Bullet" speech from April 1964, Malcolm X tells the story of a "very dark" friend who walked into a segregated restaurant in Atlanta. "He went into a white restaurant," Malcolm narrates; "he sat down, they served him, and he said, 'What would happen if a Negro came in here?'" The white waitress answered, "Why, there wouldn't no nigger dare come in here" (X 1965: 23–44). How did Malcolm's "very dark" friend manage to enter such a space with his own Blackness seemingly undetected? In his anecdote, Malcolm includes a critical detail: before walking into the restaurant, the man put on a turban (X 1965: 23–44). Clothing had racially recoded his body; the white waitress who casually promised violence to Black men did not perceive that she was talking to one. For Malcolm's friend, the turban inscribed new meanings on Black bodies.

The discussion that follows explores the meaning and power of Islamic clothing in four African American communities: the Moorish Science Temple of America (MSTA), Nation of Islam (NOI), Five Percenters, and Ansaru Allah Community, also known as the Nubian Islamic Hebrews (AAC/NIH). Of course, "Islamic clothing" constitutes an unstable, internally diverse category: What exactly makes an article of clothing "Islamic?" The four communities examined here differ from each other in their conceptualizations of Islam at large and likewise differ in the ways that they utilize clothing to embody Islam and their relationships to it. For my purposes, these communities' prescriptions for dress produce "Islamic" expressions as defined by Shahab Ahmed in *What Is Islam?*: their clothing practices reflect acts of meaning-making in terms of Islam. The artifacts with which they inscribe ideas and values on their bodies express their "hermeneutical engagement with Revelation" (2015: 356). These communities embark on projects of making meaning through resources that they have identified as Islamic. It should also be said that for the specific communities discussed here, "Islamic" serves my discussion more precisely than "Muslim." While three of the four communities examined in this chapter do self-identify as Muslim, the Five Percenters generally (though not unanimously) reject the label for themselves, while nonetheless staking a variety of claims on Islam. Five Percenters tend to resist the category of "Muslim" for its implications in their theology but continue to articulate meanings that they would understand as "Islamic" meanings, derived from Islamic sources and traditions including the Qur'an, hadith literature, classical Sufi masters, and the NOI (Knight 2011: 179–207). Whether self-identifying as Muslim or not, all four communities valorize a "knowledge of self" as critical to Black liberation from the narratives of white supremacy, identify this knowledge of self as Islamic, and embody their Islamic consciousness through fashion and the cultivation of a Black Islamic aesthetic.

In its attention to the relationship between Islam and clothing, this chapter considers ways in which these communities' clothing traditions contribute to the intersectional making of Blackness and masculinity, specifically a Black Islamic masculinity. Sherman Jackson has asserted that while anti-Muslim narratives often reproduced tropes of Muslim "hyper-masculinity," this polemical mythology ironically became a selling point for Islam in the United States, where Black masculinity was "historically threatening to and threatened by American white supremacy" (Jackson 2005: 20). In this context, Jackson explains, "Islam has represented a haven of sorts for black manhood" (Jackson 2005: 20). The myth of Muslim hyper-masculinity supported narratives of patriarchy as crucial for the advancement of Black men to equality with white men, the survival of Black women in a society that left them vulnerable, and, as Ula Yvette Taylor explains in her scholarship on women in the NOI, "building a black nation" (Taylor 2017: 178). As the movements covered in this discussion sought to construct their own ideas of Black Islamic masculinity, they mapped these ideas and values on the masculine body.

The Moorish Science Temple of America

The prophetic mission of Noble Drew Ali, founder of the MSTA in 1920s Chicago, is popularly treated as the starting point of an African American Islamic renaissance in which Black seekers increasingly looked to Islam as a mode of recovering lost African heritages and engaging possibilities beyond the white world. The MSTA, however, can be read not only as a moment of rupture from its context but also as a continuity, as it emerged in conversation with a multiplicity of discourses and movements accessible in its setting. Investigation of MSTA ideas and practices concerning clothing invites attention to a broader milieu of alternative Black religiosity and intellectual life that included Freemasonry, pan-Africanist nationalism, and a vibrant occult marketplace.

Noble Drew Ali promoted a radical rewriting of Black heritage that sought to dismantle the category of nationless, ahistorical "Negro" and recover what he presented as African Americans' true identities as "Asiatics" and "Moors." In the Moorish Science project, achieving social equality depended on possession of a proper nationality, which intersected with a rediscovery of ancestral religion, termed "Islamism." This national/religious identity became embodied through an adoption of what Noble Drew Ali understood as "Moslem" dress. Photos from MSTA assemblies present Noble Drew Ali and the men and women who followed him in a variety of turbans, fezzes, headdresses, robes, and sashes recalling imaginaries of an exotic, mystical, Islamic "Orient" that resist location in a specific Muslim setting (Gomez 2005: 261–7). The dress code materialized the MSTA argument that African Americans were not "Negroes" but properly categorized as Moorish Americans in possession of a divine and timeless history and Asiatic nationhood. While representing Noble Drew Ali's narratives of Moorish civilization, the change in clothing also produced meaningful political consequences. In a white supremacist social order, to wear "exotic" clothing linked to a larger "Asiatic" world could not only reconstruct identity for the wearer's internal narratives of self—expressing connections both to one's spiritual condition in relation to the unseen and an earthly history of Black glories—but also relocate Black bodies beyond the limits of a white-"Negro" binary. Vivek Bald's scholarship on South Asian diasporas in the early twentieth century examines the ways that in numerous contexts throughout the United States, South Asian migrants often found themselves in racially liminal positions. While excluded from membership in the "white race," they could receive greater access to white spaces than was available to Black people. Bald writes that South Asian peddlers were thus advantaged not only for the exotic Eastern "magic" that they could claim for their goods and performances, but also because they could work in areas forbidden to Black peddlers (2013: 49–93). South Asian peddlers also self-exoticized through appeals to white consumers' imaginaries of the "Orient" as an attempted survival strategy against white supremacist violence (2013: 49–93). Meanwhile, some Black peddlers took to performing "Oriental" identities, wearing fezzes and turbans and adopting accents to negotiate with, or escape from, the obstructions imposed by white supremacy (Dorman 2009: 116–42). Similarly, MSTA clothing practices can read as an attempt to transcend the confines of US racial categories and recalibrate the categorization of MSTA members.

The archive from which Noble Drew Ali drew his understanding of Islamic clothing included Black Freemasonry, which has been treated as the primary resource that informed his aesthetics (Nance 2002: 623–59). The promise of self-construction within Masonic *brotherhood*, by definition, was a gendered project. "There is hardly a more original experiment in the social (re)production of the black masculine ideal," Maurice O. Wallace writes, "than in the ritual formalizations of identity and ideality in African American Freemasonry. Probably no other cultural movement before the Civil Rights campaigns of the twentieth century has been more emblematic of the social and pyschic drama of black masculinity in the American cultural context" (Wallace 2002: 53). The production of masculinities in Freemasonry found an intersection with Islam via the emergence of Shriner Masonry in the latter nineteenth century, which led to the development of Black Shriner lodges (despite a number of court actions by white lodges) around the turn of the twentieth century ("Suit May Disband Southern Shriners": 1921). While white Shriners had appropriated imagery of an exotic Islamic East and claims of authorized lineage from Ali ibn Abu Talib as a playful jest, Black Shriner lodges provided a setting in which claimed connections to a world of timeless Black Islam could be taken seriously. In the same years that Noble Drew Ali's MSTA grew to prominence in Chicago, Muslim intellectuals such as Abdul Hamid, who asserted that authentic Freemasonry required formal conversion to Islam, could make compelling claims for their authority through references to a "Mecca-Medina" lodge in Arabia (Bowen 2011: 31–51). In part through narratives of Freemasonry having originated in ancient Egypt, and in part through the Shriners' proliferation of Orientalist fantasies that made little distinction between pharaonic Egyptian and Islamic milieus, this timeless Black Islam could absorb popular Egyptosophy as part of its discursive matrix. In her coverage of MSTA aesthetics, Susan Nance observes the presence of men wearing "King Tut" headdresses among the turbans and fezzes in MSTA group photos (2002).

Noble Drew Ali often appeared in a turban but also became famous as, in the words of one contemporary, a "small Negro wearing a flaming red fez" (Chatelain 2015: 76). Prescribed for men in the movement and recalling aesthetic overlaps with Shriner brotherhoods, the red fez became the most identifiable article of MSTA clothing in popular coverage. Media discussions of the MSTA public presence called attention to men who "flaunted their fezzes on the street and treated the white man with undisguised contempt" (Nance 2002) and proclaimed to passersby, "I am a man" (Chatelain 2015: 79). The gendered artifact of the red fez, signifying a gendered connection to Noble Drew Ali's prophetic mission, was not isolated from the broader significance of gender in his movement. While I would not exactly term Moorish Science a "nationalist" movement—Noble Drew Ali did not express aspirations for a separate Black state or Garveyite pan-Africanism, but emphasized loyalty to the US flag and MSTA members' US status as US citizens—he did share resonance with gendered rhetorics of nationalism. Collective uplift was to be achieved in part through a prescription of gender roles: masculine dignity came with the strength to publicly proclaim one's manhood without fear of white violence; feminine dignity came with modesty and protection from white violence by benevolent Black patriarchy (Chatelain 2015: 75). While echoing the Masonic technology of a masculine self as constructed through initiatic brotherhood, the MSTA red fez would also signify this Masonic genealogy's intersection with popular rhetorics of Black collective uplift, salvific patriarchy, and the recovery of Black historical consciousness that had been suppressed and subjugated in regimes of white supremacy.

The Nation of Islam

Arguably the two most widely revered icons of Black masculinity in the 1960s, Malcolm X and Muhammad Ali, articulated and embodied their visions of Black Islamic manhood as followers of Elijah Muhammad, patriarch of the NOI from 1934 until his death in 1975. As highly visible members of the Nation, Malcolm X and Muhammad Ali helped to raise the public profile of the Nation's standard dress for male members: the suit and bow tie. In the landscape of American Islam prior to the Immigration Act of 1965, when African American communities and leaders were most prominent as public faces of Islam, the bow tie became coded in many Black social contexts as "Islamic" garb and emblematic of a Black Islamic masculinity that promised, among other things, an ascension for Black men to the full privileges of patriarchy enjoyed by white men, as well as protection and security for Black women (Taylor 2017: 104–5, 114–15).

Narratives concerning clothing appear at the very beginnings of the Nation. The movement originated in 1930, when a mysterious stranger began going from door to door in the most impoverished Black neighborhoods of post-Depression Detroit, attempting to peddle silk garments. He would explain to potential customers that these silks had come from their homeland, and that they had never seen such clothing because they had been made ignorant of their own culture. Clothing became a point from which the stranger could teach on other areas in which his conversation partners had become alienated from their heritage: food and religion. When invited to stay for dinner, the stranger would eat whatever his hosts offered him, but then explain that in their homeland, people did not eat such food. Black people in the Americas suffered from frequent health issues and lived shorter lives, he explained, because they had been directed away from their natural way of life and had been taught by the Devil to eat the wrong foods. He also said that in their homeland, people adhered to Islam and recognized Blackness as divine, rather than worship a white god who had been invented by white slave traders (Beynon 1938: 894–907). The stranger, known by a variety of names but most canonically Master Fard Muhammad, became the center of a new movement that developed into the NOI. Following Fard Muhammad's disappearance in 1934, the movement came under the leadership of his student, Elijah Muhammad, who revealed that Fard was Allah, thereby raising Elijah's own status to that of Allah's Messenger (Beynon 1938: 894–907).

Male members of the Nation participated in Fruit of Islam (FOI) training, which alternately appealed to young Black men and terrified white media for its outward presentation. To *be* God meant showing and proving Black masculine godhood, both in terms of individual mastery over the body and the collective expression of uniformed Black bodies acting in disciplined coordination with each other. FOI training consisted of instruction for "men learning to be men" and the maintenance of a healthy family, but more famously included classes in self-defense and security detail. Men who worked as official security in Nation contexts wore FOI uniforms that resembled military dress regalia, with pillbox hats, the Nation's flag on shoulder patches, and Master Fard Muhammad's initials embroidered into the lapels, creating a powerful visual and affective embodiment of the Nation's "knowledge of self" and masculine Black godhood. This vision of the FOI found its ideal representation when the heavyweight boxing champion of the world wore its uniform at Nation rallies (Siegel: 2014). While polemical treatments of the Nation sensationalized the FOI as a dangerous "paramilitary" force, the notion of a "Black army" appealed to many potential converts for its promise of an empowered Black masculinity that could protect its communities from white violence (Abdullah 2012: 141–77). Zain Abdullah, who conducted interviews with former members of the Nation community in Newark, New Jersey, found multiple overlapping constructions of masculinity reflected in his informants' narratives for their membership in the Nation. Abdullah categorizes his interviews through a framework of three themes, each linked to a specific expression of masculinity: "FOI Security," which he connects to "hyper-masculinity"; "FOI Unity," meaning "communal masculinity"; and "FOI Respectability," which Abdullah describes as an "oppositional masculinity" for the ways that the Fruit "acted out a different standard of Black beauty, intelligence, and fearlessness" against pervasive anti-Black stereotypes (Abdullah 2012: 141–77).

While the prominence of Malcolm X and Muhammad Ali leads to a popular imagination of the Nation as a product of the 1960s, it bears repeating that the movement—along with its constructions of Black Islamic masculinity as expressed in clothing practices—emerged in the 1930s. Elijah Muhammad was born in 1897; as

Black Power and its signature stylistic expressions took shape in the second half of the 1960s, Elijah entered his seventies. His prescriptions for the Black Muslim man's clothing reflected a particular vision of respectability politics; he additionally expressed negative views of non-Muslim African cultures and saw no virtue in Afrocentric attempts to imitate what he called "uncivilized" and "degrading" clothing or "bushy hair the style of savages" (Clegg 1997: 240–1). The Nation constructed Black masculinity as innately divine but prescribed the fullest realization of this divinity through a filter of early twentieth-century US gender constructions and respectability politics, along with a long-standing orientalist privileging of Muslim Africa over non-Muslim Africa (Knight 2007: 112–13). While Elijah Muhammad might have been out of touch with rising elements of Black consciousness in the 1960s, his discourse of a Black Islamic masculinity resonated with youth cultures outside the masjid, leading to the emergence of a new movement beyond his control.

The Five Percenters

While Elijah Muhammad's conservatism alienated him from rising Black Power and Afrocentrism, the Five Percenter movement promoted an interpretation of Nation teachings more compatible with youth cultures. Founded in 1960s Harlem by an attritioned Nation member who had adopted the name Allah, the Five Percenters took their name from a Nation lesson asserting that only 5 percent of society, the "poor righteous teachers," could recognize the truth of Black godhood and liberate the 85 percent ("slaves of mental death and power") from the ruling 10 percent ("bloodsuckers of the poor") (Supreme Wisdom Lessons 40:13–16). The Five Percenters advocated a decentralized understanding of Black godhood: in contrast to the Nation, which taught that all Black men were gods, but that the supreme god (Master Fard Muhammad) had authorized Elijah Muhammad's rulership of the Nation as his Messenger, the Five Percenters taught that every Black man was entitled to the name Allah, with no transcendent Allah or Messenger above him (Knight 2007: 179–207). While asserting their relationship to Islam as a "way of life" rather than a "religion," Five Percenters generally deny self-identification as Muslims, since Muslims perform *submission* and *surrender* to an unseen, transcendent, supernatural god, while Five Percenters deny this god's existence and assert that they are their own gods, each his own Allah. Some Five Percenters interpret their theology through a lens informed by provocative resources in Sufism, citing premodern figures such as Mansur al-Hallaj and Ibn al-Arabi, though Five Percenter theology tends to emphasize Black men as *corporeally* God themselves, not merely the earthly "manifestations" or physical "embodiments" of an abstracted higher being or spirit. Five Percenter connections to Islam remain diverse and complex, with Five Percenters often engaging the Qur'an and Sufi traditions as resources for conceptualizing their godhood, and some Five Percenters do self-identify as Muslims, often through a NOI lens. But because every Black man is Allah (with some interpretations extending Black godhood to women) and constitutes his own portal of access to divine truth and knowledge,

Five Percenters can choose to engage Islamic tradition or other traditions (as in a Five Percenter intellectual taking the name Vishnu Allah). After Allah's assassination in 1969, Five Percenter theology and resistance to hierarchical organization obstructed the rise of any singular leader as a divinely appointed successor to his position or an institution that could effectively construct and enforce orthodoxies or codes of behavior and praxis (Knight 2007: 187–207). Five Percenter norms develop informally rather than through "official" decrees of a transcendent leader or organization.

In the community's newspapers, micropress publications, and artistic expressions, Five Percenter discourse on clothing has tended to focus more on expectations for women than men. Historically, Five Percenter media has prescribed a dress code of "three fourths," meaning that women are expected to cover three-fourths of their bodies in analogy to the portion of the Earth covered by water, including a head wrap. The head wrap and three-fourths code are often referred to as "refinement"; in Five Percenter alpha-numerics, "refinement" appears alongside "power" as the attribute for the number 5, the two coexisting in masculine and feminine complementarity (Knight 2007: 215). Masculine Five Percenter bodies do not receive the same attention as Earths' bodies in terms of dress code, though men do construct a gendered Five Percenter identity through proper head wear, namely the "crown." A standard crown format has grown codified through the years: a knit skullcap, similar to a kufi, with one tassel hanging from the top. While adhering to this template, artisans produce and market crowns in various styles and colors to the community. Among the original community, the concept of a "crown" might have been more fluid; an elder named C-Allah recalls making his own crowns in the 1960s by cutting the brims off his "cool hustler's hats" and explains that he was inspired by his contemporary, Universal Shaamgaudd Allah: "I got the idea looking at Shaamgaudd's crown, which was like a brimless hat" (The Gods & Earths Who Were There 2014: 102). As the expectations for a Five Percenter crown grew formalized, the crown itself became a reliable site of meaning-making in Five Percenters' gendered theologies: the skullcap, ornamenting the Black mind, represents the sun, while the tassel represents the Earth in orbit. As expressed in the interpretive traditions surrounding the crown, to adopt the name of Allah stakes a claim of both intellectual power and commitment to redemptive patriarchy.

The crown's tassel recalls the Masonic and Moorish Science traditions of the fez, and some Five Percenters do recall the presence of fezzes in the community during the 1960s. An elder named I-Freedom Allah remembers dressing up for his first meeting with Allah: "So, I bought me a dashiki and I had me an African fez. . . . I was nervous, but I was determined. I looked the part." Allah, however, was not impressed: "He looked at me with the dashiki and the fez on. He had the look in his face that said, 'You're trying a bit too hard'" (The Gods & Earths Who Were There 2014: 139–51). Five Percenter media nonetheless utilizes the fez as a detail in narrating the movement's formation. The elder C-Allah remembers seeing fezzes as an "aura" or sign of unity, adding, "That's how I knew that there some kind of divine change that took place" (The Gods & Earths Who Were There 2014: 67–78). C-Allah's sense of unity and "divine change" represented in the appearance of fezzes speaks to religio-racial meanings that had been inscribed upon the fez in the first half of the century. For decades prior to the Five Percent, the fez materialized a knowledge of God that was also a knowledge of self and nation, a spiritual technology that was also a political mission.

In what might be called an auto-hagiographic account, Universal Shaamgaudd Allah tells a story of fezzes to demonstrate the Five Percenters' superior truth. Universal Shaamgaudd writes that as a teenager in the 1960s, he was approached by a fez-wearing Shriner who took note of Universal Shaamgaudd's crown. The Shriner invited Universal Shaamgaudd to his home, where he attempted to impress the youth with his books and pictures, though Universal Shaamgaudd responded to each artifact by decoding its true meanings. The stunned Shriner invited Universal Shaamgaudd to teach the Shriners' children twice a week in exchange for several brownstone houses on South Oxford Avenue, which the lodge would donate to the Five Percenters. Universal Shaamgaudd said that he must take their offer to Allah, who answered, "That was no ordinary man, son. That was Satan. He was trying you as he did Jesus before you." Allah then informed Universal Shaamgaudd that he would face three more temptations from the Shriner, and that next time the Shriner would not be alone. When Universal Shaamgaudd returned to the Shriner, two Shriners had joined him. The Shriners attempted to get the best of Universal Shaamgaudd with riddles, but Shaamgaudd remained unshaken. Upon the third riddle, Universal Shaamgaudd proclaimed, "Get behind me, Satan! Have you not heard that thou shalt worship the Lord by God and Him alone shall you serve?" which caused the Shriners to fall to their knees, kiss the teenager's boots, and confess, "We bear witness, you are truly the son of Allah!" (Knight 2007: 101–2).

Five Percenters also mark truth on the body through the community's tradition of the wearing of its "Universal Flag," often called simply the Universal. The Universal Flag was designed by Universal Shaamgaudd Allah in the 1960s, reportedly as an amalgamation of two symbols that had been meaningful in his life: the NOI's flag, the "National," and the emblem of the Cross Park Chaplains, a youth gang to which he and other Brooklyn Five Percenters had belonged (Knight 2007: 91). Like the crown, the Universal Flag has become increasingly loaded with meanings as Five Percenter interpretive tradition developed from the 1970s and beyond, with the elements of the design (eight-pointed compass rose, with large 7 superimposed on a star and crescent), its color scheme (black and gold), and even the measurements of various angles have all undergone esoteric recodings. These recodings have become as critical as the Universal itself, and a proper grasp of the Universal's interpretation is often treated as a prerequisite to the right to wear it (Knight 2007: 168–73). In another resonance with the crown, elaborations of the Universal's meanings have operated as expressions and enforcements of the tradition's gendered theologies, chiefly through the spatial relation between the number 7 and the crescent moon. In popular interpretation, the 7 (which signifies God in the Five Percenters' alpha-numeric code, Supreme Mathematics) represents the Black man, while the crescent moon represents the Black woman, who reflects the Black man's light. This reading finds expression in the lyrics of formerly affiliated artist Erykah Badu, whose ballad "Orange Moon" includes the verses, "I'm an orange moon, I'm brighter than before, brighter reflecting the light of the sun" (Badu 2000). In commentaries on the Universal, the imposition of the 7 over the moon has been treated as signification of the Black man's dominance. This has led to some variations of the flag reading as insufficiently patriarchal, since Universal Shaamgaudd's original design displayed a portion of the moon remaining visible from behind the top of the 7. Later designs featured the 7 spanning the moon's full diameter and beyond, fully containing the moon within its length. While the cause of the change is not clear, Five Percenter exegetes did attach meanings to the difference. According to advocates of the "big 7" version, the design in which the moon eclipsed the 7 undermined the dominance of the Black man. Those who favored the "big moon" version countered that their preferred design was the *original* Universal as created by Universal Shaamgaudd and personally approved in 1967 by Allah himself; any change to the design, even if correct in the gender politics of its symbolism, would constitute a deviation from the authentic flag. Within the community, one also finds advocates of gender-inclusive theology in which Black women can claim godhood, and the flag's original "big moon" design—having been polemically implicated in feminism by its opponents—appears to provide a symbolic resource. In my work with the community, I observed that while advocates of androcentric theologies could be found on both sides of the flag debate, advocates of gender-inclusive theologies preferred the original "big moon" version.

The Universal Flag appears in numerous material iterations, not only as a literal flag but also wearable as a design on shirts, crowns, and jewelry. The Universal finds perhaps its most critical expression on Five Percenter bodies in practices surrounding the lapel pin. Like the NOI, Five Percenters used lapel pins bearing their flag to mark the status of initiates who had mastered the Lessons. For Five Percenters, the Universal lapel pin additionally signified that Five Percenters, who had previously worn the NOI's flag as a medallion, were no mere "offshoot" of the Nation but had fully come into their own as makers of a distinct and autonomous tradition. The Five Percenters' lapel pins expressed still more layers of meaning in the story of their initial production. It was during Allah's work with New York's then-mayor John Lindsay in the second half of the 1960s that Universal Shaamgaudd designed the flag. Allah took the design to Lindsay's administration with a request that City Hall reproduce it as a lapel pin for his Five Percenters. The pins were made by Eagle Regalia, a company that had produced other pins for the city, possibly including police badges. For Five Percenters, who had been demonized by New York media and law enforcement as a criminal gang enterprise and even a China-supported communist terror network with aspirations of detonating the Statue of Liberty and assassinating the pope, the government's production of their flag amounted to state recognition of their legitimacy (The Gods & Earths Who Were There 2014: 328–55). As there is no centralized institution to govern the production and dissemination of the Universal Flag, lapel pins vary in their design and quality. Today, Eagle Regalia continues to take orders for lapel pins from Five Percenters who prioritize its authenticity—the original flag design, cast from its original mold, coming from the same company that made pins for Allah. Eagle Regalia informed me that at some point in the company's relationship with the Five Percenters, community members insisted that Eagle had made an error in the 1960s, and a new die was made for the "big 7" design;

however, after years of the "big 7" version enjoying greater popularity, the original "big moon" design has recently experienced a resurgence.[1]

When reproduced on clothing or jewelry and worn as a claim of Five Percenter identity and authority, the Universal Flag remains a contested territory, subject to informal policing and vetting of its wearers. Five Percenter discourses often include accounts of the tests by which one earned his or her right to the Universal, and the circumstances by which someone could lose the flag, such as a failure to demonstrate mastery over the Lessons and interpretation of the Universal, or advocacy of positions deemed "heretical" (such as the "goddess" doctrine and the position that Five Percenters should self-identify as Muslims). Though the Universal frequently appears on merchandise today, Five Percenters in previous eras often expressed a resistance to selling items that bore the flag. Five Percenter media even claims that Five Percenters destroyed the store run by a controversial community member, Prince A Cuba, due to his selling the Universal in the 1970s (Knight 2007: 232). Jay Z sparked a prolonged community discussion in 2014 when he wore the Universal on a medallion, with Five Percenters alternately praising him for promoting their tradition as a sympathetic outsider, claiming that Jay Z was literally a Five Percenter himself, or criticizing him for appropriating the Five Percenter culture in service to his own brand (Autodidact 17 2014).

Like the NOI, Five Percenters generally deny the existence of an immaterial "soul" that can transcend the body, just as they deny the existence of an unseen "mystery god" that transcends the world. Five Percenter theology remains gendered as the Black man *is* Allah, with no spirit or "mystery god" to incarnate itself or occupy a body. The conscious Black masculine body, a material flow from the Black man's self-creation seventy-six trillion years ago, is itself the god. While there is an ongoing conversation as to whether Five Percenter theology can include Black women in this corporeal divinity, the privileged position genders godhood as masculine. As Five Percenter men often name themselves with attributes of divine sovereignty and sun imagery—King Sun Allah, Sun Ruler Allah, Divine Prince Allah, Lord Allah, Solar Allah, Divine Ruler Allah, Self Kingdom Allah, I Majestic Allah, etc.—the crown worn by men expresses a gendered theology and cosmology, in which the masculine intellect is the divine sun, singular source of light and center of its system, orbited and reflected by feminine earths and moons. The Universal Flag, while wearable by men and women alike, also contributes to the making of Islamic masculinities insofar as it invites a defense of masculine territory, its claim to the name of God.

Ansaru Allah Community/Nubian Islamic Hebrews

In Brooklyn near the end of the 1960s, a young Muslim named Dwight York found himself at the intersection of diverse and often oppositional communities. At his "home masjid," the famed State Street Mosque, he witnessed tensions between African American converts and South Asian immigrants and was disheartened to see Black members of the masjid defer to transnational Muslims as authoritative experts on Islam for no reason beyond the gravitas of having come from "the Muslim world." Though York regarded the NOI as insufficiently linked to the classical tradition, he respected their commitment to Blackness in contrast to his experience at State Street Mosque. But the State Street community was not only defined by a binary tension between African American converts and diasporic Muslims; the masjid was also home to a Sudanese diasporic community, through whom York learned of the nineteenth-century Sufi leader Muhammad Ahmad, who claimed to be the long-awaited Mahdi, built a community of followers (*Mahdiyya* or *Ansar*) and liberated the Sudan from both British and Turko-Egyptian oppressors. Amid these complexities within State Street Mosque and New York's Muslim communities more broadly, York also accessed non-Muslim communities, as his mother reportedly affiliated with both State Street Mosque and Yoruba revivalists.[2] As a group of Black members left State Street to follow a Pakistani member of the Tablighi-Jamaat and form the Dar ul-Islam movement, York experimented with his own Afrocentric Sufism and eventually became the center of a nascent community, the NIH. By the mid-1970s, the group had rebranded itself as the AAC, claimed affiliation with the Sudanese Mahdiyya (with York himself, renamed Isa al-Haadi al-Mahdi, claiming direct descent from the Mahdi), and became an increasingly prominent fixture in the Muslim landscape of Brooklyn, other urban centers in the northeastern United States, and chapters in the Caribbean. Male members were particularly well known for their distinct clothing and uniforms that they wore while peddling merchandise or soliciting donations on streets and subway cars. In the 1990s, the community broke from its self-identification as Muslims, leading to a series of aesthetic innovations, marked by an increasing incorporation of Masonic regalia (such as the fez) and Egyptosophic symbols (such as the ankh). Both community-produced and outsider media made frequent reference to these trajectories, allowing us to track changes in their presentation and examine the significance of clothing to their constructions of Islamic masculinities. The discussion that follows specifically examines the community's clothing practices from the end of the 1960s through the 1980s, which could be termed—with some cautionary disclaimers—as the group's "Muslim period."[3]

At the movement's beginnings, male members became distinguished from other communities in Brooklyn's alternative religious milieu for their unique dress: dashikis, tarbushes with green tassels, silver nose rings, and bone jewelry in their left ears, while women wore full-face veils in resonance with practices at the Dar al-Islam. "Their dress alone tells you a lot about the Muslim man," proclaims a 1972 community pamphlet (Nubian Islamic Hebrew Mission in America 1972: 7–8). For their distinct dress code, members became easily identifiable when peddling their literature on the street or visiting the masjids of their Sunni rivals, who could target the group in polemical literature without calling it by its name: a Mosque of Islamic Brotherhood (MIB) editorial from 1973 complains about "numerous little cults" characterized by their imitation of "primitive pagan societies" and specifically mentions "cult" followers wearing "rings in their noses, bones in their ears" ("The History of the Mosque of Islamic Brotherhood": 5, 14). In the early 1970s, as the movement emphasized its affiliation with the Mahdiyya and adopted the name "Ansaru Allah Community" as a Western counterpart to the Sudanese Ansar, its dress code incorporated the *jiblah* (short *jalabiyya*) and pillbox taj with turban. Later in the decade, men moved to a full white jalabiyya and white turban in greater conformity with Ansar in the Sudan (Ansaru Allah Community 1979: 13).

Throughout these changes, the AAC/NIH exhibit a stake in asserting multiple authenticities that had grown increasingly in tension with one another through the 1970s and 1980s, namely authentic Africanity and authentic Islam. The 1970s saw enormous transformations in American Muslim communities, Black consciousness movements, and their points of intersection. Following US immigration reform in 1965, Islam underwent recoding as a transnational brown culture, rather than a language of Black freedom struggle; proto-Afrocentric positions increasingly presented Islam as a religion of Arab cultural hegemony, and no less authentically Black than European Christian traditions; the 1975 passing of Elijah Muhammad led to the effective disintegration of the NOI under the leadership of his son, Warith Deen Mohammed, who directed the community away from the Nation's theology of Black godhood and sought greater connections with transnational Muslim networks. In the 1970s and 1980s, Black Sunni groups asserted Islam's status as an authentic Black African tradition in part by treating Islam as a "civilizing" influence for polytheistic African cultures, Saudi-supported networks promoted a Salafi vision of "culture-free" Islam defined entirely by allegiance to a specific textual corpus and methodology, and many Black seekers constructed their own visions of "African spirituality" through non-Islamic archives, such as Egyptosophy or Yoruba revivalism. Navigating the multiplicities of alternative Black religiosity in the northeastern United States, the AAC/NIH produced an embodiment of Black Islam that answered diverse critiques. Against Sunni projects that located "heartlands" of Islamic authority in nonBlack spaces such as Saudi Arabia and Pakistan, AAC/NIH polemics located an alternative center of Islamic gravity in the Sudan; against non-Muslim Afrocentrists, AAC/NIH could allow the critiques of anti-Blackness in Arab and South Asian Muslim cultures but uphold Islam as timelessly Black and prioritize Black Muslims, namely the Sudanese Mahdiyya, as custodians and renewers of classical Islamic tradition against European, Turkish, and "pale Arab" oppressors. AAC/NIH praxis materialized these dual critiques through work on the Black masculine body, emphasizing the connections of their clothing practices to Islam and Black Africanity.

Conclusions

The four communities examined here each embarked on a project of recovering an Islam that was perceived as timeless, innate, and essential to the nature of Black people. Their visions of Islam corresponded to constructions of masculinity that were likewise imagined as natural and inherently unchanging. To recover and rebuild the Black self meant a return to gender roles presumed to have existed seamlessly across and beyond history—literally *trillions* of years—prior to the rupture of transatlantic slavery. For Black men to realize their true knowledge of self as Muslims and/or gods was a gendered project.

These communities materialized technologies of Black Islamic selfhood with their bodies, developing sartorial cultures that corresponded with their notions of Islam and the signifiers that properly represented it. In cases such as the MSTA and the AAC, some of the choices could seem intuitively "Islamic": MSTA members, while drawing in part from orientalist imaginaries of an amorphous Islamic East, attempted to dress as they imagined their co-religionists dressed, with turbans, robes, and the ubiquitous red fez; the Ansaru Allah, while adopting a sequence of dress codes during the 1970s and 1980s, most consistently modeled their dress prescriptions after the Sudanese Mahdiyya. In other cases, clothing practices might not be immediately recognizable as Islamic: while women in the NOI modeled their dress prescriptions after notions of what women wore in Muslim-majority societies, men dressed in Western suits and military dress regalia. Five Percenter men wear tasseled crowns reminiscent of kufi skullcaps, though their crowns and lapel pins both trace genealogically through the NOI and Moorish Science Temple to the Black Shriners. What's "Islamic" about a bowtie or lapel pin?

Returning to the conceptualization of the Islamic offered in Shahab Ahmed's *What Is Islam?*, these artifacts become Islamic as reflections of their communities' hermeneutical engagements with the revelation to Muhammad. Ahmed reads Islamic hermeneutical engagements as encounters with a tripartite archive of Text, Con-Text, and Pre-Text. The meaning of "Text" here might be self-evident as the revelation itself; Ahmed's "Con-Text" reflects "the heterogeneous totality of the historical product of previous hermeneutical engagement . . . the entire storehouse of means and meanings of Islam" and its particular local expressions (Ahmed 2015: 360). Ahmed's "Pre-Text" consists of an "Unseen Reality or Truth that lies beyond and behind the Text of the Revelation-in-the-Seen and upon which the act, Text and truth of Revelation are contingent" (Ahmed 2015: 346). The Pre-Text is what must be true in order for the Qur'an to be the Qur'an; the Text expresses what is already known through the Pre-Text. Diverse actors locate the Pre-Text in different places: if Islamic philosophers, as Ahmed writes, consider reason to reflect the "infrastructure of the cosmos," reason becomes the Pre-Text from which the Qur'an materializes and through which it must be understood (Ahmed 2015: 348). In contrast, Ahmed identifies the Pre-Text for Sufi traditions as existence, insofar as "the Truth of the Pre-Text is accessible in and via the cosmos by existential knowing of the cosmos" (Ahmed 2015: 350). For each of the communities discussed here, the Pre-Text from which the Text issues would be the Black masculine divine, the innate connection of Black masculinity to creative Islamic godhood. While these four communities offered competing theologies that understood the precise relationship of Blackness to the divine in different ways, they shared an identification of Islam as the true religion of Blackness, location of the Islamic divine in close immanence to the self, and rejection of Christianity's "white" god, white supremacy's primary instrument in suppressing Black self-knowledge. Edward E. Curtis IV's account of the Nation defining "black identity in primordial terms," constructing Blackness through a lens of the "universal 'original man,'" and maintaining millennial hopes in a coming justice "through a proper understanding of their collective past" (Curtis 2006: 92–3) also effectively reports significant themes in the Moorish Science Temple, Five Percenters, and Ansaru Allah. The triangulation of

Blackness, masculinity, and the divine, by no means unique to these African American Islamic communities but reflecting an overlap of values with Black Israelites and other alternative Black religious traditions in the United States, constitutes a Pre-Textual Reality through which the Qur'an becomes authorized and also that to which the Text and Con-Text are ultimately subordinated. This Pre-Text informs a reading of Black bodies as sites at which Islam finds its fullest expression and clothing practices as reflections of a Black Islamic divine that precedes the sun, moon, and stars (Supreme Wisdom Lessons: 10:9).

Notes

1. Author's phone conversation with Eagle Regalia, January 2020.
2. Author's conversation with Paul Greenhouse.
3. My critical caution here concerns the ways in which this community's history has been repeatedly and somewhat carelessly mapped as a series of abrupt breaks and mass conversions between categories of Islam, Judaism, UFO religion, and Egyptosophy, among others. I suggest that closer attention to the community's trajectory and the relations between these categories within their specific local context reveals the problem of demarcating distinct "Muslim," "Jewish," "UFO," and "Egyptian" phases to be more complex than one might expect.

References

Abdullah, Z. (2012), "Narrating Muslim Masculinities: The Fruit of Islam and the Quest for Black Redemption," *Spectrum: A Journal on Black Men*, 1(1): 141–77.

Ahmed, S. (2015), *What Is Islam?: The Importance of Being Islamic*, Princeton, NJ: Princeton University Press.

Ansaru Allah Community (1979), *Humazah*, Brooklyn: Ansaru Allah Community.

Autodidact 17 (2014), "Five Percenters Outraged over Jay Z's 'Pimpin' of Their Universal Flag," *New York Amsterdam News*, April 17, http://amsterdamnews.com/news/2014/apr/17/five-percenters-outraged-over-jay-zs-pimpin-their-/.

Badu, E. (2000), "Orange Moon," *Mama's Gun*, Motown Records.

Bald, V. (2013), *Bengali Harlem and the Lost Histories of South Asian America*, Cambridge, MA: Harvard University Press.

Beynon, E.D. (1938), "The Voodoo Cult among Negro Migrants in Detroit," *American Journal of Sociology*, 43(6): 894–907.

Bowen, P. (2011), "Abdul Hamid Suleiman and the Origins of the Moorish Science Temple," *Journal of Race, Ethnicity, and Religion*, 2(13): 31–51.

Chatelain, M. (2015), *South Side Girls: Growing Up in the Great Migration*, Durham, NC: Duke University Press.

Clegg, C.A. (1997), *An Original Man: The Life and Times of Elijah Muhammad*, New York: St. Martin's Press.

Curtis, E.E. IV (2006), *Black Muslim Religion in the Nation of Islam, 1930–1975*, Chapel Hill: University of North Carolina Press.

Dorman, J. (2009), "'A True Moslem Is a True Spiritualist': Black Orientalism and *Black Gods of the Metropolis*," in Edward E. Curtis IV and Danielle Brune Sigler (eds), *The New Black Gods:*

Arthur Huff Fauset and the Study of African American Religions, 116–42, Bloomington and Indianapolis, IN: Indiana University Press.

The Gods & Earths Who Were There (2014), *True History of Allah and His 5%*.

Gomez, M (2005), *Black Crescent: The Experience and Legacy of African Muslims in the Americas*. Cambridge: Cambridge University Press.

Mosque of Islamic Brotherhood (1973), "The History of the Mosque of Islamic Brotherhood," *Western Sunrise*, September-October: 5: 14.

Jackson, S. (2005), *Islam and the Blackamerican: Looking Toward the Third Resurrection*, Oxford: Oxford University Press, 20.

Knight, M.M. (2007), *The Five Percenters: Islam, Hip-Hop, and the Gods of New York*, Oxford: Oneworld Publications.

Knight, M.M. (2011), *Why I am a Five Percenter*, New York: Tarcher/Penguin.

Nance, S. (2002), "Respectability and Representation: The Moorish Science Temple, Morocco, and Black Public Culture in 1920s Chicago," *American Quarterly*, 54(4): 623–59.

Nubian Islamic Hebrew Mission in America (1972), *A Look at The Muslim Man*, Brooklyn: NIHMA.

"Suit May Disband Southern Shriners: Whites Ask Court to Stop Shriners from Wearing Pins" (1921), *Chicago Defender*, January 1: 1.

Taylor, U. Y. (2017), *Promise of Patriarchy: Women and the Nation of Islam*, Chapel Hill: University of North Carolina Press.

The Trials of Muhammad Ali (2014), [Film] Dir. Bill Siegel, USA: Kartemquin Films.

Wallace, M.O. (2002), *Constructing the Black Masculine: Identity and Ideality in African American Men's Literature and Culture, 1775–1995*, Durham, NC and London: Duke University Press.

X, M (1965) *Malcolm X Speaks: Selected Speeches and Statements*, ed. George Breitman, New York: Grove Press.

CHAPTER 11
HOLLY WOODLAWN, TRASH QUEEN
QUEER AGENCY AND RESISTANCE IN
THE PURSUIT OF GLAMOUR
Jared Vázquez López

Holly Woodlawn was the star of Andy Warhol's 1970 cult classic film *Trash*. One scene in particular reveals the resemblance between Woodlawn's on- and off-screen character. In this scene, a social worker makes a house visit to the apartment where Woodlawn's character, Holly Sandiago, lives with her drug-addicted boyfriend. Holly and the social worker have an exchange in which the social worker attempts to "bribe" Holly by refusing to approve her welfare request unless she sells him her shoes, which are fabulous. Holly explains that she will not part with the shoes because she found them in the garbage and will never be able to find shoes like them again. When the social worker rebuttals that he knows Holly regularly finds and sells garbage and therefore there should be no issue with selling him the shoes, Holly exclaims, "the shoes are not garbage!" This unscripted line punctuates the scene and articulates her genius for making trash avant-garde. Woodlawn has worked to curate her style, and she will not part with it even if it means she would attain the financial assistance she desperately needs. Furthermore, there is a glimpse of her subjectivity and a theological anthropology in which Woodlawn grounds her sense of self, that she deserves glamour and will not ransom it away for a manner of stability that her social world demands. She believes in her own dignity. This becomes a reflection of her real-life struggle to find agency in a social world that marginalizes trans women of color and immigrants and relegates them to the literal and figurative trash bin.

Woodlawn was a Puerto Rican immigrant and transsexual woman with dreams of becoming a Hollywood movie star.[1] Though she was a poor, queer, immigrant, the image she constructed for the camera and the world was one of glamour in the style of Marylyn Monroe or Maria Montez (Negrón-Muntaner 2004: 91). Being a white-passing Puerto Rican afforded Woodlawn the ability to transform herself from a poor, queer, immigrant into a glamorous white woman who emulated wealth even though her glamour was an assemblage of the cheap and kitschy, and a few designer garments whenever she fell into temporary financial fortune. Thus by analyzing Woodlawn the sartorial becomes a site for a critique of American imperial and religious colonialism, and the ways that both fashion and art buttress that colonialism. In the words of Puerto Rican film and cultural theorist Frances Negrón-Muntaner, Woodlawn represents "a queer counterpoint to the canonized tales of 'becoming' American on a number of axes, including genre/gender, sexuality, race, and language" (2004: 89). Woodlawn's persona accomplished this through her focus on sartorial choices to emulate glamour at every chance. Her life's mantra seemed to be that "with the right wardrobe it might be glamorous" regardless of what the "it" happened to be (Woodlawn and Copeland 1992: 86). By taking a moment to critically reflect on the limits of possibility that frame the manner in which Woodlawn "became" American, one may discover that even though all subjects are seemingly conscripted into particular and predetermined fashion aesthetics or sartorial postures, each subject still possess the magic to queer that aesthetic and make it a site for queer becoming.

In this chapter I use "sartorial" in a distinct way from "fashion." I use "sartorial" when referring to the individual subject. By sartorial I mean the style of dress that one adopts, their personal style, and in particular the way that sense of personal style is an expression of their subjectivity and agency. I use "fashion" when referring to the industry of designers who create the haute couture and luxurious glamour that Woodlawn strives to emulate. Thus the focus of this chapter is on how sartorial choices reflect epistemological postures in the world and thus express a queer-of-color theological anthropology. Postures combine both actual postures (sitting, standing) and the intersectional positions in and from which we approach the world (race, gender, sexuality, class), revealing how epistemology is affected by the experiences of our material bodies. The secondary focus concerns how a queer ethos resists the normative within a world that seems to actively foreclose on individuality and limits the multiplicity of possibility for queer bodies. To make this argument, I employ the theological anthropology of Dwight Hopkins, Deleuze's notion of the stutter, my own theorizing on glossolalia (the religious experience of speaking in tongues), and José Muñoz's theory of disidentification. Thus I explore how all subjects are conscripted into particular stylized and predetermined sartorial choices, and how Woodlawn sketches a queer ethics of agency and resistance vis-à-vis the sartorial.

A Low Life in High Heels: The Holly Woodlawn Story

Woodlawn told her story in detail in her autobiography *A Low Life in High Heels* and, in doing so, presented the story of a person desperate for acceptance, individuality, and fame. Indeed, the title is not only a kitschy preamble of the hilariously tragic story the reader is about to encounter. It is also a theme that will come to dominate Woodlawn's life. Spoiler alert: Holly Woodlawn never became the star she dreamed of becoming. She lived on welfare for much of her life, missed the premiere of *Trash* because she was in jail for grand larceny, and her relationship with financial stability was on-again, off-again. Still, she boasted of having partied with the rich and famous, of having captured the interest of Hollywood royalty, and of being one of the inspirations behind Lou Reed's hit "Walk on the Wild Side" (Woodlawn and Copeland 1992: 2). It is the space between that tension of abject poverty and moments of stardom that is at the heart of this chapter and of what makes Holly Woodlawn so spectacular a woman. Negrón-Muntaner writes that *Trash* "shows off strategies of valorization and exchange with American culture brought about by migration in a colonial context" (2004: 88).

As will become evident, Woodlawn accomplished that with her life and not just her performance in *Trash*.

She was born in 1946 in Puerto Rico to a Puerto Rican mother and an American soldier of German descent who left mother and child early on. Two years later Woodlawn's mother married a Polish Jew who adopted and raised Woodlawn as his own (Negrón-Muntaner 2004: 88–9). As one might guess, Holly Woodlawn is not her real name. "Holly" is borrowed from Truman Capote's character Holly Golightly in *Breakfast at Tiffany's*, an apt choice considering Golightly's similar life of striving for glamour at all costs. "Woodlawn" is taken from the cemetery in the Bronx where many notable rich and famous are buried. "Holly Woodlawn" is a kind of comedic social commentary, one that invokes both "high and low values of what is worthy and beautiful" (Negrón-Muntaner 2004: 93). This is not hard to grasp when one reads her name slightly differently, Hollywood *lawn*. Like the title of her autobiography, her name gives foundational context to her life. Woodlawn is both desirable and glamorous and yet continually exploited and walked over. She seems to have existed as little more than a tchotchke for the rich and famous because of the proximity to the "real" and avant-garde that her presence in any space provided. But Woodlawn was much more than her social world perceived. Her very name becomes but one example of the ways in which Woodlawn lived a disidentificatory life rooted in a deep belief in her own worth and beauty. "Holly Woodlawn" would be the foundation upon which her sartorial subjectivity flourished.

Ideals of beauty were highly impactful in Woodlawn's early life. In her autobiography Woodlawn describes her early life in Puerto Rico as pleasant and joyful, and one of her fondest memories was the way that people would fawn over what a pretty child she was. Her difference set her apart, she was light skinned and a natural blonde, likely due to her German father, and she had her mother's green eyes (Woodlawn and Copeland 1992: 32). In her autobiography when she speaks of how she remembers her mother, during that time she reminisces that she looked just like Ava Gardner. This fascination with the beautiful and glamorous American actor would influence Woodlawn her entire life. From when she first began her transition to presenting more feminine after having run away from home at the age of fifteen, to her obsession with perfecting the role and look of a good house wife while living with her first long-term boyfriend (a straight man who gave her the money for her sex change which she ended up blowing on a shopping spree). It seems that for Woodlawn all that mattered was that she be beautiful and glamorous and live a life of fantasy. She had convinced herself that what she needed to attain stardom was an *image* that was grand, statuesque, and fabulous (Woodlawn and Copeland 1992: 3). The "real" was less important than the image she projected, which is why she could not be bothered with trying to hold down menial jobs. In many respects she was right. Of her old self, she remarked that Harold (her given name) was lifeless and insecure, but that Holly *is* loud, outrageous, and a voluptuous vixen (Woodlawn and Copeland 1992: 4). Behind all of this, however, Holly was sober to the reality of her situation, of the low class to which she belonged. Her beauty, her new name, and the facade of a glamorous life allowed Holly the ability to escape her identity as a poor, queer, immigrant and replace it with an idealized version of a fabulous white woman, even if, in actuality, she never attained such a status (Negrón-Muntaner 2004: 90).

Woodlawn was bold, unafraid, and relentless. No matter what life threw her way, she always found a way to make the most of it, which Negrón-Muntaner attributes to a Puerto Rican attitude that "regardless of the pain, there is always something to be enjoyed" (2004: 104). It was that boldness and attitude that allowed Woodlawn to move through countless adversities, lost jobs, homelessness, failed relationships, and the sex work she loathed, and end up in the right place at the right time to meet Andy Warhol. Upon meeting Woodlawn (1992: 117), Warhol immediately commented on her glamorous appeal and suggested she star in one of his films. What Holly was unaware of was that like other white queer artists of the time, ethnic minorities, and specifically Puerto Ricans and African Americans, were often seen as little more than objects that could be used for making art and then discarded (Negrón-Muntaner 2004: 111). But in her mind Holly Woodlawn had found her big break. Perhaps one of the saddest parts of the story is that while Woodlawn longed for real fame, to be seen as an actor in her own right, she was often only seen as a low-life drag queen whose appeal was precisely that she lacked what the larger social world counted as worthy of genuine admiration. Nowhere is this more evident than when Warhol and the Factory left Woodlawn (1992: 7) in jail rather than bail her out, which caused her to miss the premiere of the film in which she was the star, a film which added to Warhol's wealth and acclaim. Notably, Woodlawn (1992: 6) was paid a mere $25 for her work in the film.

Woodlawn's life represents the tension at the heart of the questions which drives this chapter. On the one hand, she is a poor, queer, immigrant who longs desperately to achieve the height of the American dream, wealth, and stardom and who would seemingly stop at nothing to achieve it. On the other hand is a society that does not value the aspirations of the poor, the queer, the immigrant. Woodlawn did what she perceived others had done to attain status; she worked hard to become a glamorous white woman. If she could not achieve the dream in actuality, at least she would look like she had. Despite her efforts and the crafting of a unique style that appealed to so many, she continuously ran up against limits which kept her confined to a role that society had deemed appropriate for someone in her station. Despite all her efforts, including a stint as a designer clothing model in a department store and supposed star quality, her glamorous image failed to meet the standard of what counted as valuable. However, I do not claim that the glamour that Woodlawn constructed failed her entirely. The glamorous image she assembled was an act of queer resistance that defied limits and provided her a sense of dignity when no one else would.

The Limits of Style: Our Epistemological Postures

When thinking about subjectivity, the tension around agency is forefront and is immediately reduced to the fictional binary choice between the subject's ability to self-determine and the influence of the subject's social world on their development.

Woodlawn notes this in her autobiography when she tells of her parents' discovery of her queerness. Subsequently placed in a correctional institution at the age of fifteen, she found herself in an existential quandary. She writes: "All throughout a young adult's life, he or she is taught, 'Be yourself.' Be an individual. But the truth is, my dear friends, when one is too much of an individual, then he or she is condemned" (Woodlawn and Copeland 1992: 44). This experience taught Woodlawn early on that her social world did not hold space for her queerness. That lack of space emerges from the material conditions of existence which are foundationally at play in the development of individual and communal practices. However, Woodlawn understood that she was not held captive by the constraints of her social world, but that she played an active role in the creation of her lived reality (Bourdieu 1977: 78–9). Woodlawn knew that the answer was not only to escape the correctional facility but to run away from the social word of her childhood to some place where she could carve out a space for herself (Woodlawn and Copeland 1992: 44). Woodlawn was not simply reacting to her world, but she was learning that she had agency in who she presented to the world, in the creation of who she was (Bourdieu 1977: 72–3). However, the process of production is not one sided, as Woodlawn would learn. There are external forces that impose upon the subject and the practices the subject develops in response. The subject exists in dialectic relation as does the body and the space within which the body exists; they produce each other (Bourdieu 1977: 83, 89). Thus Woodlawn's response to the shame of her queerness in the choices about what counted as glamorous and how to present herself as such was deeply informed by her real life as a poor, queer, transsexual immigrant living in Miami and New York City during the 1950s, 1960s, and 1970s. When Woodlawn ran away from home and began to present as feminine, first by shaving her legs for the first time, she was not merely changing her presentation with what was made available to her in order to *look* like a woman; she was shaping the understanding and presentation of her body in ways specific to her own bodily postures and movements, and which reflect her aesthetic sensibilities, her desires and aspirations to break free from the queerless social world of her parents and *be fabulous* (Woodlawn and Copeland 1992: 51).

In order to unpack the question of agency a bit more, I turn to the theological anthropology of Dwight Hopkins. Hopkins understands agency as being comprised of two aspects, spontaneity and intentionality. The unpredictable or spontaneous demonstrates that the self has the ability to have intention and cross the boundaries of the social mythologies that maintain communal order. The individual is capable of transgressing the borders of self and community because the self is, in essence, a reflective being that possesses the ability to know itself (Hopkins 2005: 109). However, if the communal order is governed by industrial complexes like that of "high art," haute couture, or even religion and the institution of heterosexual marriage, which utilize the force of influence by those with the greatest capital (like Warhol, or the elite fashion houses, or the Catholic Church in which Woodlawn was raised) to ensure adherence to organizing mythologies, then it begs the question of the limits of individual intention. Force, in the case of religion, for example, operates through discourses of the ineffable (what goes without saying) and social pressures to adhere not only to what is socially aesthetically pleasing but to that which reifies the binary construction of gender and sexuality (Bourdieu 1993: 134).

The force of the binary constructions that is at work in limiting possibility is evident in Woodlawn's experience of living with a straight man as his wife (a lie they told the landlord to avoid suspicion). Woodlawn met Jack while trying to make ends meet as a sex worker. What began as a trick ended up with Jack and Woodlawn living together. Woodlawn describes the process of becoming even more feminine to please Jack and notes that the more feminine she became, the more Jack treated her like a real person (Woodlawn and Copeland 1992: 72). At home, she strove to emulate the traditional 1960s housewife, apron and all, but Woodlawn's transformation also had affects in the world outside of their apartment. As a boy she got harassed, but being so naturally feminine in stature and manner when she presented as a woman, she got catcalls and whistles. Woodlawn quickly learned that she could manipulate the world around her by how she showed up in that world. A poignant example is when she first met Jack's parents. Though they were not thrilled that Jack and Woodlawn were living together out of wedlock, they warmed up to her as soon as they met her. She captivated them, and the secret, she reveals, was all in the eye makeup (Woodlawn and Copeland 1992: 74). Once again, Woodlawn defied the social constructions that sought to limit her by employing her sartorial choices as her weapon against that social world. It might seem that Woodlawn capitulated to the binary that Hopkins's theological anthropology depends on. However, when examined through a queer-of-color critique, it is evident that Woodlawn's queerness is in fact operating as a defiant act of self-determination. Woodlawn played to the binary and her social world in order to create for herself a reality that allowed her to exist as the woman she knew herself to be.

The challenge to spontaneity is rooted in the recognition of the force and active role that the power structures that govern the social world of the individual produce. Even what are perceived to be spontaneous acts and unpredictable movements are in fact the effects of a series of contextual conditions that necessarily offer the possibility of only a limited number of acts (Bourdieu 1977: 85). Thus Woodlawn constructed an image within the confines of what her social world considered glamorous, and she assembled glamour from whatever was at her immediate disposal. It would seem then that the subject can act, but the action is limited by the conditions under which that subject develops. If this is the case, then it seems that there cannot be unique and unpredictable actions that arise from a blank slate of intention and that somehow originate from outside the self and community. There can only be response to the world itself. Yet Hopkins wants to argue that it is indeed possible for the self to "affect the processes that affect the kind of selves we become" (2005: 108). Hopkins would have us accept that in the production of the subject one can affect the conditions of that production, but this kind of manipulation of the conditions of production would require too large an effect on the part of the individual. The conditions are produced on a communal scale and thus would seemingly reside beyond the reach of the singular subject.

The dialectic relationship between the subject and their social world, spontaneity and intention, reveals that there is no sartorial decision that is in any way wholly "unique" (Bourdieu 1977: 96). Woodlawn constructed her womanhood by emulating the glamorous styles of starlets like Marylyn Monroe, or even the Ava Gardner-esque beauty of her mother, and she constructed her image by rummaging through trash and using what others have discarded. Her real life and her character in *Trash* seem to reflect each other at the nexus of the trash bin. In the film Woodlawn's character was known to collect garbage and sell it to make ends meet. Sometimes, however, she would find a particularly glamorous article of clothing which she would keep for herself. In her real life, Woodlawn too would use the scraps she found to make herself look as glamorous as possible, like when she used her friend's old and used makeup in a cheap motel in Georgia on her way to New York (Woodlawn and Copeland 1992: 51). Thus by focusing attention on real activities with which all subjects themselves interact rather than simply trying to describe practices as if anyone can stand outside of their social world, the ways in which the social world that Warhol created in his Factory, and the implications for the ways in which Woodlawn moves through the outside world and constructs her own subjectivity begin to reveal themselves. Warhol and Morrissey, the writer and director of *Trash*, are not mere external observers capturing a subject in its natural habitat, as it were. Warhol could not hope to understand all of the factors at play within Woodlawn and the character she played in his film because he himself was a player and thus implicated in the game. Warhol lacked the control he presumed to possess. His and Morrissey's gaze through the camera lens transferred influence as observer onto the observed, and vice versa (Bourdieu 1977: 116). For Warhol to see himself as simply an objective artist capturing Woodlawn's character in film missed the manner in which his body, social class, and actions as an artist interacted dialectically with Woodlawn's and with the social world of the Factory in the production of meaning, and by extension with Woodlawn's sense of self and his own (Bourdieu 1977: 119–21).

Hopkins's theological anthropology seems to fear a "passive incarceration" of the subject that would result in a "nonperson limbo" (2005: 108). But to argue against an overly active agency is not to suggest that the self is an automaton devoid of any agency. It is simply to question the degree to which agency is ascribed to the self in an anthropology that begins with a reliance on the organizing binary mythology of male and female. Woodlawn was seen as glamorous by many, but the moment they discovered that she was "a man," the facade fell apart. Woodlawn might have been accepted by the avant-garde art community, but she was rejected by the larger social world that rejected queerness, and transness, as a legitimate way of being. Indeed, it would seem that, even for Hopkins, Woodlawn does not quite fit the available scripts. The subject exists in a dialectic relationship with the social world so that while the subject is in one sense determined by its world, it also affects the world that produces the conditions for the recognition of the subject (Bourdieu 1977: 89). Certainly, the subject has an agential quality, but that agency is bound up and subject to the limits of its social world which determines the conditions for the development of the self (Bourdieu 1993: 135). Woodlawn may have successfully emulated a glamorous white woman, but the larger social world in which she existed failed to recognize her as such, nor did they or the art community of the Factory bestow on her the privileges of that identity.

Woodlawn was not ignorant of Warhol's exploitation of her, but rather than blaming him for her inability to rise to the top, she accepted it as her responsibility. What Warhol gave her was social capital. What she did with that capital was hers to decide (Woodlawn and Copeland 1992: 24). This is clear when she proclaims, "Sure, I was still a poverty-stricken low-life, but now I was a *famous* low-life, bathed in adulation. I had proven that I could be truly fabulous" (Woodlawn and Copeland 1992: 17). In the Factory the force upon Woodlawn was the artistic vision of Warhol and Morrissey that longed to capture the grimy, the degenerate, the bottom of society, but which allowed Woodlawn only a certain kind of glamour and prevented her from breaking out of the mold Warhol had created for her. Therefore, the question must be posed as to the nature of spontaneity, and how we understand the operation of the unpredictable and spontaneous. To what extent can an individual be spontaneous when their body has been disciplined to produce particular effects that ensure the preservation of that which governs the community in which they exist?

In the search for the self she longs to be, Woodlawn transgressed the social norms and organizing mythologies of gender and sexuality, which have become "central to the hermeneutics of the self" (Halperin 1990: 26). The transgression of Woodlawn was that she disturbed the idea of "true" sexuality through her confession of who she knew herself to be, a woman, and the camouflaging of who the world said her body revealed her to be, a man. For Woodlawn (1992: 73), the transition from male to female was slow and gradual. She remarked that it was easier to move through the world as a pretty girl than a queer boy. Yet, she also confessed that the decision to have a sex change operation was neither easy nor obvious; she struggled with anxiety about what the right choice was, about what it meant to live authentically as herself. She writes, "I never once felt like a woman trapped in a man's body. I felt more like a man trapped in high heels!" (Woodlawn and Copeland 1992: 94). Indeed in her autobiography she repeatedly referred to herself as man and woman, depending on the context and the story she was telling, rather than drawing a line in the sand and making a permanent linguistic switch to woman. Woodlawn interrupted the idea of both uniform heterosexuality and transsexuality by her confession and secrecy, by the way she spoke about herself (Foucault 1978: 69). By both speaking and not speaking "truths" about herself, her queer confession revealed the social anxiety around sex thus drawing focus on the very thing that organizing mythologies are meant to keep hidden, that gender and sexuality are constructed. In a theological view, confession's operative function is that it compels discursive practices about the very thing that it also demands remain unspoken (Foucault 1978: 58). Similarly, Woodlawn's queer confessions through her sartorial assemblages, whether as housewife or movie starlet, compel us to confront the unstable nature of sexuality in ourselves. That which has been deemed taboo and unspeakable is forced into the public discourse precisely by the demand of secrecy. Woodlawn troubled this; the confession of herself which simultaneously required secrecy of that which must remain unspoken in order for her to be accepted as a glamorous woman (Butler 2011: 85).

Deleuzian Disruptions: Holly Woodlawn's Sartorial Stutter

Woodlawn's sartorial posture was a moment of interruption to the idealized versions of glamour and gender. In this way we might say that she mimicked a Deleuzian stutter. For Deleuze the stutter is more than an interruption of speech. The stutter does not merely affect language; it introduces language. The stutter becomes integral to language itself and is not foreign to language but constitutive of it. By becoming stutterer, the speaker makes language itself stutter (Deleuze 1997: 107). Language should not be confused with speech. We might think of speech as being subject to our usage whereas language exists beyond or in spite of usage, in a Heideggerian sense. The equilibrium of language as a system is disrupted in the stutter. Different from multilingualism where different systems are mashed together and conflated, the stuttering disruption of language engenders the emergence of another nonlanguage within the system of language itself. This is a language that was not preexistent but one that emerges in a contextual moment of what seems like a chaotic happening of language (Deleuze 1997: 110). Warhol and Morrissey attempted something like this in their filmmaking. For *Trash* Morrissey has to explain to Woodlawn that there were essentially no scripted lines, which caught her off guard. Morrissey explained that he would provide her with an outline of a scene, but that it was up to her to make up the dialogue as they went along. Woodlawn (1992: 6) remarked that this was a good idea, being paid simply to let Morrissey film whatever gibberish flew out of her mouth, but it was not mere gibberish. Woodlawn's performance was praised for the way it performed "realness," so to speak. Similarly, Woodlawn's sartorial aesthetic was not mere gibberish; she was not merely wearing garbage. In this sense gibberish is a form of Deleuzian stutter. The stuttering of language is the place where it undermines the presumed givenness of language through three components of the stutter: decomposition, deterritorialization, and pushing to the limit (Hardcastle: 9). Thus the materiality of language can be understood as the force that language has on bodies insofar as the power of naming to restrict what a person can do, the way that it affects a person (Hardcastle: 11). Woodlawn's sartorial aesthetic and performance in both film and life accomplished this very disruption.

One way to think about the sartorial stutter is through the notion of camp, and the particular sense of camp expressed in Susan Sontag's well-known claim that camp which knows itself to be camp is less satisfying. There is a naiveté to camp that gives it its power. Similarly, to imagine the stutter as mere vocalized gibberish misses its productive nature. Here I refer to the schizophrenic type of nonsense found in the gibberish of Lewis Carroll, a nonsense that is not mere surface but functions to question that which was presumed "mere surface" with no more need of excavation. Woodlawn (1992: 163) described the actors of Warhol's Factory as fools whose job it was to act like lunatics. But Woodlawn's performance was more than foolish lunacy. She knew she was being ridiculous and thus deployed a performance rooted in the ridiculous as methodology that reworked normative values and therefore rendered critics powerless over her agency as a subject (Negrón-Muntaner 2004: 104). She does this in both film *and* life. However, in life she seemed to believe her sartorial ostentatiousness was serious; in real life she wanted to be taken seriously. There was a naiveté in Woodlawn's real life which made the campy aesthetic of her life that much more appealing. She was "real."

One example of her naive nature was when she finally went to see *Trash*. After a day of shopping at Bergdorfs and being made over at the salon at the expense of a wealthy friend from the art world Woodlawn shows up to the theater decked out in a red sequin dress. With a small entourage in tow, she arrives at the theater in a limousine. The several hundred patrons who were serendipitously there to see the film that evening went wild when Woodlawn arrived. They swarmed her asking for autographs, and she felt like the movie star she dreamed of becoming (Woodlawn and Copeland 1992: 24). She lived that evening as if she had not just been in jail and adorned in rags hours before; this was where she was supposed to be. That sense of naiveté in her lived sartorial performances calls into question the presumed ideological and theological order of our social world and disrupts the limitations placed on her marginalized body as a poor, transsexual, immigrant (Deleuze 1979: 287–8).

Like Deleuze's conception of the operative quality of the stutter, in a theological frame, the glossolalic event (the religious experience of speaking in tongues) produces an effect that reveals a new territory that can then become populated with liberative potential to break free from oppressive structures. Speaking in tongues disrupts the normalcy of the world and brings about a break in the routine of the given, of the hegemonic. More than this, speaking in tongues erupts when one has given up on the attempt to control language; it is a surrender to let language be what it is without the need to understand within the confines of intelligibility (Vázquez 2016: 63). Glossolalia may sound to be little more than nonsensical gibberish to the listener, but if we understand glossolalia through a primary concern with the atmosphere created by the "starting and stopping, a repetition of sounds, a tension, a disfluency" and what the effects of such an atmosphere are, then we may begin to realize that it functions as a liberative site where the weight of the demands to conformity begins to dissipate (Hardcastle: 20). When one is left speechless, unable to express in normative terms who one is, glossolalia erupts and speaks for the subject. Similarly, Woodlawn's most glamorous moments seem to be a glossolalic break from those moments of failure and ridicule she experienced throughout her life. The stutter even disrupts and resists the interpretations that might be offered in an attempt to recapture sense. Thus it is possible to imagine another manner of the function of queer sartorial expressions, they are stutter, and they are glossolalic. In this sense Woodlawn's sartorial aesthetic gave voice, so to speak, to her desire and aspiration to be allowed to be all that she knew herself to be, a glamorous woman. In this way Woodlawn's sartorial stutter operated as a survival strategy to preserve herself in a social world that too often was ready to discard her.

Queer Sartorial Ethics: Subaltern Bodies Resisting Colonization

Critics and praisers of Woodlawn tended to focus on her ties with Warhol and her transness but consistently ignored the reality that her success as a performer of camp was built upon her ethno-nationality as a Puerto Rican immigrant (Negrón-Muntaner 2004: 92). Reviewers who praised her "high camp style" failed to link her "outstanding performance to her ethnicity or transcultural identity" (Negrón-Muntaner 2004: 106). This reveals a problematic reality for subaltern bodies that do not fit into the script of white-supremacist-hetero-patriarchal ways of being and its cast of identities deemed as valuable. Woodlawn's body, except perhaps her ability to pass as white, did not fit into the articulations of identity formation and the Western model they are grounded in because that script was not written for her (Muñoz 1999: 7). The body/subject of the white, heterosexual, male fits the script so well not because he is fulfilling some universal or *a priori* way of being. He fits the script because the script was written for him and by him. Similarly, the body of the white, *homosexual*, male finds himself in proximity to his heterosexual counterpart, able to camouflage his queerness with "masculine" performance and/or wealth. Furthermore, while *white* gay camp causes us to witness the superficiality of sex, Woodlawn's camp grounded in US/Puerto Rican identity causes us to bear similar witness to ethnicity/race, class, and language (Negrón-Muntaner 2004: 110). Sex and the sartorial are intimately intertwined, but so too are race, class, language, and religion.

Woodlawn's change of name from her given male name to her female name is one way to trace the migratory experience of Puerto Ricans. The migration from the island to the US mainland during the mid-twentieth century was often one accompanied by shame. Puerto Ricans, both straight and queer, and particularly those in diaspora have historically been associated with trash (Negrón-Muntaner 2004: 113). Thus for Woodlawn to migrate from queer Puerto Rican male to glamorous white female required a new name, and it would need to be a name that signaled the "appropriate" class, race, gender, and sexuality (Negrón-Muntaner 2004: 93). The shame in these intersecting identity markers created a tension for Woodlawn, wanting to affirm that Puerto Ricans are beautiful, and yet also leaving parts of that shameful identity behind to be who she longed to be (Negrón-Muntaner 2004: 95). Writing about Puerto Rican migration to the United States, Lawrence La Fountain-Stokes (2009: ix) writes, "Sexuality is a key factor shaping and defining Puerto Rican migration to the United States." By this he means that alongside gender, class, sex, race, education, religion, etc. sexuality is a determining factor in both the motivations for migration and in the particular set of survival strategies that are produced by immigrants. La Fountain illuminates the entanglement between US and Puerto Rican economies, politics, social discourses, and transnational migration patterns, as they relate to queer identity, and how queer cultural productions interpret and are reflective of the individual life, social relations, and the sociopolitical conditions of the two states that the migrant vacillates between. Woodlawn is emblematic of this vacillation. Through her performances in film and in life she did not necessarily raise herself entirely out of her lowly position and into the higher realms of class and refinement. Instead, she "[brought] pieces of . . . highness to the lows of queer world-making" thus remaining in a queer liminal space (Negrón-Muntaner 2004: 94).

Personas such as Woodlawn represent a kind of intentional political voice that reflect the quotidian experiences of Puerto Rican diaspora, and what it means to tease out the complex identity of Puerto Rican, American, and queer. La Fountain illustrates the complexities of diasporic life for queer folk by demonstrating that their work is not simply a kind of lamentation over the difficulties faced in a migratory existence. Their work is also productive. Woodlawn represents the experiences of a colonized people and how those people develop strategies that not only serve as survival mechanisms but alter the American cultural landscape itself. The site of their artistic work in places like the streets of New York provides the discursive and physical location for the enactment of "interventions [that] offer new social visions and spaces for Puerto Ricans and other queer people of color" (La Fountain-Stokes 2009: 132). This is the work of queer cultural production and queer sartorial aesthetics, the emancipation of terrains that lie within the realm of the colonizer through transgressive performances in order to offer the possibility of reformulating both one's cultural heritage and the culture of their social world.

José Muñoz proposes disidentification as an articulation of how bodies that do not fit the script cope with that inability. *Disidentification* is the collection of "survival strategies the minoritarian subject practices in order to negotiate a phobic majoritarian public sphere that continuously elides or punishes the existence of subjects who do not conform to the phantasm of normative citizenship" (Muñoz 1999: 4). Disidentification is not about merely assimilating to the dominant demands of identity or conversely resisting and counteridentifying (Muñoz 1999:11, 22). It is about reframing categories, eliciting permanent structural changes, and "negotiating the flux of discourse and power" rather than some essentializing choice between two polar opposites (Muñoz 1999: 11, 19). The manner of disidentification takes various forms. It is simultaneously a hermeneutic process of production and mode of performance that oscillates between reception and production (Muñoz 1999: 25). By centering his explication of disidentification in culture producers like drag queens, films and filmmakers, writers, and artists, rather than simply theory, Muñoz focuses strategies of survival on the practices and performances of material bodies and how they find ways to rescript their own subjectivity through productions of themselves that recast their bodies and identities within larger hegemonic cultural narratives. Thus rather than conforming to a respectability politics in order to overcome "ethnic abjection," Woodlawn preferred to confront and dare shame by showing off her chocha (vulgar Puerto Rican slang similar to pussy) to the world; in other words, she lived as a woman unabashedly (Negrón-Muntaner 2004: 89). For even while Woodlawn aspired to be a glamorous Hollywood superstar, she knew exactly how the dominant social world perceived her and her lack of social status. Rather than wallow in shame for it, she reveled in her lowliness, and for that she is remembered as a cult icon of one of the most popular art houses of the last century.

Woodlawn is an example of how the sartorial becomes a strategy for the disruption of dominant scripts of gender, sexuality, ethnicity, race, and class. Negrón-Muntaner compares Woodlawn's autobiography with that of Esmeralda Santiago's *When I Was Puerto Rican*. In particular Negrón-Muntaner compares the covers of the two books as they relate to the story on the pages within; Santiago's displaying a peasant girl and Woodlawn's displaying her glamorous face fully done up and accessorized. The first seems to evoke a longing to reconnect with the lost "real" version of herself, the other a celebration of her unreal self as a male Puerto Rican *and* a female American. In representing herself thus Woodlawn revealed the "instability of transcultural subjects" who struggle with futile attempts to "correct ethnic, racial, or gender shame through linguistic performance" which amounts to drag (Negrón-Muntaner 2004: 89). Here Woodlawn's inner conflict is revealed. She did not want to be just another Puerto Rican drag queen, seemingly denying the similarity and significance of her performances to those of her Puerto Rican queer peers (Negrón-Muntaner 2004: 92). Rather, Woodlawn wanted to be more; she longed to be a glamorous person in her own right.

For Woodlawn, cross-dressing offered a way to counterbalance her gendered ethnicity allowing her to be more than just another "queer male body of color, the 'no body' of America" (Negrón-Muntaner 2004: 92). If we replace the queer Puerto Rican immigrant with the gender nonbinary subject, for example, and the United States with the fashion industrial complex, then we will begin to identify strategies of sartorial resistance for a broader queer community. The sartorial becomes a migratory bridge between queer gender/sexuality and heteronormative hegemony. Woodlawn demonstrated the possibility of sartorial disruption along a multiplicity of axes—gender, sexuality, race, ethnicity, and class. In *Trash* and in life, Woodlawn's confession of herself as woman through the sartorial demonstrates that style is indeed a generative site that provides moments of rescripting, a chance for queer bodies to disrupt the hegemonic flow of conscription into socially constructed and prescribed identities. It is precisely the disidentification of the ethno-national or transcultural queer subject that engenders a sartorial politic of resistance and re-imagination.

Note

1. Though it is not the current term most accepted for transgender individuals, "transsexual" was how Woodlawn described herself. I will use transsexual in reference to Woodlawn to honor how she understood and described herself, but also because it evokes a particular moment in the development of how the social world interpreted queer bodies.

References

Bourdieu, Pierre (1977), *Outline of a Theory of Practice*, trans. Richard Nice, Cambridge: Cambridge University Press.

Bourdieu, Pierre (1993) "Haute Couture and Haute Culture," in Richard Nice (trans.), *Sociology in Question*, 132–138, London: Sage Publications.

Butler, Judith (2011), "Gender is Burning: Questions of Appropriation and Subversion," in *Bodies That Matter*, 81–97. New York: Routledge, 2011 (reprinting).

Deleuze, Gilles (1979), "The Schizophrenic and Language: Surface and Depth in Lewis Carroll and Antonin Artaud," in Josué V. Harari (ed.), *Textual Strategies: Perspectives in Post-structuralist Criticism*, 277–95. Ithaca, NY: Cornell University Press.

Deleuze, Gilles (1997), "He Stuttered," in Daniel W. Smith and Michael A. Greco (trans.), *Essays Critical and Clinical*, 107–14, Minneapolis. MN: University of Minnesota Press.

Deleuze, Gilles and Claire Parnet (1987), "Many Politics," in Hugh Tomlinson and Barbara Habberjam (trans.), *Dialogues II*, 124–147. New York: Columbia University Press.

Foucault, Michel (1978), *The History of Sexuality, Vol 1: An Introduction*, trans. Robert Hurley, New York: Vintage.

Halperin, David (1990), *One Hundred Years of Homosexuality*, New York: Routledge.

Hardcastle Jones, Kelly *Deleuze's "Stuttering": Decomposition, Deterritorialization, and Pushing Language To Its Limit*, University of Guelph (Unsure if this is an unpublished thesis). https://kellyhjones.files.wordpress.com/2014/03/deleuzes-stuttering.pdf

Hopkins, Dwight N. (2005), *Being Human: Race, Culture, and Religion*, Minneapolis: Fortress.

La Fountain-Stokes, Lawrence (2009), *Queer Ricans: Cultures and Sexualities in the Diaspora*, Minneapolis, MN: University of Minnesota Press.

Muñoz, José Esteban (1999), *Disidentifications: Queers of Color and the Performance of Politics*, Minneapolis, MN: University of Minnesota Press.

Negrón-Muntaner, Frances (2004), "From Puerto Rico with *Trash*: Holly Woodlawn's *A Low Life in High Heels*," in *Boricua Pop: Puerto Ricans and the Latinization of American Culture*, 87–114. New York: New York University Press.

Vázquez, Jared (2016), "Tongues and the Revelation of Being: Reading Pentecostal Spirituality with Heidegger," in Kenneth J. Archer and L. William Olivero, Jr. (eds.), *Constructive Pneumatological Hermeneutics in Pentecostal Christianity*, 51–65. New York: Palgrave MacMillan.

Woodlawn, Holly and Jeff Copeland, (1992), *A Low Life in High Heels: The Holly Woodlawn Story*. New York: Harper Perennial.

CHAPTER 12
FASHIONING A GLAMOUR
MAGICAL EMBODIMENT IN CONTEMPORARY WITCHCRAFT
Kristen J. Sollée

> Most witches, self-identified or not, have been very beautiful. I identify mostly with the word *enchantress*. . . . I am going to put a spell on you when I walk into the room.
>
> —Bri Luna

Glamour is a glimmering thread that ties self-proclaimed witches of the present with accused witches of the past. Through the ritualized use of clothing and cosmetics, contemporary witchcraft practitioners are fashioning their bodies as sites of resistance, liberation, and magic-making. By harnessing glamour spells to hex, heal, conjure, and banish—to shape-shift their inner and outer worlds—they are engaging with the history and aesthetics of witchcraft and reckoning with cultural associations between femininity, adornment, and evil.

To undress the visual legacy of the witch, this chapter interweaves scholarly and popular perspectives on witch-hunting and witch fashion, elements of spellcraft, and interviews with contemporary witchcraft practitioners. Our exploration begins by examining the origins of the witch archetype, leaps forward onto the witchiest couture runways, veers back into the past to uncover the role of glamour magic in the witch hunts, and concludes with the words of witchcraft practitioners who spell out how they manifest their aesthetic magic.

Fashioning the Witch: Early/Modern Origins

The witch looms large in Western visual culture. We see her in the glut of pointy-hatted hags on Halloween, in pentacle-clad pagans during Midsummer rites, in eldritch robes casting spells on screen. The witch is as much of the physical realm as of the metaphysical realm, straddling the liminal space between fact and fiction, the literal and the literary. There is no single way that witches appear, as perceptions of the witch have been shaped and reshaped across continents,cultures, and epochs.

In the ancient world, witches were creatures conjured by mythology, associated with the demonic, child-eating *lamia* of Greek lore, and the winged, clawed, Roman *strix* (Hutton 2017: 68–9). The witch was equally "a traditional literary trope of some versatility and antiquity" (Andrikopoulos 2020: 7). She is the nubile Circe in Homer's *Odyssey* and the hag necromancer Erictho in Lucan's *Pharsalia*.

In the Middle Ages, witches began to pique Christian interest as theologians examined the nature of evil and Satan's most seductive servants. Augustine of Hippo wrote of Circe transforming Ulysses's men into beasts, as well as "landladies of inns, imbued with these wicked arts" who performed similar acts to passersby (Böer 2012: 466). Thomas Aquinas proposed that demons had the ability to deceive men's eyes (Almond 2014: 76), which would become a bedrock belief about witches, too (Almond 2014: 120–8). But it wasn't until the Renaissance bloomed that witches seemed to proliferate among the European populace, taking on a visible new role in art, popular culture, and politics.

See her dance with demons in a ring, cone cap pointing skyward, skirts brushing the ground

See her command a cauldron in a wimple, shifting the weather with herbs 'round her waist

Between the fifteenth and seventeenth centuries, witches were wreaking havoc with their dark magic: blighting crops, laming livestock, killing babies, and inflicting *maleficia*. The witch's destructive magic was believed to emanate from her body, and she had the ability to inflict destruction on other organic bodies, too. "Like the maternal body, the witch's body is locked into a controlling, dominating relation with the bodies of others; it is the seat of her power," contends Diane Purkiss (1996: 129).

Although many men were prosecuted by the Catholic, Protestant, and secular authorities for the crime of witchcraft, about 70–80 percent of the thousands of accused witches in Europe and North America were women (Rowlands 2013: 449). To examine how we see witches, then, has long been synonymous with how we see wicked women, for "the stereotype of the witch represents early modern Europe's profound fear of female deviance" (Hults 2005: 15).

See her burst forth from her bodice, trumpet sleeves at her elbows, bestowing a kiss on the Devil's backside
See her face crossed with wrinkles, hair a wild bird's nest, deep in the woods with her coven unclothed

As witches became increasingly feared and despised by clergy and community alike, the witch's malevolent aims and attributes were fleshed out in grotesque detail in demonological writing (Williams 2013: 75). "The discourse of witch-hunting was often verbal," affirms art historian Linda C. Hults. "It was also visual, in the form of public spectacles surrounding the torture and punishment of accused witches; illustrations for treatises and pamphlets; theatrical designs and costumes; and paintings, prints and drawings by prominent artists" (2005: 14). Drawing from demonology and popular folklore, the witch was introduced into visual culture as a perverse maiden, a murderous mother, and a cannibalistic crone. The body horror and embodied power of the witch made her a widely interpreted artistic trope throughout early modernity, lasting well past the witch hunts and into the present.

Although witch-hunting began to wane in the early eighteenth century, representations of the witch did not disappear. "The moral codes of the Reformation and Counter-Reformation years, which punished fornication and adultery, forbade swearing and regulated dress, [fell] into disuse," explains Lyndal Roper. "The baroque imagination, which had made witches fearsome and required their actual death, had finally faded away" (Roper 2006: 251). Nevertheless, the witch continued to captivate imaginations, becoming known less and less through her direct persecution and more through creative execution.

Fashioning the Witch: Sorcière Couture

> The original witches were benevolent but because people didn't understand them they bullied them. We're left with a bad image of them.—Rei Kawakubo

In the twentieth century, the witch emerged as a fashion icon. Valerie Steele, fashion historian and director of the museum at FIT, suggests that part of the witch's enduring appeal in fashion lies in "the charisma of evil" and her wicked role in folklore. "The image of the witch is a very important image in fairy tales, really almost as important an image as the princess, and increasingly, I think is perceived as being more of a sexy, fashionable image than the princess," Steele says. "You compare the younger, Lolita-like princess with the older maleficent witch who is sexually mature and a phallic figure" (Sollée 2017: 108). This seasoned sensuality is particularly appealing to those looking for armor or agency in their sartorial choices. "Witch fashion" has thus become an all-encompassing moniker for revealing or concealing, retro or contemporary, ornate or austere—but always engaged with conceptions of feminine power.

In 2004, Comme des Garçons designer Rei Kawakubo described her fall collection to editor of *Vogue International* Suzy Menkes, uttering the words "witch" and "magic" (Menkes 2004). Kawakubo said she "was thinking about witches. . . . Witches in the original sense of the word, in the sense of a woman having power" (Frankel 2015). The clothes Kawakubo produced were Victorian mourning-inspired with layers of black ruffles and beads, feathers and bows. On the runway, models wore a streak of bright red lipstick on half their mouths, with hair twisted into snake-like shapes atop their heads.

Kawakubo's designs were an exercise in severe femininity. They evoked an era when the color black was ubiquitous in mourning wear (Steele and Park 2008: 28) and witches appeared in the newly minted gothic novel to heal the sick, divine the future, cast erotic spells, and raise the dead (Mulvey-Roberts 1998: 254). Witch fashion frequently overlaps with Gothic fashion, and this stylistic crossover is apparent in multiple elements of the Comme des Garçons collection. As Catherine Spooner notes, "restricted, heavily layered [garments], often with elaborately twisted hair, indeed suit our preconceptions of the Gothic" (2005: 3).

In 2007, Alexander McQueen looked to the witch in his collection "In Memory of Elizabeth Howe, Salem, 1692" after discovering that a distant relative had been hanged in the Salem witch trials. The show featured flashy occult motifs like glittering, celestial headpieces, and a red neon pentagram on the runway but was dominated by a New England Puritan aesthetic offset with pops of beading, mesh, and leather (Mower 2007). As with Kawakubo's witch-inspired collection, McQueen's clothes were predominately black, the hue most often utilized in witch fashion because of its mysterious and multifaceted connotations.

"She exemplifies the dark ages, the primitive, the superstitious, the unenlightened," writes Diane Purkiss of the witch. "It is right for her to wear black, because her black clothes show she is from the deep, unknown past. She also represents the dark forces of unreason which may return at any moment to menace civilisation" (1996: 277).

See her summon on the runway, sartorial spells within her hips
See her slink in lace and leather, the past a presence beneath her heels

By 2013, the ascendancy of witch fashion was heralded by *The New York Times* in an article cheekily titled "Witches Lose the Warts." The *Times* singled out black-on-black witchy clothes in recent collections by designers Yohji Yamamoto, Gareth Pugh, Ann Demeulemeester, Rick Owens, and Cushnie et Ochs. Hedi Slimane's Saint Laurent debut was also cited, with its wide-brimmed hats and flowing capes which took stylistic cues from 1970s California occultists like artist Marjorie Cameron and Fleetwood Mac chanteuse and purported witch Stevie Nicks (La Ferla 2013).

Along with Puritan and Victorian dress, the styles of the 1960s and 1970s are part of the witch fashion arsenal. Popular interest in witchcraft saw a resurgence in the period as the Wiccan religion and its witch-identified adherents multiplied in the United Kingdom and the United States, and books on witchcraft proliferated (Hutton 1999: 273). The 1960s and 1970s was also a time when the witch archetype solidified as a "martyr mascot for the women's movement," after members of the guerilla theater group WITCH (Women's International Terrorist Conspiracy from Hell) dressed in black shifts and pointed black hats for their well-publicized feminist political action campaigns (Sollée 2017: 53–4).

See her shimmer in psychedelia, scarves a-ripple in the wind
See her stalk the streets at midnight, sister of the moon she is

Perhaps the most relevant point the *Times* piece made about witch fashion came in a quote proffered by *Fashionista.com* senior editor Hayley Phelan. Commenting on the unifying aesthetic of witch fashion, she proposed that such clothes seem to be "celebrating a kind of beauty . . . that maybe appeals more to other women than to men." Unlike the witch who haunts early modern visual culture, crafted solely by and for men, the witch of contemporary fashion is designed predominately for women, regardless of the designer's gender identity. Disparate styles may constitute witch fashion, but the witch projects a singular brand of bold femininity no matter in what costume and time period she appears. Or, as Carly Cushnie of American fashion house Cushnie et Ochs puts it, "The witch is the ultimate bad girl. You want to be her."

Amid a renewed public push for gender equality ushered in with the mainstreaming of the #metoo movement, the witch is still widely considered to be the "ultimate bad girl"—or, just as often, a feminist. "Vulnerable women used to be suspected of witchcraft. Now witchiness is a sign of strength," declared a *Washington Post* headline (Bonos 2017). "Are Witches the Ultimate Feminists?" asked *The Guardian* (Kelly 2017). "The Witch Continues to Enchant as a Feminist Symbol," *The New York Times* echoed (Guadagnino 2018). This newfound celebrity accounts for the continued popularity of witch fashion but has also provided visibility to fashion-conscious practitioners of witchcraft. For many modern witches, glamour isn't merely an aesthetic practice but a magical one, and their stylistic choices are more than skin-deep.

Glamour (Magic) and Its Discontents

Scroll through the millions of posts under the #witchesofinstagram hashtag on Instagram, and you'll alight upon impeccably styled spellcasters holding court. Amid tableaux of kaleidoscopic altar spaces brimming with tarot cards, carved candles, and hand-crafted herbal remedies, these witches frequently wear stock elements of witch fashion: a fringe shawl from the 1970s, a black Victorian mourning veil, a somber Puritan cotton dress. Their clothing may bear a time stamp of the past, but their presentation is very much of the present. "Social media platforms, particularly Instagram, have transformed the visual witch aesthetic into a culturally resonant identity marker," posits Tara Isabella Burton (2020: 117). No longer the sole province of vivid myths and epic poems, woodcuts and paintings, or even film and television, witches are now highly visible online.

At first glance, witches of the digital realm may seem to be merely eye candy, but many are explicitly using fashion and makeup in their witchcraft as an intentional practice. Bri Luna is one such witch. As the creative director and founder of *The Hoodwitch*, Luna has painstakingly built and curated an online community offering "everyday magic for the modern mystic," which boasts nearly a million followers. Old Hollywood glamour, vintage 1960s and 1970s occult aesthetics, impossibly ornate nail art, and a slice of BDSM seduction are juxtaposed with eclectic and accessible rituals and spells, meditations, astrological advice, tarot spreads, and book recommendations for further study. *The Hoodwitch* is equally a space for witchcraft as it is witch fashion.

For years, Luna worked as a makeup artist and esthetician and parlayed this experience into the visual branding of her site. In 2019, she collaborated with the cosmetic company Smashbox to create the Crystallized Collection, a line of makeup inspired by crystals and nature-based magical practices "to celebrate beauty rituals inspired by the transformative quality of crystals." Some of the products are made with actual quartz, and each one reflects Luna's occult knowledge.

"Glamour is one of the oldest and certainly one of the most powerful forms of magic to me," Luna declares. "The word glamour in itself is powerful, a captivating and illusory spell to have an undefined or unspeakable quality or qualities that lure and/or attracts people into your realm without their understanding of why. . . . This is an art form, knowing yourself, learning how to play up those qualities and embodying that fiercely and unapologetically" (Herstik 2019). This art form is precisely the practice linking witches like Luna with accused witches of the past.

The origins of *glamour* are equal parts mundane and magical, with roots in the Scottish word *grammar*, meaning learning or knowledge, and *gramarye* meant occult learning or magic (Patton et al. 2004: 39). It wasn't until the mid-nineteenth century that glamour took on its current association with fashion. Prior to that, it was a distinct type of deceptive magic that witches could wield. Using glamour spells, early modern witches had the supposed ability to deceive the eyes of anyone they pleased, making victims believe what they were seeing or feeling was real.

See her now (or see her never) cloaked in words to do him harm
See her shift like changing weather, image working like a charm

Glamour magic is referenced in at least two translations of popular witch-hunting manuals, French jurist Nicholas Remy's *Demonolatry*, first published in 1595, and German Inquisitor Heinrich Kramer's *Malleus Maleficarum*, first published in 1487. Remy writes generally about demons and witches and how they cast their "magical portents and glamours," by "confus[ing] the imagination of a man" or "caus[ing] an actual object to assume the apparent shape" to suit the spell in question (Levack 2015: 94). Kramer, however, is more specific about the gender of the spellcasters he describes. He draws attention to the men who suddenly felt as if their penises were missing, when, in fact, their senses had merely been deceived by a fiendish sorceress. "A glamour is nothing but a certain delusion of the senses, and especially of the eyes," he explains (Kramer 1928: 52).

Witches or not, the idea of women deluding men's senses well predates the witch hunts. In the Christian Bible, there are multiple instances of fashion and cosmetics tied to female duplicity and immorality. The archetypal fallen woman Jezebel "painted her eyes and adorned her head" before her murder, and the city of Jerusalem is likened to a heavily made-up woman to put into context how depraved it has become. "Why dress yourself in scarlet and put on jewels of gold?" asks Jeremiah. "Why highlight your eyes with makeup? You adorn yourself in vain. Your lovers despise you; they want to kill you."

The untrustworthiness of adornment is part of the bedrock of Christian thought. "From the Old Testament to the medieval *danse macabre*, clothing is associated with earthly vanity and constructed as a medium of deception and a marker of humanity's 'fallen' state," Catherine Spooner asserts. She points to the "frequently misogynistic nature" of this belief, and the attendant associations between adornment and "feminine duplicity, vanity, and sensuality" (2005: 2).

Femininity, adornment, and evil were well-worn subjects of theological and demonological debate by the time witches became the focus of Christian persecution. In the 1612 witch-hunting manual, *On the Inconstancy of Witches*, Pierre de Lancre describes the sorceresses that Satan chooses to copulate with at the witches' sabbath as "pompously clothed" (Levack 2015: 385). One 1630 witch trial confession from the German region of Sauerland depicts the Devil as providing "beautiful clothes" for the witches who join him in debauched celebrations at the sabbath (De Blecourt 2013: 96). And an English treatise from 1616 specifically aligns glamour magic with women's use of cosmetics, proposing that "painted women" were likely to be witches or prostitutes (Wygant 2007: 19).

> *See her as the Devil's darling, bestial colors upon her lips*
> *See her change her visage daily, enchanting each and every stitch*

Glamour retained its uncanny connotation well after the witch hunts, carrying the dark magic and deviant femininity of the early modern sorceress within its syllables. "The lingering meaning of spells and witchcraft continued to be found in the idea of glamour as the dangerous secret of those outside respectable society," Elizabeth Wilson explains, "the *femme fatale* of the decadence and the *fin de siècle* was a manifestation of this, sometimes literally diseased and deathly" (2007: 99).

After feminist representations of witchcraft began to bubble up in the 1960s and 1970s, film and television of the 1990s began to explicitly reframe femininity, witchcraft, and glamour as positive attributes wielded by women. Tracing glamour's magical lineage, Rachel Moseley interrogates the "double-edged term glamour" as it applies to representations of fictional witches, and how "the root of the word 'glamour' reveals a relationship between feminine allure and magic, witchcraft and *power*."

Moseley looks to teen witch films like *The Craft* and television shows such as *Charmed* and *Sabrina the Teenage Witch* wherein "a profound but contradictory link is posited between femininity and magic in which femininity is produced as superficial and deceptive charm, mysterious and unknowable essence, *and* as power." In the representations Moseley analyzes, witches have shed their early modern skins: they aren't diabolical daughters of darkness, but nor are they liberated women with full agency, either. They are ambivalently feminist at best, and glamour proves to be both "a sequined corset and glittering prison" for them (Moseley 2002: 404). But where fictional witches may falter, modern witches prevail.

Modern Glamour Magicians

I usually don't pre-plan any of my looks. It's all intuitively done.—Amy Mills

"Fashion alchemist" Gabriela Herstik, author of *Inner Witch* and *Bewitching the Elements*, is a glamour magician who believes beauty should be the subject of exaltation. Part of her witchcraft practice includes curating and posting a variety of occult-themed fashion shoots online that correlate with her spellwork offline. "For me, fashion is a way to embed meaning and intention into my everyday life because you have to wear clothing whether you like it or not," Herstik explains. "It's a way for me to deepen my everyday life through color, through talismans I wear, through crystals I put on or carry with me, even the specific clothing I wear can alter my mood."

Each time Herstik gets dressed is a ritual unto itself. She keeps items of clothing she plans to wear on her altar to charge them with intention before putting them on. She uses sacred smoke to spiritually cleanse her clothing of unwanted entities or energies. She uses color magic correspondences to choose which hue her clothing should be (green for money, pink for self-love, red for Venus devotionals). Sometimes she prays over her pieces to bring her good fortune or draws sigils (symbols charged with specific magical intentions) on the tags of her clothes or the soles of her shoes for protection. "If I'm leading a ritual I will probably wear something oversized, flowy, and black because I need to be able to move around, I need to be able to breathe," she details. "But if I'm doing a ritual at my house by myself, I will probably either be naked or wearing some kind of lingerie."

Herstik's relationship with undergarments and BDSM accouterments has been part of her devotional practice with the Roman goddess of love, beauty, and sex. "Since I'm dedicated to Venus, most of my rituals end up with some kind of sex magic," Herstik says. "Figuring out that I enjoyed wearing lingerie was the beginning of me starting my relationship to Venus. It's very intrinsically tied. . . . I definitely feel like Venus appreciates the vibe of it."

Herstik's glamour magic pervades both sacred and profane aspects of her life. Her glamour magic is not reserved for taking part in witchcraft rituals but is employed even in mundane, everyday activities like going to work or hanging out with friends. In these situations, just as in her ceremonial magical practice, Herstik uses fashion to modify her mood or her gender expression and manifest her will. "Changing clothes can alter your experience of your day," she explains. It's a way for me to express myself creatively and subvert norms through what I'm wearing . . . which I feel like is intrinsically tied with magic and witchcraft in general."

To Herstik, glamour magic is nothing like the kind of magic conceived of by demonologists in early modern times but a technology influenced by the past that can transform the present and future. "Glamour magic means owning who I am, taking responsibility of the way I am seen by being intentional with the clothing I wear," Herstik says when asked to define the practice. Glamour magic means "using fashion as a way to shape the way people see me, the way I experience and move through the world, and how I feel while I do it" (Sollée 2019).

See her kneel with dagger drawn, clad in black upon the ground
See her bound in red, red ropes, a crush of roses as a crown

Like clothing, the use of cosmetics can also be a vital part of spellwork for modern witches. Dakota St. Clare emphasizes the importance of makeup for "femmes of all stripes" in a publication about enchantments and glamour magic. "Each individual item which one applies to their face is an opportunity for a magical act," St. Clare writes. "The application of makeup and the utilization of magic are both some of the highest expressions of one's autonomy, agency and personhood" (2018).

Makeup plays a central role in musician, designer, and luthier Amy Mills's witchcraft practice. Mills details how she incorporates sigils into her makeup that may look like decorative filigree to the untrained eye but are designed with much more in mind. After creating a heart-shaped sigil for professional success one day, she immediately drew new opportunities when she inscribed it atop her foundation and paired it with a "witch demon" look and went out to a club (Sollée 2019).

St. Clare's publication illuminates how to apply eye makeup, lipstick, foundation, and bronzer in magical ways as a purification rite, as an "invocation to the Sun," to "[ward] off the evil eye," for "shaping one's words," and to "see the truth in all things." This kind of magic, St. Clare explains, is particularly the province of queer individuals who desire to embody demonized aspects of femininity and consciously seek to challenge patriarchal and heteronormative associations between feminine aesthetics and evil. "It's the transformation of the mundane into the magical which forms the core principal of folk magic, which has always been kept alive by femmes," they write.

See their cheeks with symbols swirled, painted to protect their form
See their lips a golden sheen, calling in the force of Sun

In modern witchcraft circles, glamour magic is frequently couched in terms of survival and as a tool to move through trauma and reclaim one's body. Meredith Yayanos reveals the process she undergoes when deciding what clothing to wear to psychotherapy:

> I spend a long time deciding what I'm going to wear, not out of anxiety or vanity, but because every item of clothing I choose on Therapy Day is consciously selected to pull up a particular thread of narrative. Every outfit I wear helps me to sort out what part of myself I want to invite to the front, to be most present and focused during the session. Sometimes I wear the cuddly knits, like long distance hugs, that my mother makes for me. Other times, like a berserker preparing for battle, I'm armoured up in spikes and leather. (Yayanos 2019: 156)

Yayanos's words serve as a reminder that there is often more than meets the eye in how a witch appears. Nevertheless, the cultural links between femininity, fashion, and frivolity persist, plaguing many witches—particularly those who showcase their work online.

"I'm not just a fucking Instagram girl," Bri Luna exclaims when asked about negative reactions she has received for her glamorous presentation. "Yes, I'm fucking stylish and I love beauty, but don't discredit the fact that I'm an actual practicing witch" (Sollée 2018). In an age when feminine adornment is still devalued, glamour is still viewed with suspicion. And yet, it is glamour magic practices that allow contemporary witches to grasp the agency that witches of the past were denied. Where accused witches once had little say over what became of their bodies, self-identified witches can freely transform their bodies through the medium of fashion.

Countering persistent sexist narratives about femininity, adornment, and witchcraft, Pam Grossman emphasizes that glamour is indeed one of the most potent forms of magic in the modern witch's grimoire. "The fashion witch is self-possessed, first and foremost," Grossman writes. "She controls how much of herself she shows and shares. Whether others consider her anatomy a monstrosity, or a thing of majesty is of little concern. She knows her body is her own. And that is true power" (2019: 119).

A Glamour Fashioned: Past Is Presence

Twenty years into the new millennium, witch fashion has arguably reached its apex. Commodified and cannibalized, the witch has become a wildly popular product (Burton 2020: 117). She's infused into the garments of couturiers and fast-fashion retailers who aim to offer a whiff of witch essence to a public ravenous for all-things-occult. But, like feminism, which has been "'glammed' up to become more palatable to a wide, popular audience" (Hearn 2020: 1), the archetypal witch has arguably been glammed up, so she might appeal more widely too. This is readily apparent in the aforementioned designer's collections, which are mostly preoccupied with the sleek eroticism of the witchy maiden, occluding a wide swath of witch imagery that is too fearsome or aged. There were no demonic crones with dimpled folds of flesh and flagging breasts to be found on Kawakubo's, McQueen's, Cushnie's, or Slimane's runways, after all.

Writer Kate Guadagnino is equally concerned with what will happen to the witch when faced with increasing commercialization and co-optation. "How, though, to perform the trick of growing fashionable but not diminished?" she asks in *The New York Times*. "Much has been said about the ongoing commercialization of feminism, but the symbol of the witch is perhaps not so easily corrupted, retaining both an earthiness and a hardness, one born of an instinct for self-preservation" (2018). This debate begs yet another question. Does the assumption that the witch even *can* be corrupted by the popularization of witch fashion fall victim to the same sexist mindset that underpins cultural contempt for adornment? Instead, might not the archetypal witch retain her awesome power not in spite of her glamour, but because of it?

Shifting focus away from the glamorous armor of witch fashion to the protective glamours worn by modern witches can help transform popular conceptions of glamour from artificial and fraudulent to freeing and fantastic. As contemporary glamour magicians rehabilitate patriarchal ideas of glamour, they are, in the process, giving depth to a surface designation. They are inciting those who gaze upon them to honor the magic that haunts the folds of their clothes and the powder in their compacts. They are underscoring that intentionality in dress can help manifest one's desires and aid in overcoming trauma.

Glamour was once "a witch's weapon" in early modern times (Wygant 2007: 19), and it remains just as much so today. Centuries, ideologies, sensibilities, and cultural contexts may separate self-proclaimed witches of the present and accused witches of the past. But for years, the former have often revived and reframed the lore of the latter for magical and spiritual sustenance and practice (Hutton 1999: 415). Sartorial spellwork is one such practice. Where a glamour was once believed to be an illusion cast by a witch to deceive or harm others, glamour is now a magical mode of adornment crafted by a witch to empower or protect herself. And where the destruction of a witch's body was once a public spectacle, now a witch standing visibly in her power is a sight to behold.

See her don a second skin, calling in her self-possession
See her painted with her will, rising, rising to accession

References

Almond, Philip C. (2014), *The Devil: A New Biography*, Ithaca, NY: Cornell University Press.
Andrikopoulos, Giorgos (2020), "Witches in Greece and Rome," in Johannes Dillinger (ed.), *The Routledge History of Witchcraft*, 3–18, London: Routledge.
Böer, Paul A. St. (2012), *Augustine of Hippo: The City of God*, Edmond: Veritatis Splendor.
Bonos, Lisa (2017), "Vulnerable Women Used to be Suspected of Witchcraft. Now Witchiness Is a Sign of Strength," *The Washington Post*, October 27, https://www.washingtonpost.com/news/soloish/wp/2017/10/27/vulnerable-women-used-to-be-suspected-of-witchcraft-now-witchiness-is-a-sign-of-strength/.
Burton, Tara Isabella (2020), *Strange Rites: New Religions for a Godless World*. New York: PublicAffairs Books.
De Blécourt, Willem (2013), "Sabbath Stories: Towards A New History of Witches' Assemblies," in Brian P. Levack (ed.), *The Oxford Handbook of Witchcraft in Early Modern Europe and Colonial America*, 84–100, London: Oxford University Press.
Frankel, Susannah (2015), "Rei Kawakubo: Fashion's Great Iconoclast," *Dazed*, October 3. http://www.dazeddigital.com/fashion/article/26740/1/rei-kawakubo-fashion-s-great-iconoclast.
Grossman, Pam (2019), *Waking the Witch: Reflections on Women, Magic, and Power*, New York: Gallery Books.
Guadagnino, Kate (2018), "The Witch Continues to Enchant as a Feminist Symbol," *The New York Times*, October 31. https://www.nytimes.com/2018/10/31/t-magazine/witch-feminist-symbol.html.
Hearn, Alison and Sarah Banet-Weiser (2020), "The Beguiling: Glamour in/as Platformed Cultural Production," *Social Media + Society*, Jan-March 1–11.
Herstik, Gabriela (2019), "How the Hoodwitch Is Making Witchcraft More Inclusive," *Dazed*, April 10. https://www.dazeddigital.com/beauty/soul/article/43969/1/how-the-hoodwitch-is-making-witchcraft-more-inclusive.
Hults, Linda C. (2005), *The Witch as Muse: Art, Gender, and Power in Early Modern Europe*, Philadelphia: University of Pennsylvania Press.
Hutton, Ronald (1999), *Triumph of the Moon: A History of Modern Pagan Witchcraft*, Oxford: Oxford University Press.
Hutton, Ronald, (2017), *The Witch: A History of Fear, From Ancient Times to the Present*, New Haven: Yale University Press.
Kelly, Kim (2017), "Are Witches the Ultimate Feminists?" *The Guardian*, July 5. https://www.theguardian.com/books/2017/jul/05/witches-feminism-books-kristin-j-sollee.

Kramer, Heinrich and James Sprenger (1928), *The Malleus Maleficarum*, trans. Montague Summers. http://www.malleusmaleficarum.org/downloads/MalleusAcrobat.pdf.
La Ferla, Ruth (2013), "Witches Lose The Warts," *The New York Times*, March 6. https://www.nytimes.com/2013/03/07/fashion/witches-have-a-fashion-moment.html.
Levack, Brian P. (ed.) (2015), *The Witchcraft Sourcebook*, 2nd ed., London: Routledge.
Menkes, Suzy (2004), "The Collections/Paris: Dark Romance at Comme des Garcons; a Futuristic Miyake," *The New York Times*, Mar 5. https://www.nytimes.com/2004/03/05/news/the-collections-paris-dark-romance-at-comme-des-garcons-a-futuristic.html.
Moseley, Rachel (2002), "Glamorous Witchcraft: Gender and Magic in Teen Film and Television," *Screen*, 43(4): 403–22.
Mower, Sarah (2007), "Fall 2007 Ready-To-Wear Alexander McQueen," *Vogue*, March 1. https://www.vogue.com/fashion-shows/fall-2007-ready-to-wear/alexander-mcqueen.
Mueller, Cristina. "I'm A Real Witch, and I Spend $7,855 A Year On My Beauty Rituals," *Glamour*, October 31. https://www.glamour.com/story/bri-luna-hoodwitch-what-it-costs-to-be-me.
Mulvey-Roberts, Marie (1998), *The Handbook to Gothic Literature*, New York: New York University Press.
Patton, et al. (2004), *Glamour: Fashion, Industrial Design, Architecture*, New Haven: Yale University Press.
Purkiss, Diane (1996), *The Witch in History: Early Modern and Twentieth-Century Representations*, New York: Routledge.
Roper, Lyndal (2006), *Witch Craze: Terror and Fantasy in Baroque Germany*, New Haven: Yale University Press.
Rowlands, Alison (2013), "Witchcraft and Gender in Early Modern Europe," in Brian P. Levack (ed.), *The Oxford Handbook of Witchcraft in Early Modern Europe and Colonial America*, London: Oxford University Press.
Sollée, Kristen J. (2019), Interview with Gabriela Herstik and Amy Mills.
Sollée, Kristen J. (2018), "The Hoodwitch's Bri Luna is Making Witchcraft More Inclusive," October 3. https://bust.com/feminism/195187-the-hoodwitch-bri-luna-interview.html.
Sollée, Kristen J. (2017), *Witches, Sluts, Feminists: Conjuring the Sex Positive*, Berkeley: Stone Bridge Press.
Spooner, Catherine (2004), *Fashioning Gothic Bodies*, Manchester: Manchester University Press.
St. Clare, Dakota (2018), *Femmecraft: Witchery for Femmes of All Stripes*, Brooklyn: Black Hand Press.
Steele, Valerie and Jennifer Park (2008), *Gothic: Dark Glamour*, New Haven: Yale University Press.
Williams, Gerhild Scholz (2013), "Demonologies," in Brian P. Levack (ed.), *The Oxford Handbook of Witchcraft in Early Modern Europe and Colonial America*, 69–83, London: Oxford University Press.
Wilson, Elizabeth (2007), "A Note on Glamour," *The Journal of Dress, Body and Culture*, 11(1): 95–108.
Wygant, Amy (2007), *Medea, Magic, and Modernity in France: Stages and Histories, 1553–1797*, London: Routledge.
Yayanos, Meredith (2019), "The Harpy," in Katie West and Jasmine Elliott (eds.), *Becoming Dangerous: Witchy Femmes, Queer Conjurers, and Magical Rebels*, Newburyport: Weiser Books.

CHAPTER 13
INTERVIEW WITH DAMCHO
Otto von Busch

Damcho is a multimedia artist who has exhibited and performed in numerous solo and group shows in Europe and Australia, as well as being the recipient of several awards. From early on in her practice, Damcho's work has explored the notion of boundaries and sought ways to subvert this concept. While being informed by feminist thought, it is her spiritual contemplations—which are grounded in formal studies in Buddhism, including living ten years as a nun, holding Tibetan monastic precepts—that motivate and often narrate her art and research. When Damcho returned to making art after her decade as a Buddhist nun, her practice aligned with the re-awakening of her sexuality and body awareness. Taking inspiration from the materiality of the rubber trees' serum (latex), her postgraduate autoethnographic research has been conducted under the banner of Bodhi Unbound—"Bodhi," meaning "awake" (also referencing "body") and "Unbound," connoting a delimiting of restrictions. Damcho is currently a Master of Contemporary Art candidate at the School of Art, University of Melbourne, Australia.

OTTO: Could you start with how you got in contact with the latex scene?

DAMCHO: I was in London and I was going through a difficult period. And so a friend said, let's go to this alternative handcraft market, which was people selling kinky things. We went there and the first store I came across was a latex couture stall. And there was this woman who's been making latex clothing for something like twenty-five years and was from the Royal College of Art, where I was working at the time. We made a really lovely warm connection. So when I was faced with her racks of black latex gear, which I would usually have found intimidating or would have been a bit shy about approaching—not knowing where to start in considering the outfits—I felt disarmed by her and I just started looking through things and then decided to try a few things on.

The first piece I tried on was a black studded corset, and it felt liberating! It made me feel embraced. It made me feel empowered. It made me feel exposed. It was a combination of so many things. Putting it on felt very ritualistic, and it strongly reminded me of being a monastic again. But this time it felt like I had the power. Like I was the one that created the rules around these kind of "robes" or uniform. I wasn't subjected to someone else's dictation. I immediately got hooked on the sensation and possibilities and you know, latex isn't cheap, but she gave me a good deal. Then soon after, there was a pop-up shop sale at another latex store in London and quite quickly, I started to build on my latex wardrobe. I also started learning how to also make my own latex garments.

OTTO: So you understand latex culture through a lens of Buddhism? Can you say something about "Bodhi Unbound"?

DAMCHO: Yes. When the seduction of latex wearing first grabbed me, the paradox of its capacity to simultaneously restrict and provide relief and release struck me as something akin to the experience of being a Buddhist monastic. As a nun, I was frequently aware of the inhibiting nature of the precepts and the prescribed conduct for a nun, whilst also seeing these restrictions as opportunities for transcendence or as a vehicle to awaken to my true nature. So, for me, what resonated was that element of restriction also allowing possibility for transcendence, or you could say of the boundary being the territory that you can also transcend. There's a Sanskrit word for this awakening: "bodhi." In Buddhist terminology we frequently hear bodhi coupled with the word sattva which means being; "awakened being." Or bodhi plus citta, which means mind or heart; awakened mind. Bodhi is pronounced "body," so when paired with the word unbound, to me suggests the potential of awakening from the restrictions of form or the preconceptions related to the body. I hope it might also allude to the potential of awakening from within this vehicle that we inhabit.

OTTO: And what is this relationship to embodiment you seek in the work you do with skin and latex?

DAMCHO: Yeah, I think it is because we relate to the body in many ways, but when you're identifying the perimeter of the body, you look at the sheath that encloses it, the skin, the outer layer, that shows the structure of our form and houses what we identify with as "self." And in that sense, I think the body can be viewed as the home where wisdom, where the potential for enlightenment resides. Through identifying with what is enclosed, the body can be viewed as a temple. I think that the territory of the body and the way that the body is enclosed, can highlight that aspect. The form (body) is the vehicle in which our mind and enlightened potential, and wisdom is housed. So when we're talking about the body being enclosed, we're actually just dressing the perimeter of the body. The latex itself, or the robes, are simply the dressing or the ornamentation on what you might call the temple of the body. So they highlight the form in which these things take place and in which they reside. It's only the outer shell of it.

OTTO: But robes are often loose and draped to make the body shapeless in ways, or at least very differently from latex as a second skin. So is there also an idea about the tension between these two?

DAMCHO: Yes, absolutely. Both of them deliver an identity. Neither of them are apologetic in their presence, I guess. You're right about the robes: they are very loose fitting. My lower garment [*shamtab*] was just a tube of fabric, which is folded in a particular way, thus identifying the lineage from which my ordination came. And it's tied with a rope, a belt with a bow in it. As a part of the many pieces of monastic robes, there's also a draping shawl [*zen*] across the shoulder over the top of that. So the form is shrouded by layers and layers of lengths of cloth. And every time I put the robes on, it was a reminder of the precepts that

I'd taken. But it did nothing to help me identify with the body. It only helped me to identify with the lineage I was part of and the choices I had made to become a nun.

Latex, on the other hand, is a very physical punctuation to the form of the body. So that for me immediately gave a site for a dialogue between the container and the contained. With the robes, that dialogue was much more ephemeral. I really lost touch with my body through the process of wearing robes and keeping the precepts, whereas putting the latex on was a way in which I found a territory through which that dialogue could start to take place again.

OTTO: You have used the image of the mirror in Buddhism in relation to latex. Could you explain some more about that?

DAMCHO: As an analogy in Vajrayana Buddhism, the mirror is used to signify the nature of our mind in that it reflects everything that comes before it, but it does not get stained or caught up in those reflections. So the mirror might be reflecting something ugly or something beautiful or something distressing or something soothing, but the mirror itself is unstained by anything that comes before it, and yet it is there as a witness to it. We could project anything onto it and it remains neutral. However, we often get caught in judging the image that we see reflected in the mirror.

The idea of a connection with latex came as it can also have a very shiny and reflective surface when it is polished with gloss. And further to that, I became aware of how that surface received the projections and judgments of others onto me. Like assuming I was submissive or dominant or assuming I was a sexual object or things like that. But then on the inside, it became a mirror for me as well. So my internal experience of it was because it had a sense of amplifying my form of making me feel hyper feminine, of making me feel objectified. It became a mirror back to myself about how I actually behave in those situations or how I feel in those situations. And there, I also tried not to be stained by the projections, but to remain clear, but perhaps more like a two-way mirror. You know, as it just has these dual connotations of reflecting from both inside and outside.

OTTO: There's something very physical with latex that is different from other materials, as it retains the humidity of the body and it doesn't insulate. It is a material that amplifies the skin as you experience temperatures different or stronger. And with the skin being our largest organ, latex can sometimes be like a magnifying glass between the skin and the world. Is there also something about the material qualities of latex, and its affect on sensation, that is of interest, that is, it's not about what others see and think, but something that is in our sensation of being in the world?

DAMCHO: Yes, absolutely. Because the Buddhist meditation teachings explain that we've got multiple senses through which we can be mindful and aware, such as sight, hearing and touch, etc. The touch sensation is something that we become so familiar with, that we become used to, such as the drape of the clothes on our body or the wind blowing on our skin. But for me, when I put on the latex, it becomes this amplification of the sensation of touch. It brings with it a heightened sensation of the body in relation to space. So temperature becomes amplified, breezes become amplified. Someone stroking you, or not, those things become amplified. And that pressure on the skin, of having that constant hugging of the latex, provides a continual awareness of the boundaries of the body. So I found that a particularly stimulating invitation to become mindful of the body in a heightened way.

OTTO: Coming back to the question of boundaries, unboundedness and bondage, and relation between tension and release, does that relate to your Buddhist perspective?

DAMCHO: Yes, in fact, one of the most physically liberating sensations that I have experienced in recent years has been simply the latex catsuit being taken off! The moment the zip is pulled down, the body meets the world anew. First, the body is encapsulated in this heightened sensory bound state. But the moment that it's released from that, the unbound-ing brings an even more elevated sense of the boundary of the body. In this sense, it's like it's been freed. For me, every time that is repeated, it actually reminds me of loosening from the restrictions of the precepts. So I guess it's a repetition of one of the ways in which I experienced a sense of freedom being returned to my life when I stopped being a nun.

OTTO: It reminds me of Oscar Wild's quote that you give a man a mask and he will show his true face, that a freedom comes from covering up. Is there something about the restriction of the body that may allow a type of emotional freedom?

DAMCHO: My experience of being a nun wasn't always easy, given the difficult relationship that I (and some others) had with our teacher. But despite that, there were times when I felt I could live within a set of very rigid constraints and still feel complete and whole and at home with myself.

But unfortunately, the traumatizing nature of the situation with the teacher meant that there weren't the conditions to safely continue on that path. Rather than leading to freedom, the restrictive conditions were damaging.

Whereas with the latex, the restrictive nature is a self-inflicted experience. For me, it wasn't masochistic, but a self-dialogue that I set up in order to contemplate structures of restriction. And I guess the boundaries and territories that wearing latex creates become a playing field on which transgressions can be explored. Whilst being a monastic, there was so much rigidity in what could and couldn't happen. Exploring the transgression of boundaries is just a way of coming to know our own mind, our own temperament and the possibilities of assumptions versus freedom. It was a much more rigid playing field as a monastic, whereas with latex these territories are actually open for you to explore.

OTTO: We discussed earlier the notion of latex as a second skin, and I'm just curious if there's also a connection to another sense of self? If it evokes another layer of self?

DAMCHO: I think that the notion of the mirror relates here again because through the reflection on this second skin, you could say there could be as many second selves, as there are people perceiving us. The human form is a site for projection. We project onto each other's forms and appearances all the time.

But I would say the latex makes it more poignant, and that goes back to the latex being an amplification of the boundaries at the site of the body. It is the mirror onto which countless projections can be cast. As for it being a second self or soul, I think it can relate to, as you mentioned earlier, the skin being a special organ of the body, a larger organ than the heart. We all experience the sensations of the heart and what it can do and how it feels, as well as how it performs its biological functions. We experience that in different ways, but for me it's a very fertile but hidden, essential organ that I carry with me. In the same way, the skin produces the sense of knowing that I'm here, I exist through the sense of feeling physical form, in space, in this body, in this world. Without touch, without the perimeter of the body's form, you drift.

Actually, there was a contemplation that monastics are told to do when you experience desire or attraction to someone else: you're supposed to visualize them being skinned alive. So they become a mass of blood and flesh and muscles and fat and bones. That contemplation never worked for me. Because even if I felt desire towards somebody else, it was actually a heartfelt connection I felt for their inner being, rather than their body. But without the skin that held that person together, there would be nothing to desire.

OTTO: There's something fascinating about just that metaphor of a person being skinned alive, a person you feel desire to. And their inner anatomy and blood and all of that comes to mind. I'm thinking of the projection of desire, and its working with the second skin of latex, what dreams you project onto that mirror. If you will see that image of latex skinned, what would be beneath that? So just like if there's organs and blood and all of that in the human body, what is under that skin that holds together your projection of your desire?

DAMCHO: Right. So the question becomes how do you then unpick what your projection is. You have to skin your own projection. That fleshy body under your desire. It's interesting. Some of the most fun times I had in London were going to "Rubber Cult," a latex fancy dress party, where people would just wear the most brilliant costumes and masks. So the entire body is re-identified with another identity altogether, dressed in latex in some really very striking outfits. But rather than those becoming a solidified identity through which we would relate to someone else, you're left with reconsidering another person afresh. Some people are covered head to toe in latex and wear contact lenses, so you're unable to connect with anything of the "original" body—I guess like someone in a zentai suit, though with added personality of the costume—but you're left with a voice and eyes and that's all that is there to relate to of that person. It's something exceptionally freeing in communicating afresh with somebody when you don't know who's under that skin, that costume. You've got no idea of who they are, or their back story. It's just the outer skin that is presented and rather than the form being deceptive, I found the interactions in those settings very open and deeply relatable. Perhaps it's that thing with what Oscar Wilde said about the mask. People were very real with each other, but you've got no idea who each person is outside of such a setting.

OTTO: So under the latex mirror skin, is there a different kind of realness? A masquerade can also offer that, but it seems you suggest this is a masquerade, more embodied in a way.

DAMCHO: One of the paradoxes of latex itself is that it appears to be plastic or of not being natural. It's not a woven, breathable fabric or anything, but it appears futuristic and otherworldly. But I sometimes consider it as the serum of a tree that it has been tapped from. And so it's one of Mother Nature's inner expressions that we're wearing on the outside. Quite early on in my experiences with latex, I developed a poetic material relationship with it being something that anchors me to earth. So when you talk about a second skin, it actually felt like not another skin, but something that was just picking up and just drawing from within the earth, something that's already there. Yes, this special skin of latex is something deep coming up to the surface, through the serum of the rubber tree. And so, the second skin emerges from within.

CONTRIBUTORS

Editors

Otto von Busch is Associate Professor of Integrated Design at Parsons School of Design, USA. He holds a PhD in design from the School of Design and Craft at the University of Gothenburg, Sweden, and has taught and exhibited work internationally on the topic of empowerment and vitalism in fashion.

Jeanine Viau is Associate Lecturer of Religion and Cultural Studies at the University of Central Florida, USA. She holds a PhD in theology with a concentration in women's studies and gender studies from Loyola University Chicago and has taught and published on contemporary Catholicism, queer studies in religion, and feminist theology.

Chapter Contributors

Fiona Dieffenbacher is Assistant Professor of Fashion at Parsons School of Design, USA. She holds an MA in fashion studies from Parsons, where she teaches a range of fashion courses. Her research is located at the intersection of dress, embodiment, and materiality, with a particular emphasis on the "space in between" theory and practice.

Nicola Masciandaro is Professor of English at Brooklyn College (CUNY), USA. He holds a PhD in medieval studies from Yale University. Some recurring themes of his research and writings are labor, mystical sorrow, individuation, decapitation, anagogy, commentary, and love.

Liz Wilson is Professor of Comparative Religion at Miami University of Ohio, USA. She earned her doctorate at the University of Chicago Divinity School, specializing in Indian Buddhism. Her publications illuminate questions of power and identity in South Asian Buddhism and Hinduism using analytical lenses from gender studies, sexuality studies, family studies, and gerontology.

Kodo Nishimura is a global makeup artist and Buddhist monk, born and raised in a serene Buddhist temple in Tokyo and a graduate of Parsons School of Design in New York. His makeup works have appeared in national shows such as *Miss Universe*, *The View*, and he has done makeup for celebrities such as Chloe X Halle and Christina Milian.

Contributors

Mark Larrimore is Associate Professor of Religious Studies and directs the Religious Studies Program at Eugene Lang College of Liberal Arts at The New School, USA. He is the author of *The Book of Job: A Biography* (2013).

Joseph Walser is Associate Professor of Religion at Tufts University, USA. He holds a PhD in history of religions from Northwestern University and has taught and published on the religions of India and China.

Hassanah El-Yacoubi is a PhD candidate in religious studies at the University of California Riverside, USA. Her research focuses on the intersections of Islam, gender, and fashion. She is also a leading modest fashion influencer creating cross-cultural and inter-religious understanding through female entrepreneurship and empowerment.

Benae Beamon is Visiting Assistant Professor in the Department of Women's and Gender Studies at Bucknell University, USA. She holds a PhD in social ethics from Boston University and has taught and published research on Black studies, queer and trans studies, Christian ethics, and Black artistic expression.

Tanya White is Assistant Professor of Fashion: Materials and Fabrications at Ryerson University, Canada. She holds a PhD in design from Glasgow School of Art and has taught and published work internationally on creative practice in textiles and fashion.

Shekinah Morrison holds a BA in humanities and cultural studies from the University of Central Florida, USA. She is currently pursuing women's rights advocacy through volunteer work with a special interest in advancing the understanding of intersectional feminism and misogynoir in the corporate sector.

Michael Muhammad Knight is Assistant Professor of Religion and Cultural Studies at the University of Central Florida, USA. He holds a PhD in religious studies from the University of North Carolina in Chapel Hill, specializing in Islamic studies, and is the author of fourteen books, including *Metaphysical Africa: Truth and Blackness in the Ansaru Allah Community* (2020).

Jared Vázquez López is a PhD candidate in theology, philosophy, and cultural theory at the Iliff School of Theology and the University of Denver, USA. He has published on Pentecostalism and philosophy, and his dissertation research examines Pentecostal religious practice, transnationalism, and queer identity in Puerto Rico and Puerto Rican diaspora in the United States.

Kristen J. Sollée is an arts and *occulture* journalist and a part-time lecturer at The New School, USA. She holds an MA in East Asian studies from Columbia University with a concentration in gender studies and material culture. Her books exploring the witch archetype have been featured in *The Guardian*, *National Geographic*, *NYLON*, and *NPR*.

Damcho is a multimedia artist who has exhibited and performed in numerous solo and group shows in Europe and Australia, as well as being the recipient of numerous awards. When Damcho returned to making art after her decade as a Buddhist nun, her practice aligned with the re-awaking of her sexuality and body awareness.

INDEX

9/11 attacks 92

Abdullah, Zain 151
Acaranga Sutra 79
acela ("unclothed") 79
Adam and Eve 27–8
Aden, Halima 98
Adriel, Jean 40
aesthetics 135, 136
aesthetic state 123
affective response 136
Affect Theory, Shame and Christian Formation (Arel) 127
Afrocentrism 152
Afro-diasporic communities 113
Ahmad, Muhammad 157
Ahmed, Leila 92
Ahmed, Sara 73, 112, 113, 122, 136, 138, 140, 141
Ahmed, Shahab 147, 159
Ali, Muhammad 150, 151
Ali, Noble Drew 148–50
Ali ibn Abu Talib 149
Allah 152, 153, 155
Allure 101
American Academy of Religion 1, 9
American Eagle 97
American Islam 150
Amida Sutra 69
anaesthetic 135, 136, 138
anatomical bodies 45
ancient India 78–9, 87
Anderson, Benedict 52
anorexia 124, 130
Ansar. *See* Mahdiyya
Ansaru Allah Community (AAC) 147, 156–9
anthropology 3
anthropotechnics 5, 15, 73
anti-aesthetics 135, 136
apostle Paul 29, 31, 32
Aquinas, Thomas 177
al-Arabi, Ibn 152
Arab women 97
Arbery, Ahmaud 101
Arel, Stephanie 127, 130
Aristotle 6, 34 n.2
Aruni Upaniṣad 87
ascetic emulation 119, 122–5

asceticism 117, 118, 124, 126
ascetic practices 75, 80, 81
ascetic training 10
Atman (the soul) 55, 61. *See also* soul
Augustine of Hippo 177
autoethnography 75, 134, 136, 137, 139
avant-garde 4, 39, 162, 168

Baba, Meher 37–48, 48 n.4
    connections with persons of glamour 39–40
    God Speaks 44, 47
    highest of high fashion 41–4
    sensitivity and human warmth of presence 44–5
    soul at play 45–7
    spelling silence 40–2
    style 37–8, 44, 47
Bachelard, Gaston 42
Badu, Erykah 154
Bailey, Van 111
Bajracharya, Chanira (Kumārī) 58, 63
Bald, Vivek 149
"The Ballot or the Bullet" (speech) 147
Barfield, Owen 6
Barnard, Malcolm 22
Barthes, Roland 77
BBC 63, 65
beauty 16, 41, 47
becoming 23, 24, 34
being 6, 19, 24, 28, 41, 45, 79
Bell, Quentin 25
Berger, John 28
Berro, Zahraa 97
Bhabha, Homi 2
Bhagavad Gita ("Song of God") 60–1
Bhikkhus 81, 82
"big 7" design 155–6
bklyn boihood 111
Black, Brian 86
Blackness/Black culture/Black life 6, 101, 106, 107, 109, 110–13, 134, 144, 147, 148, 151, 159, 160
    African American communities 147, 150, 160
    Black Africanity 158
    Black consciousness 152, 158
    black flesh 111, 113, 114
    Black Freemasonry 149

Index

Black Islamic masculinity   148–52, 156–60
Black liberation   147–8
Black Lives Matter Movement   101
Blackness as divine   151, 152, 159, 160
Black (black) people   101, 113, 151, 158
Black Power   152
black queer   107, 109–14
black queerness   107, 108, 110, 111, 113, 114
Black Shriner   149
Black Sunni   158
black transness   75, 109
Black women   148, 150, 154, 156
bodhi   189
Body Dressing (Kaiser)   24
body(ies)   6, 15, 16, 19–25, 28, 29, 33, 34, 75, 77, 82, 84, 85, 88, 95, 103, 110, 112, 113, 173, 188, 189, 191
  Black   101, 106, 110, 112–14, 149, 151, 160
  Black queer   113, 114
  of Christ   129
  deformed   125
  emaciated   83, 117, 118, 120, 123–5, 127, 129–31
  female   103, 120, 130
  fleshy and fleshless   121, 127
  masculine   83, 84, 148, 156, 158
  physical   24, 29, 32
  shape   123
  subaltern   171–4
  trans   113, 114
body image   117, 118, 121–3, 126, 131
Bordo, Susan   121
Boutet de Monvel, Bernard   39
Brahmins and thread   85–8
Brancaccio, Pia   82
Branson, Toni   108, 109
Brooke, Anthony   39
Brown, Robert   84, 85
Browne, Thom   20, 21, 34
Bucar, Elizabeth   96
Buddha   81–8, 89 nn.14, 21
Buddhism   66–70, 86, 188–90
Buddhist meditation teachings   190
Buddhist monastic robes   80–5
Buddhist monks   67, 68, 71, 78, 80, 81, 86, 88
Buddhist temples   68, 69
Burke, Edmund   119
Burroughs, William   129
Burton, Tara Isabella   180
Bynum, Caroline   130
Bynum, Catherine Walker   118

Calvin, John   24
Calvinism   24
Camerlengo, Laura   97

Cameron, Marjorie   179
capitalism   140
capitalist domination   99
capitalist market economies   98
Carlyle, Thomas   48, 143
Caro, Anita de   39
Carrington, Andre   110
Carroll, Lewis   170
Cartesian Dualism/split   5, 19, 24, 27, 34, 34 n.2
Catholicism   2
Catusparisat Sutra   89 n.21
Caudalie   101
Celtic Christian church   25
Celtic culture   25
ceremonial choreographies   67
Ceres, Vatican Sala Rotunda   83
Chaker, Isra   96
Chamaa, Nora   102
Chanji   38
Chan-Malik, Sylvia   94
Charmed (TV show)   182
Christian Bible   181
Christianity   6, 24, 78, 88, 126, 159
Christian shame   127
class   52, 163, 164, 168, 172–4
clothes/clothed/clothing   4, 5, 9, 15, 20, 21, 24, 25, 27–9, 32–4, 45, 52, 53, 77, 78, 82, 84, 95, 97, 98, 107, 108, 110, 112, 114, 137, 143, 150–1, 158. *See also* dress/dressing
Clotilde   47
CNN   65
collective judgment   24
Collins, Steven   86
colonialism/colonization   162, 171–4
Comme des GarÇons   178
commodification   99
Common Era   84, 88
Communist Party   53
concealed   143
consecration (*diksa*)   80
consumerism   3
contemporary India   78
contemporary witchcraft   176
conventional beauty   135
Cooke, Miriam   93
Cooper, Brittney   110
corporeal emulation   74
corporeal visibility   103
Corpus (Nancy)   125
cosmetics   176, 181–3
Craft, The   182
Critical Aesthetics and Postmodernism (Crowther)   119
cross-dressing   174
Cross Park Chaplains   154

199

Index

"crown" concept   153
Crown Your Occasions   98
Crowther, Paul   119, 123, 126
Crystallized Collection   180
cultural difference   73
cultural impressions   122
cultural practices   62, 99
Cultural Revolution   53
Cummings, Hakeemah   101
Curtis, Edward E., IV   159
Cushnie et Ochs   179, 180, 185
cyborg   8, 9

D'alessandro, Jill   97
Damcho   144, 188–93
DapperQ   109, 112
darshan   53, 59
Dar ul- Islam movement   157
death and funerals   31, 69
deathly form   118–25
deep dress/dressing deeply   7–11, 16, 73–5
Dehija   84
de Lancre, Pierre   182
Deleuze, Gilles   144, 163, 170–1
Demeulemeester, Ann   179
Democratic National Convention (2016)   100
Demonolatry (Remy)   181
Demoting Vishnu: Ritual, Politics, and the Unraveling of Nepal's Hindu Monarchy (Mocko)   62
de Perthuis, Karen   46
Derrida, Jacques   128
Descartes, Rene   34 n.2
Dhammapada   86
dhutanga   81
Digambara Jain   78
Digha Nikaya   82
disidentification   45, 113, 138, 144, 163, 173
disordered eating   125
divine/divinity   7, 15–17, 37, 41–3, 46, 47, 53
  entities   10
  feminine   53–4, 60
Dolce Vita, Anita   109
drag   10–11, 11 n.1
dress/dressing   5, 10, 15, 16, 20, 24, 25, 34, 73, 74, 95
  codes   94, 148, 153, 157, 159
  form(s) of   34, 52, 53, 81
  head   94, 97
  Islamic   94, 98
  modest   3, 94, 96, 97, 103
  "Moslem"   148
  practices   7, 9, 29
  religious   2–4, 19
  rural and ethnic   52
  style of   53

women   96
work   27
drug culture   127
dualism   7, 8
Du Bois, W. E. B.   6
Dürer, Albrecht   78
Durgā-Taleju   51, 52, 56, 58

Eagle Regalia   155
early Christian church   24
early Pasupatas   80
East Asia   80
Edenic naturalness   78
education   139–41
ego. *See* self
Egyptosophy   149, 158
ELLE Women in Hollywood event (2018)   20
Ellis, Carolyn   134, 139
Ellison, Ralph   107–8
embellished techniques   33
embodiment/embodied practice/embodied
  soul   2, 16, 19, 20, 25, 27–9, 32–4, 45, 46, 52, 54, 92, 111, 113, 117, 125, 127, 158, 189
emotional freedom   191
emotions   73–4
entrepreneurial tactics   73
Entwistle, Joanne   25
ephemerality   4, 70, 96, 107, 111, 130, 190
epistemology   94, 103, 138, 163, 165–9
erotic   77, 78
ethic of honor   107–11, 113, 114
ethnicity   65, 117, 172–4
Ethnographic I, The (Ellis)   134
ethnography   19, 137–9
Ettinger, Bracha   119, 128, 129
Eurocentrism   7, 95
Europe   98
expressive sublime   126

fabrication   33
Fanon, Frantz   112
fashion   1, 15–16, 22–3, 27, 34, 38, 44, 46–8, 48–9 n.15, 70, 73, 75, 77, 107, 111, 139, 140, 143, 144
  alchemists   144
  concept of   3
  contemporary   3, 19
  divinity of   41, 46
  events   74
  market   97, 98, 102
  media   96, 97
  modest   74, 96–9, 101, 103
  Muslim   97, 102
  religious   52, 78, 79
  scholarship   5, 19
  studies   3, 7, 19, 20, 34, 108

styles   96, 122
theory   19
Fashionista.com   179
fashion-style-dress   8, 10, 16, 25
female deities   54
female monks   70
female Muslim corporeality   102
Female Nude, Art, Obscenity and Sexuality, The (Nead)   120
feminine adornment   176, 181, 182, 184–6
femininity   144, 178, 180, 182, 184, 185
fez   148–51, 153
Filigenzi, Anna   81
fine art   119
Finkelstein, Joanne   108
Five Percenters   144, 147, 152–6, 159
Fleetwood Mac   179
Floyd, George   101
Form & Fashion   134
Forum of Women, Law, and Development   62
Frame, John   25
Freire, Paulo   134
French Revolution   53
Freud, Sigmund   7
Fruit of Islam (FOI)   151
future body as ultimate dress   29–32, 34

Gandharan art   82, 83
@garbsandcarbs   97
Gasteren, Louis van   37–8
gay marriage   69
Gay Science, The (Nietzsche)   41
gender   94, 102, 130, 150, 152, 155, 167, 169, 170, 172–4
   equality   180
   expressions   111, 112, 183
   fluidity   130
   identity   180
   normative aesthetic   109
Gender Blender (podcast)   111
gestural realities   110–11
Giovanni, Nikki   108, 114
glamor/glamour   16, 38–41, 43, 46, 143, 144, 162, 165, 168–70, 174, 176, 186
glamour magic and its discontents   180–4
glossolalic events   144, 163, 171
Gnosticism   24, 35 n.4
God   24, 25, 27–9, 34, 42, 45
goddess Durgā   54
goddess Vajra Devi   54
God Help the Child (Morrison)   134, 135
God-Man, The (Purdom)   40
God Speaks (Baba)   44, 47
"God's True Cloak" (Rilke)   11
Gombrich, Richard   86
Gossett, Che   109

Gothic fashion   178
GQ   20
Grossman, Pam   185
Grunewald Christ   127
Guadagnino, Kate   185
Guardian, The   61, 180
El Guindi, Fadwa   94
*guṇa*s (strands of existence)   51, 53, 60, 61
gymnosophistai ("naked philosophers")   79

Hakeem, Neelam   97
al-Hallaj, Mansur   152
Hamid, Abdul   149
Hanson, Karen   27, 29
Haraway, Donna   8, 9, 11, 73
Harding, Luke   61
Harper's Bazaar   101
Harun, Aysha   101
Hayden, Robert   113
Hazlitt, William   20
Heavenly Bodies Exhibition (2018)   1–2, 11, 32
hegemony   107, 109, 110, 112, 113, 158, 174
heroin chic fashion model   117, 119, 123, 125, 126, 129, 131
Herstik, Gabriela   182, 183
high fashion   2, 41–4
hijab   73, 91–4, 96, 97, 103
Hijaz, Anwar   102
Hinduism   54, 55
Hindu monarchs   52
Hindu philosophy   51, 60
H&M   97
Hollander, Anne   28, 77, 82, 83
Holy Spirit   32
Holy Trinity   25, 27
Hoodwitch, The   180
hooks, bell   134, 140
Hopkins, Dwight   163, 166–8
humanity   7, 42, 43, 47, 110, 114
human rights   61, 62
hyper-masculinity   148

identity   4, 5, 20, 21–3, 29, 34, 42, 43, 189
   Black   159
   Buddhist   81, 82, 88
   cultural   2, 95, 96
   formation   24, 25, 27, 92, 94
   human   47
   Muslim   93–5, 98, 103
   national   52
   "Oriental"   149
   queer   172, 173
   religious   93, 94, 148
   social   85, 86, 88, 95
   trans   107
   visual communication of   53

Index

Idrissi, Mariah   97
imagined community   52
IMG   98
Immigration Act (1965)   150
immortality   5, 8, 29
incarnation   10, 15, 16
India   74, 80
Indian asceticism   88
Indra Jatra   51, 59, 63
Infinite Abaya   102
"In Memory of Elizabeth Howe, Salem, 1692"   179
inner experiences   3, 5, 7, 8, 10
inner life   5–11
Inner Witch and *Bewitching the Elements* (Herstik)   182
"insides" and "outsides"   20–2, 24, 34
insignia   81, 85–8
Instagram   97, 101, 102, 180
integrated model   24–7
In the Wake: On Blackness and Being (Sharpe)   113
Islam   93–5, 100, 103, 158, 159
Islamic Arabia   95
Islamic clothing   94, 98, 147–9
Islamic culture   94
Islamic practices   102
Islam in America/American Islam
    African American Islam   144, 147–9, 158
    American Muslim communities   92, 102, 158
    American Muslim women   97
    authentic Africanity   158
    authentic Islam   158
Islamism   92, 148
Islamophobia   100

Jackson, Sherman   148
Jacobs, Marc   20
Jain monks   82
James, William   8, 74
Japan   67, 68, 70
Japan Buddhist Federation   68
Jasmine and Marigold   98
Jay Z   156
Jesco, Jackie   59
Jessawala, Eruch   39, 47
Jesus   88
Jim Crow South   106
Jones, Catrina   108, 109
Junky (Burroughs)   129

Kaiser, Susan   23, 24, 34, 52
Kant, Emmanuel   124
Kantian Sublime: From Morality to Art, The (Crowther)   126
Kardashian, Kourtney   3
Kardashian West, Kim   3
Kathmandu   51, 52, 54–8

Kawakubo, Rei   178, 179, 185
kenosis   127
Khan, Ghazala   100
Khan, Humayun   100
Khan, Khizr   100
Khoja-Moolji, Shenila   100
Kodo Nishimura   65–71
Kooiman, Mary Jane   77
Kramer, Heinrich   181
Kristeva, Julia   118, 119, 122, 128–30
Kumārī of Kathmandu   52
Kumārī of Patan   51, 58
Kumārī(s)   15, 16, 51–63
    rituals and lives of   54–9
    shakti, divine female power   54
    today   61–3
    tricolor symbolism   59–61
    visual information exchanges   52–3
kumkum   57
Kushan Era   84, 85

Lady Gaga   20, 21, 34
La Fountain-Stokes, Lawrence   172, 173
Lalitavistara   81
latex culture   144, 188–93
Lewis, Reina   96
LGBTQ
    community   67, 69
    events   70
    rights   69
"Life update + why I stopped supporting a certain brand" (YouTube video)   101
Lindsay, John   155
Lintott, Sheila   124
living goddess   52, 54–8, 61–3
L'Oreal   43
Low Life in High Heels, A (Woodlawn)   163–5
Luna, Bri   180, 181, 184

McCarthy, Julie   58
McClendon, Emma   2
McGovern, Nathan   86
McIntosh, Peggy   134
McQueen, Alexander   179, 185
Mahamaudgalyayana   86, 87
Mahavira   79, 80
Mahdiyya   157–9
Maitreya   85, 88
makeup   16, 65–71, 93, 183, 184
Malcolm X   147, 150, 151
Malleus Maleficarum (Kramer)   181
Manandhar, Razen   62
Manifesto (Matchabelli)   40
Mani   38
Man Ray   39
Maoists   62

202

Index

Marc Jacobs menswear suit   20
Maria Carmi. *See* Matchabelli, Norina
Maroba, Boka   109
Martínez-Toledo, Luis Iván   31
masculinity   85, 88, 113, 144
Masonic technology   150, 153
Matchabelli, Norina   37, 39, 40
material culture   19, 20, 34
materiality   20, 27, 31, 33, 112, 129
matrixial borderspace   128
Meachi   70
medieval crucified Christ   117, 119, 123, 126, 127, 129–31
Menkes, Suzy   178
Merton, Thomas   144
Met Cloisters   2, 11, 32
#metoo movement   180
Metropolitan Museum of Art   1
Middle East   95, 98
Miller, Daniel   21, 22
Miller, Monica   112
Mills, Amy   182, 184
Minakshi temple, Madurai   53
mind/body split   5, 24
"Minding Appearances" (Kaiser)   24
Miss Universe   65, 66
Mocko, Anne   62, 63
modern glamour magicians   182–5
modernism   119
modernity   7
Modest Fashion Movement (MFM)   74, 91–3, 96–103
modesty   28, 96, 97, 103, 150
Modist Ghizlan Guenez   98
Mohammed, Warith Deen   158
Moore, Brenna   16
Moorish civilization   148–9
Moorish Science Temple of America (MSTA)   147–50, 159
morality   117, 118, 123
Moran, Terry   59
more fully clothed   32–3
Mori, Riyo   66
Morrison, Shekinah   134–40
Morrison, Toni   134
Morrissey   168–70
Moseley, Rachel   182
Mosque of Islamic Brotherhood (MIB)   157
Mounier, Emmanuel   28
Muhammad, Elijah   150–2, 158
Muhammad, Fard   151
Mulasarvastivadin monastic code   85–7
Mulmi, Subin   62
Muñoz, José Esteban   144, 163, 173
Museum at the Fashion Institute of Technology   2
Muslim fashion

brands   92, 102
entrepreneurs   98, 99, 102
fashionistas   97
lifestyle   92, 93, 102
models   91
modest fashion   91, 93
"Muslim New York Fashion Week"   91–2
style arbiters (*see* fashionistas)

nagina ("naked")   79
Nag Sadhu yogis   78
naked asceticism   79–80, 82, 83, 85
nakedness   27–9, 32–4, 77–80, 82–4
Nance, Susan   150
Nancy, Jean Luc   125
Nation of Islam (NOI)   147, 148, 150–2, 155–9
Nead, Lynda   120
@neelam_   97
Negrón-Muntaner, Frances   162, 163, 165, 173
neoliberal consumer culture   98
neoliberalism   102
Nepal   51, 52, 54, 55, 57, 62
Newars   54
"new cycle of history"   92
New York Fashion Week (NYFW, 2017)   109
New York Times, The   179, 180, 185
Nicks, Stevie   179
Nietzsche, Friedrich   41, 143
Nike   99
North India   81
Nubian Islamic Hebrews (NIH). *See* Ansaru Allah Community (AAC)
nudity. *See* nakedness

observance (*vrata*)   80
Olivelle, Patrik   86
Ó Murchadha, Felix   28
online content   74
On the Inconstancy of Witches (Lancre)   182
ontological recognition   21
oppression   95, 96, 100
Orientalism   95, 103
"Oriental"   149
Oriental woman   95
Orsi, Robert   2
Other Foundation   109
Ottoman period   98
outer life   7, 10
Owens, Rick   179

Pakistan   81
pamsukula   81
Pancha (five) Buddha   55
Paris Fashion Week   3
Parsons School of Design   65, 66
Patika   82–3

203

Index

"Payasi Sutra" 82
pedagogical strategies 75
penis 84–5, 89 n.14
PFH Modest Fashion Convention 91, 96
Phelan, Hayley 179
Philosophical Enquiry into the Beautiful and Sublime, A (Burke) 119
Picard, Max 40
Picture of Dorian Gray, The (Wilde) 3
piercings 135
Plato 24, 31, 34 n.2
platonic dichotomy 21
poetic language 15
polysemic 96
POPSUGAR 101
post-Revolutionary China 53
Powers of Horror (Kristeva) 118
Pradhan-Malla, Sapana 61
pravrtim 88
precarious deformity 118–21, 125–7
Prince A Cuba 156
Protestant Christianity 86
Protestant Reformation 19, 86
psychotechnical artistry 74
Ptolemy 79
public education 75
public nakedness 79
public university classroom 74, 75, 139
Puerto Rican diaspora 172, 173
Pugh, Gareth 179
Purdom, C. B. 40
Pure Land Buddhism 70
    Pure Land school 65
The Pure Land Churches of America 69
Purkiss, Diane 177, 179

Queer Eye: We're in Japan (TV program) 65
queer theory/queerness 166–8, 172
    queer aesthetics 109
    queer agency and resistance 165, 166
    queer community 174
    queer confession 169
    queer sartorial ethics 171–4
Queer Phenomenology (Ahmed) 112, 136
Qur'an 147, 152, 159, 160

race 102, 162, 163, 172–4
racism 106, 112
"The Rainbow Sticker" 68
rajas 60
reclothed 27–9
Red Guard 53
Reed, Lou 163
refinement 153
reformed theology. *See* Calvinism
religion 1–3, 19, 75, 77, 85, 96, 144, 158, 166

religious
    art 129
    belief 19, 34
    culture 5, 6, 10, 53
    regalia 74, 78
Remy, Nicholas 181
respectability politics 152
resurrection 31, 129
R/Evolution 109, 112
Rhi, Juhyung 83
Rilke, Rainer Maria 11
Rivera, Gabby 112
Rizer, Maggie 32, 33, 35 n.11
Rolland, Romain 7
"Romanesque Arches" (Tranströmer) 1
Roper, Lyndal 178
Royal College of Art 188
royal power 52
"Rubber Cult" 192
Ruggerone, Lucia 110, 112
Rumi 15
Russian Doll (Autumn/Winter '99 Couture show) 32, 35 n.11

Sabrina the Teenage Witch (TV show) 182
Said, Edward 95
Saint Augustine 24
St. Clare, Dakota 183, 184
Saint Laurent 179
Samkhya 60
Sanderson, Alexis 80
Santiago, Esmeralda 173
Sanyogita Devi 39
sartorial
    choices 163, 167
    practices 92–5
    spellwork 186
    stutter 170–1
Sartor Resartus (Carlyle) 48, 143
sattva 60
Saunders, Kenneth James 86
School of Art, University of Melbourne 188
Schopen, Gregory 85–8
Scott, Walter 41
second skin 3, 15, 189, 191–3
self 15, 16, 22, 28, 34 n.1, 52
    affection 74, 107, 108, 110, 111, 113, 114
    Black 158, 159
    construction 25
    determination 108, 109, 111, 114, 167
    and other 27, 29
    presentation 24, 25, 53, 60
    revelation 75, 107, 108, 111, 113, 114, 134
    sense of 21, 108, 168, 191
semiotics 22
sexuality 66–8, 167, 169, 172–4, 188

Index

Shaikley, Layla   97
"Shaking It Off "   79
shakti   54
Shakya, Rashmila (Kumārī)   57, 59, 61, 63
shame   28, 86, 127, 137, 166, 172–4
Shams, Mona   97
Shapin, Steven   24
Sharpe, Christina   110, 113
Shriner Masonry   149
silence   40–4, 48
Silent Models   41
Simmel, Georg   7, 8
skin   77, 189–93
Slaves to Fashion (Miller)   112
Slimane, Hedi   179, 185
Slim for Him (Kreml)   125
Sloterdijk, Peter   5, 73
Smashbox   180
social equality   148
social media   97, 101
Soelle, Dorothee   15
Sontag, Susan   170
soul   2–7, 10, 16, 19–25, 29, 33, 34, 44–7, 55, 56, 73–5, 143, 144, 156
    fashion-dress-embodied soul   25–7, 34
Souls of Black Folk, The (Du Bois)   6
South Asia   53, 78
South Asian diasporas   149
Southeast Asia   80
South India   81
spiritual body   32
spiritual infinity   46
spirituality   2, 3, 10, 75
spiritual practices   9, 10, 16, 74, 75
Spooner, Catherine   178, 181
SS Conte Rosso   48 n.4
SS Conte Verde   39
Stallings, L. H.   111, 113, 114
Stallybrass, Peter   27, 28
Stanford University   65
starving/fasting   83, 124, 125, 130
State Street Mosque   156, 157
Steele, Valerie   178
stereotypes   93, 100, 102, 151
Stevens, Don   44
Stoicism   35 n.9
style   16, 24, 107–11, 165–9
Style Is Freedom   108
subjectivity   6, 7, 19, 24, 34, 34 n.3, 107–9, 113, 139
    colonial   2
    Muslim   93, 95, 97, 99, 100, 102
    political   52
    queer   109
    social   108
    trans   110

subject-object interactions   74
"Sublime Hunger: A Consideration of Eating Disorders beyond Beauty" (Lintott)   124
Sublime Object of Ideology, The (Zizek)   119
sublime/the sublime   130
    emaciation   117, 118
    emulation   75, 117–32
    hunger theory   124, 129
    sublimation   119
    visions   118–21
Sufism   152, 157, 159

Tablighi-Jamaat   157
Tagore, Rabindranath   143
Taleju   54
tamasa   60
Tantric Buddhism   54
Tarde, Gabriel   8
tattoos   135
Taylor, Breonna   101
Taylor, Ula Yvette   148
Teufelsdröckh, Diogenes   37, 48
Théâtre des Bouffes du Nord   3
theological anthropology   168
Theory of the Leisure Class, The (Veblen)   144
Theravada Buddhism   70
thinspiration project   125
This Monk Wears Heels (Kodo Nishimura)   65
tika ceremony   62
Times   179
Titthiyas   81, 82
traditional schooling   139–40
transatlantic slavery   158
transcendental formlessness   118–21, 127–31
transformation   73, 74
transness   109, 114, 168
trans people   109, 110–12, 114
transphysical   32
trans style   109, 113, 114
Tranströmer, Tomas   1, 7
Trash (1970)   162–4, 168, 170, 171, 174
Tree, Isabella   57, 59
tricolor symbolism   59–61
Trinitarian theology   16
trinity knot   25, 35 n.5
tripartite color symbolism   51–3
triperspectivalism   25
Triquetra. *See* trinity knot
Trump, Donald   100
Tulloch, Carol   25
turbans   39, 94, 97
Turner, Terance   3

unclothed. *See* nakedness
unconventional beauty   135
United Kingdom   98

205

Index

United Nations Population Fund   65
United States   74, 91–4, 97–100, 103, 106, 148, 149, 158, 160, 174
Universal Flag   154–6
Universal Shaamgaudd Allah   153–5
"the unlimited itself"   7–9
upasampada (full) ordination   81
Uruvela Kassapa   87
US immigration reform (1965)   158

Vajrayana Buddhism   190
Van der Goes, Hugo   78
Veblen, Thorstein   144
Vedic learning   85, 87
Veiled Collection   102
veiling practices   92–7, 99, 103
veneration   10, 54, 55
Viau, Jeanine   134–41
Viktor and Rolf   32, 33, 35 n.11
visibility   96–101, 107, 108
visual
   communication   52–3
   culture   118, 121, 129, 176, 177, 179
   iconography   117, 132
   patterning   123, 127
Vogue   101
Vogue International   178
von Busch, Otto   188–93

"Walk on the Wild Side" (Reed)   163
Wallace, Maurice O.   149
Ward, Graham   130
Warhol, Andy   162, 165, 168–71
Washington Post   180
Ways of Seeing (Berger)   28
Weil, Simone   47
West, Kanye   3
Western culture   92, 96, 99, 103
   art   82
   gaze   95, 98
What Is Islam? (Ahmed)   147, 159

When I Was Puerto Rican (Santiago)   173
white supremacy   112, 148–50, 159
"White Supremacy in Modest Fashion" (2020)   101
WhoWhatWear   101
Wiccan religion   179
Wilde, Oscar   3, 143, 191, 193
Wilson, Elizabeth   8, 16, 74, 99, 140, 143, 182
Wilson, Nicole   108
Wise Systems   97
witchcraft practice   183–5
"Witches Lose the Warts"   179
witch fashioning
   early/modern origins   176–8
   Sorcière Couture   178–80
witch-hunting   176–8, 181
women abuse   62
women of Muslim faith   73, 74, 91–6, 98, 99, 101–3
   monolithic Muslim woman   93, 95, 100, 103
   Muslim womanhood   93–6, 99, 100, 102, 103
   Muslim women   73, 74, 91, 93–5, 98–102
Women's International Terrorist Conspiracy from Hell (WITCH)   179
Woodlawn, Holly   144, 162–74
Woodward, Sophie   136–7
Wright, N. T.   31, 32

Yaeger, Lynn   20, 21, 34
Yale University   65
Yayanos, Meredith   184
YEEZY uniforms   3
yogic practice   60
York, Dwight   156–7
Yoruba revivalists/revivalism   157, 158
Young, Serenity   84
YouTube   101

@zahraa_hberro   97
Zizek, Slavoj   119, 125, 129